HARVARD HISTORICAL MONOGRAPHS

LIII

PUBLISHED UNDER THE DIRECTION
OF THE DEPARTMENT OF HISTORY
FROM THE INCOME OF
THE ROBERT LOUIS STROOCK FUND

COPYHOLD, EQUITY, AND THE COMMON LAW

CHARLES MONTGOMERY GRAY

HARVARD UNIVERSITY PRESS

CAMBRIDGE, MASSACHUSETTS · 1963

Distributed in Great Britain by Oxford University Press, London
Library of Congress Catalog Card Number 63–11420
Printed in the United States of America

TO

HANNA HOLBORN GRAY

ACKNOWLEDGMENTS

I am indebted to Professor W. K. Jordan of Harvard University for overseeing these studies when they took the form of a doctoral thesis, and to Professor David Berkowitz of Brandeis University for a perceptive reading at that stage; to Professors Samuel E. Thorne and John P. Dawson of the Harvard Law School for their helpful criticisms; to the Society of Fellows of Harvard University, both for giving me the opportunity to work into the field of legal history and for supporting the research for this book; to the History Department of Harvard University for making its publication possible; and to my wife for many things.

C.M.G.

CONTENTS

COPYHOLD, EQUITY, AND THE COMMON LAW

INTRODUCTION

This book consists of three studies centered around the question of how copyholds were adopted into the family of interests in land protected by English royal justice. The first study proceeds from the long-recognized fact that the Chancellor afforded protection to copyholders before the courts of common law did. I deal first with the question of whether the Chancellor's intervention was a pre-Tudor phenomenon, and then with the further question of how the Chancellor was persuaded to take copyholders under his wing. A subsidiary topic in the first study deals with the roles of the Star Chamber and Court of Requests in copyhold matters. I attempt to justify treating these courts in a subordinate way by arguing that they were probably ancillary to the Chancery and of little importance for the fundamental legal change.

In the second study, I try to infer the date at which the common-law judges decided that the copyholder's interest merited protection by writ of trespass. A later step, extension of the action of ejectment to copyholders, is also dealt with. I go on to discuss the grounds on which the judges were persuaded that writs should lie for wrongs to copyholders which previously had been thought irremediable at common law.

My third study is also about the courts of common law. It deals with a necessary consequence of the judges' decision to afford protection: the elaboration of a body of legal doctrine concerning copyholds. The study is approximately bounded by the end of Queen Elizabeth's reign. I limit myself, as it were, to the first draft of a new chapter in the law of real property. There are two reasons for this limitation. First, the final draft of the chapter—the rules, founded on traditionally cited cases, which governed the courts' handling of new cases from roughly the mid-seventeenth century until copyhold dwindled and died in the nineteenth—is amply on record. Secondly, on numerous points the first draft is markedly different from the final one. Especially if unprinted reports of cases are used to supplement the traditional corpus in print, one sees that Elizabeth's judges, struggling unguided with a new and thorny field of law, produced a great deal of irresolution, as well as many starts and suggestions which, whatever their merits, were in time forgotten. In the third study I try to give a picture of conflicting judicial approaches to those issues that were least easy to settle.

In this introduction, I shall try to accomplish two things. First, I shall explain what a copyhold is and thereby show why the tenure originally lay outside the reach of the common law and, for a shorter time, even beyond the more vaguely delimited grasp of the Chancellor's equity. Secondly, I shall attempt to place these studies with respect to their emphasis, hypotheses, and limitations, and with respect to earlier writings on the legal history of copyhold.

I

An understanding of the legal nature of copyhold and its antecedents is involved with, but not equivalent to, an understanding of the manorial economy and the practical nature of English peasant tenure. Those who write in legal terms can hardly avoid the charge of legalistic distortion, while those who write in economic terms are likely to be vague about the ultimate, if rarely invoked, legal facts on which practical relations depend. Since these studies are about the professional arguments and decisions of lawyers and judges, I must start out by defining and explaining copyhold in legal terms. I must at the same time admit that what follows makes unclear distinctions look clear and gives a theoretical cast to ideas which were not thought about theoretically on the level of village and manor. In effect, I shall give a lawyer-like account of the origins of copyhold while acknowledging that lawyerly language is inadequate for describing complex historical change. The statements that follow would, I think, seem acceptable to, say, a mid-fifteenth-century lawyer. Given the limitations of legal language for historical purposes, I think they are faithful to modern knowledge of late medieval agrarian history. They would not, however, seem acceptable to most sixteenth-century lawyers. As I shall show in the second study, confusion over the origins of copyhold was a factor in the emergence of its new legal status.[1]

A copyhold is a villein tenement new-made. Medieval English law distinguished villenage as a tenure from villenage as a personal status: a free man could hold his land by villein tenure as well as by free tenure. For purposes of legal exposition and in order to avoid the complications introduced into the law of landownership by questions of personal status, let us assume that a piece of land is held in villenage by a free man and then ask what it means to say he holds in that tenure. The answer is that the tenurial language here has reference primarily to the services he owes his lord for the land. The tenurial language does not refer primarily to the man's "estate" in the land.

"Estate" is usually defined as a quantity of interest. A fee simple is the maximum estate, or quantity of interest, a man can have in a piece of land, because if he has a fee simple the land will descend to his heirs-general as long as he has heirs. It will escheat to the lord only upon failure of heirs. The fee simple is as close to absolute ownership as a feudal-tenurial system can get. The free alienabilty of land held in fee simple was established at an early date. The next largest estate is the fee tail, where the land is inheritable only by the heirs of a man's body, either his issue generally or a special class of his issue (male, female, begotten upon a particular woman). The hierarchy of estates then declines through the life-estate and the term of years, to end in estates at will and at sufferance.

Tenurial language—as, for example, to say that a man holds in fee simple or, synonymously, to himself and his heirs—commonly has reference to estate. But to say a man holds in villenage essentially has reference to services. It means he renders unfree services. Then what sort of services are unfree? This question cannot be answered with full precision. In general, if the tenant owed a good deal of indefinite and supervised agricultural labor, his service was unfree. Other duties thought of as degrading and villein-like could also count as evidence that a tenure was villenage. The courts would look at the facts of service and infer the tenure: there does not seem to have been an altogether simple test.

Suppose, then, that a free man is found to hold a piece of land by villein services, and hence "in villenage." What does this tell one about his legal position generally and his estate in particular? According to the settled medieval law—let us say the law of 1300—it means that the common-law courts will not protect his possession against his lord. Even against a mere stranger, one who enters without the lord's command or countenance, the tenant in villenage would appear to have no common-law redress.[2] His common-law potentialities are, in short, the same as those of a man who, without regard to the kind of services he pays, has an estate at will. It is therefore convenient to classify villein tenants as tenants at will. But this classification is only appropriate in a common-law context: from a manorial point of view, to know that a man holds in villenage is not informative as to the quantity of his interest.

It is not surprising that the medieval courts withheld protection from villein tenure, but neither was their position inevitable. There is an indication that the free man holding by inferior services almost won common-law standing in the thirteenth century.[3] The logic of denying him standing on the ground of his services, looking neither at his personal status nor the quantity of interest apparently conveyed by his grant, is not compelling. Still it is not surprising the courts took the position they did. Though an occasional free man might hold in villenage, most villein tenements were held by villeins. Lawyers naturally thought of an area in which landlords were entitled to manage their relations with characteristically servile tenants and to exercise the private jurisdiction that went with landlordship. The anomalous case, where unequivocal freedom of person combined with unequivocal servility of tenure, would hardly change a fundamental habit of distinguishing the common law's area of concern from the jurisdictional preserve of private landowners.

From a manorial vantage point, villein tenure looks very different. The manor itself is a hard concept to define. A manor is a territory—or, better, lest neat districting seem implied, a congeries of lands—that goes by the traditional name of the manor of such and such; it is an agricultural community in a world of intermingled open fields, shared commons, and labor services on the lord's demesnes; it is a variegated private jurisdiction. For our purposes, the jurisdictional aspect is most important, for the manorial court protects the villein tenant and his rights arise under its law.

The tenants of the manor, free tenants often and villeins invariably, owe suit of court as part of their service. The suitors, or the homage as they are often collectively called, are there to find facts and declare the law according to whatever arrangement is customary. The law of the manor is properly called the custom of the manor. It is no less law for being custom. The common law itself cannot be defined except in terms of custom: it is the custom of the king's courts; or it is the common custom of the realm; or, indeed, it is law insofar as law is custom, insofar as it is neither enactment nor the natural precepts universal to rational creatures.

Rules affecting unfree tenure are a conspicuous part of the body of manorial custom. It would be equally true to say that manorial custom includes rules affecting the lands traditionally held by such tenure, a segment of the manor which tends to remain continuously identifiable and acquires the name of customary land. The custom defines the character of a villein tenant's interest, but this does not prevent his interest from being substantially analogous to the interests of other men who hold by free services, who hold common-law, as opposed to customary, land. Assuming that it is customary for the lord of the manor to grant customary land to men and their heirs for villein services, and a tenement is so granted, then the tenant has an estate very like a fee simple, a customary fee. This means that manorial custom must determine who will have the land when the first grantee dies. Possibly, though by no means necessarily, custom will come up with the same rules of primogeniture among males and coparceny among females as govern the inheritance of most common-law land. Custom will also have to provide a procedural law appropriate to the protection of an estate of inheritance. It will need something analogous to the writ of *mort d'ancestor,* by which dispossession from one's immediate inheritance is remedied at common law, and something analogous to writs of entry and writs of right, by which remote disseisins can be overcome. Indeed, manorial procedure, and, moving outward from the procedural heart, substantive law, naturally would and did imitate the professionally elaborated law of Westminster. "Plaints in the nature of novel disseisin," of *mort d'ancestor* and of entry in the per and cui, of formedon in remainder, and the rest, became commonplace in manorial courts. Juries were used alongside the traditional homage. The stewards who presided frequently had some legal training. At the same time, similarities between manorial procedure and Westminster procedure, custom and common law, should not be overemphasized. The manor was not a perfect legal microcosm. Villein tenure and its successor, copyhold, retained peculiarities.

A description of villein tenure serves to describe the main configurations of copyhold, and much of what follows, though said of copyhold, may be taken as supplying further details to the description of villenage. The transition from the one to the other, which belongs to the later fourteenth and fifteenth centuries, is best understood if one imagines the lords of manors setting out to preserve the legal relationship which had always existed between themselves and their villein tenants, while altering, or accepting the historical alteration of, certain practical features of the relationship.

When peasants were personally villeins, they could have had little choice except to acquiesce in the treatment which their lords' grace, directed and softened by tradition, accorded them. As many of them became personally free, they must have taken heart to demand that their positions as small landholders be at least clarified, even though in essentials those positions remained unchanged. The growth of more businesslike habits on the part of landlords—the disposition to keep careful manorial records and to hire better-trained stewards—contributed a perhaps still larger share to a new atmosphere of legal exactitude. In this atmosphere, it became standard usage to preserve the proceedings of manorial courts in writing. The record of those proceedings was more than a record of litigation. Like Parliament, the courts were not so much organs of a special function as occasions for varied activities, including routine transactions between lords and their tenants and among the tenants themselves. If a piece of customary land was to be granted to a man, or transferred from one man to another, the conveyance was usually made in court, in the witnessing presence of the homage. Grants and transfers made out of court were commonly presented in court by the homage as a whole or by witnesses. When such procedures became customary, they tended to become conditions for the validity of the transactions under manorial law. If a court roll was kept, a grant made or presented in court would be entered on the roll along with other matters. The kind of interest the grantee had, his manorial estate and the conditions of his tenure, became matter of record. Then, to reinforce the tenant's certainty, as if to make him feel the more like a holder of common-law land, it becomes the practice to make a copy of the parts of the court roll which affect his property and to give him that copy. He now has an evidence of title analogous to the deeds which a common-law owner would normally possess. He comes to be called, after the kind of evidence he has, a tenant by copy of court roll, or copyholder, in contradistinction to a common-law tenant by deed, or by charter.

The new ways of keeping titles and transactions clear and the new terminology do not by themselves alter the realities of a man's tenure. A man could be a copyholder in the literal sense and still be thought of as a tenant in villenage. The change which affected those realities and tended to dissociate the names was the widespread commutation of labor services into money rents. Commutation obliterated the old basis for distinguishing free from unfree services. To preserve the old legal status of holders of customary lands, it was necessary to find an appropriate formula for making grants. The device arrived at was to grant the land in whatever estate the grantor desired and custom warranted—for example, to A and his heirs—and then to add "at the will of the lord according to the custom of the manor." This formula, entered on the court roll and the copy, made two things clear. The phrase "at the will of the lord" made it clear that from the point of view of the common-law network of relationships only an estate at will passed from the grantor. The rest made it clear that from the manorial point of view a fee, life-estate, or whatever, had passed.

The preservation of the legal substance of villein tenure under the guise of copyhold may be seen in such a light that it seems entirely natural, or in another light which makes it something of a historical puzzle. Gradual readjustments without fundamental change is the way things happen, the more so in tradition-bound societies. On the other hand, one ought to ask why, with the waning of personal villenage and the commutation of labor dues, the old system did not more frequently give way to leasehold arangements between landlords and small cultivators. Historical inertia is probably the main key to the existence of copyhold, but it is still worth enquiring whether the customary system did not under the circumstances have palpable economic advantages.

The best reason for a landlord to desert customary demises and go over to short-term common-law leases for years was that such leases might be renegotiated frequently to bring what the traffic would bear, whereas customary tenures were usually for life or hereditary. In addition, a lord might wish to avoid the trouble and expense of court-keeping, though the right to hold court was of course an ancient dignity. Several reasons counted in favor of continuing the old ways. For one thing, insofar as there was a tendency toward leasehold, it was not on the whole a tendency toward short-term, frequently renegotiable, leases. As between, say, leasing for twenty years and letting by copy for life, the choice might be so nearly a matter of indifference that the landlord would naturally continue the traditional way of doing things. A preference for long-term commitments, without regard to the legal arrangement, may be explained in part by the desirability of giving the tenant reason for careful husbandry and maintenance, in part by prevalent conditions of bargaining between landlords and tenants, and in part by social factors which caused landowners to avoid the role of business-like merchants of leases. Secondly, the landlord has an obvious advantage when his tenant is without legal protection independent of the lord and his agents. Finally, even a scrupulous lord who would not use this advantage derives some benefit from the usual incidents of copyhold. The economic effect of these incidents was to make it uncertain at the outset of a tenancy what the lord's profits from the customary relationship would be. Copyholds were characteristically not paid for by rent alone, but by a fine given to the lord at the beginning of the tenancy, plus rent. Moreover, because a new fine fell due whenever a new tenant came to the land by conveyance or inheritance, the grantee who lived longer or held on to his land longer would do the better as against the lord. It is true that leaseholds were also commonly paid for by an initial fine, plus rent. Once purchased, however, the lease was the tenant's chattel property for the duration of the term. Once the lord had received the fine, he had received all that the parcel of land would yield, save for the fixed rent, up to the expiration of the term. But if the land was let by copy, the lord had a distinct chance of realizing more from the parcel of land than a single fine, plus rent, for if the land was conveyed or inherited he would receive a new fine. Besides the dues given when the land was transferred, the lord could anticipate the possibility that the tenant would forfeit his land by breaking one of his customary obligations. The tenant would either lose his tenement or redeem it. (The causes of forfeiture commonly warranted by custom were failure to render rent and other services, such as suit of court; waste; making unwarranted conveyances by common law forms; and felony.) Windfalls have their attractions.

If, in a bad year, a copyholder was unable to pay his rent, his liability to lose family lands would hang over him and perhaps enable the lord to exact something extra in better times, whereas a renter's deficiencies, after the expiration of the lease, are personal debts, which may not be so easily collectible. A customary tenant with a stake in the land, however feeble from the point of view of common law, has a motive to cultivate the soil carefully and to maintain the buildings, which is to the lord's advantage, and which the tenant's liability to forfeiture will reinforce. In sum, one may wonder whether most large landowners would have made more money out of short-term leases than out of the numerous but uncertain possibilities of the customary system. The survival of a great deal of copyhold later on, the countless chances to rent by common-law lease which lords apparently passed up in favor of reletting by copy, must also be explained in part by men's realism about their economic advantage.

Pressures from tenants also help to explain why villenage was transformed rather than replaced. In the key years toward the end of the fourteenth century, free peasants were in a notoriously favorable bargaining position. The peasant might see advantages in holding a lease guaranteed by the common law, certain and predictable with respect to its total cost, and not committing him too far ahead. On the other hand, given the choice, men may easily be tempted to make a long-term arrangement now on what seem favorable terms in preference to risking an unknown future. The legal weakness of a copyhold outside the manor might appear to be offset by the value of an estate for life or of inheritance within the manor, the more so when lords were impoverished of tenants and therefore likely to prove reliable. Though leaseholders had the common law's protection, that protection was remote and expensive and, before the middle of the fifteenth century, not fully adequate. Although, before that time, the leaseholder could recover specific possession of the land against the lessor, he could recover damages only against a stranger.[4] The copyholder, by contrast, had the remedies of the manorial court, which, to the extent that they were effective in fact, were more comprehensive. A peasant who was in a good position to bargain but lacked the capital to buy a freehold might therefore serve himself and his family best by purchasing a copyhold, and men with long-standing vested interests in villein tenements would hardly want to give them up for new relationships.

Because copyhold evolved out of villein tenure by easy steps, because the transition was a realignment of the *status quo* intended to preserve the *status quo,* the change had no immediate consequences in the king's courts at Westminster. The courts of common law merely left things where they stood: no writ lay for villein tenants against the lord and those claiming through him, so no writ lay for copyholders. As some thirteenth-century judges seem to have considered a position more favorable to personally free tenants in villenage, so in the late fourteenth century there is at least one suggestion of a way to protect copyholders.[5] But all the evidence indicates that nothing more came of this attempt than of the earlier one. The common law had to move a considerable distance from the origins of copyhold before it could admit the tenure to protection. Legal history had to be forgotten and distorted and subordinated to legal theory.

The Chancellor was to intervene between lord and copyholder well before the common law did. As will appear in the first study, the evidence will permit, if not endorse, the view that equitable intervention in copyhold matters started early in the fifteenth century, hard upon the emergence of copyhold proper as a widespread tenure. The evidence will also permit the view that the Chancellor did not take notice of copyholders' complaints until the threshold of the sixteenth century. If in fact the Chancellor was deaf to copyholders for a considerable time, his reluctance, like that of the common law, is explicable by the conservative character of copyhold. If the Chancellor would not provide relief, it means that it was still natural to think of a lord's obligation to treat his tenants fairly and honor manorial custom as a charge on his private conscience rather than a charge on the public conscience which the Chancellor represented. Equity may have needed to gain a perspective in which a lord who evicted a copyholder contrary to the custom, or contrary to his own grant, or to the tenant's unjust loss, would appear like other offenders against institutionalized conscience.

If the affinity between villenage and copyhold had needed confirmation in the days when one was splitting off from the other, certain technical features of the tenure would have provided it. Later, when copyhold arrived at legal protection, the historical meaning of these features was blurred, and they received ingenious constructions.

Although in many manors copyholds were granted as estates of inheritance and were in fact inherited, the heirs of copyholds did not enjoy the easy succession of common-law heirs. The lord's right to a fine from the heir was involved with a procedure which marks the tenure's inferiority. The fine was not simply a financial due, but the price of a new grant for life, no different in principle from the fine given by the original grantee. The heir was obliged to present himself as such, to be authenticated as such, in many cases, by the homage, to pay his fine, and then to receive what came to be called admittance to the tenancy. Later law was to conceive admittance as in essence a form, albeit one which must be observed, rather than as a qualification on the estate's heritability. Originally, however, the heir's admittance was probably thought of as a new grant, even though the custom put the lord under a strong obligation to make such grants to heirs. But if admittance is conceived as a new grant, the heir does not take by hereditary succession in a strict sense and is at least nominally dependent on the lord's favor. Probably, however, the original meaning of admittance was obscured at an early date by customs which recognized the heir's right to enter immediately after his ancestor's death, even though his possession would become wrongful if he delayed obtaining admittance too long.[6]

As the heritability of copyhold was qualified in keeping with its humble status, so was its alienability. To transfer a copyhold, it was necessary to surrender it to the lord with a request that he regrant it to the alienee. The term *ad oeps,* "to the use," came to be used in these transactions: a tenement would be surrendered into the lord's hands to the use of A, and A would then pay his fine and obtain admittance. Surrender and admittance were later construed as customary forms by which a conveyance from surrenderor to surrenderee was made. It came to be held that the surrender passes no interest to the lord. The original thought must have been that a villein tenant had no strict right or capacity to dispose of his land, but must literally give up the tenement and ask the lord to grant it to someone in his stead.

The conveyancing procedure of surrender and admittance had the advantage of providing an easy way for copyholds to be devised. The tenant would surrender his land to the use of his will, continue to occupy it at the lord's grace for life, and declare by testament who should have it thereafter. This indirect method of bequeathing land parallels the only medieval device for disposing of normal freeholds by will: a feoffment to the use of one's will and testamentary declaration of the uses. Subsequent law, again by applying the principle that surrenders give the lord only the power and duty to go through the form of admitting the alienee, made copyholds to all intents directly devisable, subject to observation of the customary forms.

If surrender and admittance set customary land apart from common-law land, conveyancing procedure also provides an example of the many analogies between the two kinds of land. As freeholds in most circumstances had to be conveyed by livery of seisin—manual transference of a stick or clod symbolizing transfer of the land on or near which the parties stood—so copyholds were usually conveyed from surrenderor to lord, or lord to grantee, by the handing over of a verge or wand. "Tenants by the verge" was an alternative name for copyholders.

One exception to the procedure of surrender and admittance should be mentioned. Manorial custom often permitted copyholders to make short-term leases, on the order of one year, by word of mouth or deed, just as if they had been common-law tenants. Such customs exempted the copyholder from the liability to forfeiture normally incurred for attempting to convey a copyhold by common-law lease or feoffment, an attempt which would imply the intention of disseising the lord. In addition, the lord might license the copyholder to make a common-law lease for a longer period, thereby waiving his claim to the forfeiture. By asking a price for such licenses, lords could augment their manorial incomes.

In sum, copyhold emerged out of villenage changed in appearance and in dignity but the same tenure at its legal core. The original connection was slurred over, forgotten, and disputed in the sixteenth and seventeenth centuries, when, in the Chancellor's wake, the common law extended its protection to copyholders. Common-law protection was to be achieved by the idea of prescription, the idea that customary tenants should be supported in their estates as those should be who have enjoyed a privilege in fact from time out of mind. Common-law protection was to be limited, however, to the procedures and remedies of the action of trespass and its offshoot, ejectment. This limitation reflects the fact that in the Middle Ages the privileges enjoyed by villein tenants in their manors were indifferent matters to the royal judges. The actions copyholders never won—writs of right, writs of entry, and possessory assizes—were developed to protect the only privileges to occupy and deal with land the central courts were originally interested in, though ejectment later had to be invented for leaseholders. After copyhold arrived at protection, and the real actions more or less contemporaneously fell into disuse, these old common-law actions remained theoretically available to someone at all times. The person entitled to recover a piece of land by these actions was said to have the freehold in the property, even though the identical land was safely held by a copyholder in fee. The freehold was a heritable and alienable interest, even though its owner could not occupy and use the land as long as the copyholder had heirs. As long as the manor remained intact, the lordship of the manor and the freehold in customary land would normally coincide. An exception to this would occur if the lord let the manor for a term of years. The freehold and right to the real actions would then be in the lessor while the lordship, according to the common custom, would go to the lessee for his term, enabling him to grant copies. Thus, in the end, the common law might find itself defending a number of superimposed properties in the same customary land: freehold, leasehold, copyhold. In the Middle Ages there had been comparable layers of interest, but they were sharply divided by lines of jurisdiction and procedure.

2

Insofar as these studies seek to establish facts, their procedures are simple enough. Only their limitations need be pointed out. The first study attempts primarily to establish when the Chancellor began to protect copyholders. It succeeds in setting out arguments for adverse views on this question. I base these arguments mainly on petitions to the Chancellor through the reign of Henry VIII. These documents are preserved in and indexed by the Public Record Office. Printed sources supplement this evidence to some extent. The petitions that can be dated before the accession of Henry VII have been previously investigated, by Alexander Savine in 1902.[7] It seems to me, however, that Savine was too confident of the relevance of his evidence and failed to see its problematic implications. I therefore reconsider all his documents. I then extend the investigation of Chancery petitions through the reigns of the first two Tudors, dealing with documents which were not available to Savine in indexed form. I do not go beyond Henry VIII because I think it is clear that equitable protection for copyholders was established well before the end of that reign. By relying on the Record Office index, I may have missed some copyholders' petitions from within the delimited period. I have, however, made a point of looking up not only those petitions which the index actually describes as concerning copyhold, but also those which are indefinitely described as concerning land and which do not obviously fall under some common and quite different category of Chancery case. Records of decisions in Chancery cases before 1535 are not preserved, unless by chance a decree is endorsed on the petition. It might be worth looking into Orders and Decrees for the last years of Henry VIII's reign, but in the interest of more promising lines of inquiry I have not taken the time to do so. By the time Orders and Decrees start it seems clear that the copyholder was well taken care of. Pleadings in Chancery cases beyond the initial petitions are frequently preserved and frequently used in my arguments. For my brief treatment of the Court of Requests and Star Chamber I have also depended on the Record Office indices. In the case of Star Chamber proceedings, there are still masses of unindexed material, which might of course do violence to my suggestions. In the notes, I have given abstracts of pleadings preserved in the Record Office. Although this practice is no substitute for full reproduction of the documents, they are available in comparatively accessible form in the archives. The volume of this book would be expanded unduly by including an extensive collection of documents which by nature contain a great deal of repetitious and conventional verbiage. On the other hand, I hope that the abstracts, together with occasional commentary on detailed points in the cases, will be a more satisfactory guide to the sources than bare citation.

At the center of my second study is the question of when the common-law courts decided to allow actions to copyholders. The materials I use toward answering this question are for the most part in print and well known. They were used by the principals in a controversy over dating the legal protection of copyholders waged at the end of the nineteenth century. Of the parties to that debate, I. S. Leadam and W. H. Ashley,[8] I am much closer to Ashley. I have made no attempt to refute Leadam point by point. I hope it will be clear from my treatment of much of the same evidence that Leadam frequently misinterpreted the legal sources. The pivot of Leadam's position was his discovery that the Domesday of Enclosures of 1517 does not reveal an appreciable number of copyholders among the evicted. This fact is wholly consistent, however, with the probability that in 1517 copyholders were solely and sufficiently protected by the Chancery and the Conciliar courts. It should not lead one, as I suspect it did Leadam, to look at the common-law evidence through the assumption that protection must have been established by 1517. In putting common-law intervention considerably later, Ashley was in my judgment entirely right. I only attempt to look at more evidence than Ashley did, and to make a more exact guess as to the turning point. To these ends, I have used some unprinted evidence found among the law manuscripts in the British Museum. This material is slight in amount, but possibly decisive.

All statements based on unprinted law reports are subject to the limitation that more material may always be found. Most of the conclusions of my third study are based on such sources. I have not looked beyond the manuscript collections in the British Museum, though I believe I have searched those fairly thoroughly for the sixteenth and early seventeenth centuries. There is no reason to suppose that other manuscript reports, entirely unofficial documents, will not be found elsewhere. Further discoveries might supplement my evidence and modify my conclusions, just as the unprinted cases and reports used here qualify the printed law reports. My third study owes its existence mainly to my discovery that an account of copyhold questions in the Elizabethan courts based on the books would be quite different from one based on both the books and the manuscripts I know about.

In all three of these studies, I have concerns which are not reducible to such straightforward questions as when the Chancellor or the common-law judges decided to intervene, or, in the third study, what positions the Elizabethan courts took on certain technical and definable copyhold issues. Part of the first study is devoted to the grounds on which the Chancellor may have been persuaded to protect copyholders. This problem is closely involved with the further problem of the scope of his protection, the facts that had to be proved before any remedy would be allowed, and the remedy or remedies granted. I ask whether a definite theory is discoverable in virtue of which copyholders were held entitled to equitable redress and which by its nature would have implications for the scope of the court's protection. This inquiry depends in part on a speculative attempt to imagine how copyholders' complaints would appear to the Chancellor, and in part on some tenuous indications which my documents give. Although the pleadings from the reigns of Henry VII and Henry VIII which I use are poor, and perhaps contradictory, evidence, they do contain some features which call for explanation, and the explanations which seem most natural correspond with answers one would tend to give *a priori* to questions about the rationale and scope of the copyholder's standing in equity. If we could start from confident assumptions about the ways in which the Chancellors decided cases, about the traditions which assisted them in discriminating those claims which a court of conscience ought to hear from those best left to the consciences of individuals, it would be easier to reconstruct the manner in which copyholders won a remedy and the character of their equitable rights. In the absence of sufficient general knowledge on this subject, I hope that my tentative suggestions on the history of one aspect of equitable jurisprudence may have some slight value for a wider understanding of the Chancery. In stopping at the end of Henry VIII's reign, I have left untouched later documents which might illuminate the grounds and legal character of copyholders' position in equity. Although the common-law courts became the center of the tenure's history after the middle of the sixteenth century, the Chancellor continued to exercise a supplementary and concurrent jurisdiction. The study of Chancery pleadings, as well as Orders and Decrees, might profitably be carried forward.

In the second study, I am concerned in part with why the common-law judges decided to reverse their previous practice and allow copyholders standing. Motives may be imagined, although an urgent need to insure fundamental justice and to check rural depopulation can hardly be counted among them: the Chancellor was probably already accomplishing these ends. Whatever motives are suggested, they can have done no more than concur with lawyerly reasons. I accordingly devote considerable space to an attempt to reconstruct the intellectual problems presented to the courts by copyholders' claims, the arguments whereby the difficulties were resolved in the copyholder's favor, and the shifts in perspective which made the favorable arguments look more important than the adverse ones. We have no record of a full-dress argument of a case in which the issue of whether or not to allow a copyholder's claim is squarely raised. The process of reconstruction is therefore highly speculative. It depends on faint hints from the sources and on the mere effort to think through the problems in terms of some verisimilitude. A degree of assistance is provided by a small body of early writing on the history of copyhold. It seems possible that the effects of lawyerly logic were reinforced by historical views, however erroneous, current among lawyers.

The third study also involves a certain amount of reconstruction of reasoning. On the whole, however, the materials make it clear how the various issues I deal with were argued. There are many full-scale reports. I have found manuscript reports of numerous cases which give much more exhaustive accounts than printed reports of the same cases. I have reproduced such manuscripts, as well as those of cases not printed at all, in the notes. My principal concern in the third study, beyond establishing the record of argument and decision, is with the bearing of the histories of the issues selected for treatment on the larger history of English jurisprudence. In the first place, copyhold law provides perhaps the best available picture of Elizabethan judges engaged with a new field of law. It is possibly an advantage that this field falls within the area of real property, which was so much the heart of professional interest in that period. It seems to me useful to try to characterize what is distinctive about the way a new field was handled in the prevailing jurisprudential climate, and the development of that field may provide a significant indication of what the climate was. Subject to the hazards of general characterization from so narrow a base, I find in my materials some warrant for believing that Elizabeth's judges acknowledged a high allegiance to legal principles and legal logic somewhat remote from practical necessities. The new field of copyhold law seems to have had more of the quality of a mystery to be searched for its intelligible secrets than of an amorphous object to be reduced to clarity as quickly and consistently as possible.

Reflection on these impressions is complicated by a pattern which seems discernible in the histories of several particular issues. If mere settlement of inevitable problems was not given pre-eminent value, the process of searching out correct solutions seems in several cases to lead away from answers which suggest themselves rather naturally towards higher levels of consistency not unblemished by legal pedantry. Perhaps a difference between the spirit of the earlier Elizabethan courts and that of the courts at the opening of the seventeenth century is reflected in this apparent pattern. Perhaps it only reflects the cumulative criticism of approaches. One should not fail to qualify all such observations and speculations with the emphatic point that patterns can be seen only amid many cross-currents apt to deceive. Characterization of the way in which the judges conceived and did their job is a delicate matter. Confident statements cannot be made from the basis of so narrow an experience as the studies reported in this book provide.

CHAPTER I

THE PROTECTION OF COPYHOLDERS IN EQUITY

I

It has long been recognized that the Chancellor protected copyholders before the common-law courts intervened in their favor.[1] Although it is difficult to say by how far equity was ahead of law, there is still every reason to uphold this view. Almost certainly, there was a time when a grant *ad voluntatem domini secundum consuetudinem manerii* was held by the common law to create only an ordinary tenancy at will, but seemed to the Chancellor to carry heavier consequences. Under appropriate circumstances, this grantee or his successor, though as remediless at common law as a mere tenant at will, could obtain some sort of Chancery decree insuring his continued possession, or at the least preventing loss of his investment.

Alexander Savine, the first student of copyhold cases among the early Chancery proceedings, was inclined to place the Chancellor's intervention well back in the fifteenth century. Other writers have followed his authority.[2] Although Savine's conclusion is supported by a little evidence from outside the Chancery proceedings and certainly cannot be disproved, its tenuousness ought to be appreciated. A brief reconsideration of Savine's cases will therefore be undertaken.

With very few exceptions, no records of decisions in Chancery cases before 1535 survive. This means that conclusions about the early rules of equity must usually be based on one of two types of inference. First, if petitions to the Chancellor, or bills, stating claims of the same sort occur frequently, it may be inferred that they make a good *prima facie* case. Secondly, if pleadings for the defense have survived, and they answer to the merits of the complaint, it may be inferred that the bill was not thought clearly demurrable for substantive insufficiency. That is to say, if the defendant denies some of the material facts, or, admitting them, seeks to excuse himself by advancing further facts, it may be inferred that in the judgment of counsel the bill did not fail to state a good equitable claim. Since, however, Chancery procedure did not force the common law's strict choice between a demurrer and a plea to the merits, and defendants frequently took both courses, reliable conclusions cannot be drawn merely from failure to demur.

For the purpose of discovering how the Chancellor treated copyholders' claims, one must depend primarily on the frequency of bills complaining of expulsion by the lord of the manor or someone to whom he has conveyed the holding in question, of refusal to admit the heir or surrenderee of a copyhold, or of the lord's unwillingness to do justice in his manorial court.

Savine discovered eleven cases prior to the accession of Henry VII, the date at which his study stops. If there are any more, I have not found them. Of the eleven cases, five are manifestly useless for determining whether or not copyholders were protected in their customary estates against the will of the lord. These five are bills to compel persons holding copyholds to the use of others to carry out the trusts.[3] That is to say, a copyhold has been surrendered to the use of X to the use of Y, X has been admitted tenant, and Y is suing to compel X to make estate. The uses limited upon a surrender, which might or might not oblige the lord in equity to make admittance accordingly, are a quite different matter. Inasmuch as the trustee's obligation to fulfill his trust is personal and conscientious, there seems to be no reason why the Chancellor should concern himself with the nature of the trustee's interest. Copyholder or freeholder, he ought still to do what is in his power to see that *cestui que use* has the benefit of the land in whatever way he prefers, whether by taking a conveyance or being suffered to occupy the land and take the profits. The surrenderee to uses ought to make a new surrender to the use of *cestui que use* upon request, even if the lord is free to refuse admittance, or to expel whoever is admitted at any time.

Of the remaining six cases in Savine's collection, two may perhaps be discounted on the same ground as the bills to enforce trusts of copyhold. That is to say, they involve complaints which can be put in familiar classes of Chancery cases, and which quite conceivably could have been remedied without regard to the nature of the petitioner's interest in the land and without prejudice to the lord's arbitrary rights over copyholders.

In one of these two questionable cases,[4] the defendant is the clerk of a manorial court. It is alleged that he failed to enter on the court rolls a conveyance which would entitle the complainant to a copyhold, and the object of the suit is to compel him to perform this clerical act. The claim may be classified as a bill to repair a deficiency in evidences, a very common sort of Chancery case. The complainant seems to be in essentially the same position as a person entitled to freehold lands who, because of some defect in his documents of title, cannot assert his right. The complainant here cannot petition for and obtain admittance against the probably conclusive evidence of the court rolls. Even if it were certain that copyholders had no equitable recourse against their lords, there would be no strong reason why the Chancellor should not require a clerk to perform his office conscientiously. Though the lord were held free in conscience to put out copyholders at will, there is no reason why an uninterested third party such as the clerk should be free by negligence or malice to endanger another man's interest, albeit a legally fragile one. Only if one assumes (and the assumption is not unreasonable) that the Chancellor would not intervene in manorial affairs at all unless he held the lord liable to respect customary estates does this case count as evidence that copyholders were significantly protected in equity. The defendant's answer, which is preserved in this case, does not affect this analysis. The clerk simply says that he did enter the surrender in question and that the complainant can find it if he makes search.

The other case of dubious meaning[5] is more obscure and more complicated. The defendant is not the lord, but one Nicholl, who is alleged to be in possession of a copyhold to which the complainant is entitled by descent. Nicholl is said to have bought the reversion after the death of the complainant's ancestor, and to have entered when that ancestor died. If the copyhold was heritable, the lord ought not to have granted the reversion. If, in granting it, he intended to exericse his will against the complainant and in Nicholl's favor, Nicholl's right to the land would be as good as the lord's right to disregard customary titles, and the case would be significant for the copyholder's basic security. Instead of putting his case on this ground, however, and asserting a right adverse to the lord, the petitioner states a cause of action which is common in the Chancery. He alleges that Nicholl has constantly threatened to "beat and mayhem" him, so that he is afraid to enter upon the tenement or "pursue" for it. The claim may therefore be assimilated to those in which a person entitled at common law asks the Chancellor's help because the adverse party's intimidating conduct, power, influence, or bribery obstructs the normal course of the law. It seems perfectly possible that the Chancellor could hold that the lord had no duty to respect customary estates, and at the same time that a person in Nicholl's position was obliged to refrain from the use of terror. Nicholl might be entitled as the beneficiary of the lord's will and yet not be free to use the threat of force to prevent the complainant from taking his case to the manorial court and doing what he could to convince the lord that his was the better customary right and hence the better claim on the lord's favor.

On the other hand, it may be argued that if the Chancellor would intervene in this case he would probably also compel the lord to respect copyhold estates. The bill, like most of those in similar cases involving common-law rights, asks that the substance of the matter be tried in the Chancery, that Nicholl be examined concerning the property dispute. Suppose that he were so examined and it were found that by the custom the estate was heritable and the complainant entitled. One would then expect the Chancellor to make a decree enjoining Nicholl from intermeddling with the land. Such a decree would imply that when the lord granted the reversion to Nicholl he either could not or would not violate the custom, either that he intended to violate it and thereby failed in an equitable duty, or that he had no such intention but merely made a mistake. Unless the lord were examined, there would be no reason to conclude that his will was to observe the custom in all particulars. If Nicholl relied in the Chancery suit on his better customary right alone, there would be no occasion to examine the lord. In that case, the decree must either be based on the consideration that the lord's will is irrelevant, or on the consideration that since Nicholl relied on the custom alone he in effect admitted that he did not enjoy the favor of the lord except insofar as it was consistent with the custom. The problems raised by this line of reasoning would of course not exist if the Chancellor would go no further than to require Nicholl to give surety against hindering the complainant from manorial process. On the whole, it seems possible that the claim in this case could be good without regard for the copyholder's rights against the lord, but doubts can be raised.

The bill against Nicholl contains two other features of unclear significance. The petitioner says he requested the steward to restore him to the tenement and that he offered to pay double the accustomed fine if restored. Secondly, he claims to have offered to pay Nicholl the sum which the latter gave for his interest. These allegations do not seem to add to his claim on any theory. The application to the steward seems to have been an attempt to secure his assistance privately, not a regular manorial proceeding. Perhaps the two offers to pay unowed money do little credit to the strength of the complainant's title. The case is generally confusing; its one clear feature is its similarity to many Chancery cases having nothing to do with copyholds.

Savine's four remaining cases are all in point, but not altogether free of complications. One of them may not belong to the fifteenth century at all.[6] It is addressed simply to the Archbishop of Canterbury, who might as well be one of the archbishops who held the Chancellorship after Henry VII's accession as an earlier one. The case involves land in the manor of Great Hormead, Hertfordshire, and the bill reveals that the lord was the Earl of Oxford. However, except for the years 1471–1485, when they were deprived for political reasons, the Earls of Oxford owned the manor throughout the fifteenth century and most of the sixteenth.[7] If there is any reason for cataloguing the documents under Henry VI, I am unaware of it.

Whatever the date, the case is good evidence of the lord's liability in equity. The bill alleges that one of the three complainants was wrongfully expelled from a copyhold by the farmer of the manor, who is defendant. The other two complainants claim that in the course of this eviction certain of their goods were wrongfully appropriated, and that the defendant and his adherents "lie in wait to beat and slay [them] so that they dare not abide in their houses." The defendant answers these three charges separately. As to the taking of the goods and the lying in wait, he excepts to the Chancellor's jurisdiction, saying that these matters are determinable at common law, and then proceeds, as is common in Chancery cases, to deny the substance of the allegations. As to the eviction, he significantly does not except to the jurisdiction. He answers by alleging that the first complainant, who was tenant, refused to pay the services, wherefore the understeward, at the lord's command, entered, after which he let the land to the defendant for years. The implication of this answer is that the lord's right of entry, upon which the defendant's title to possession depends, had to be justified by the custom. Because the copyholder, by withholding his services, committed forfeiture, the lord was entitled to enter; hence, by implication, the lord would have had no right of entry, in contemplation of equity, if there had been no forfeiture.

The initial bill in another case[8] is plainly based on the theory that the lord must observe the custom. It alleges simply that the lord, defendant, has refused to admit the petitioner to a copyhold which should be his by virtue of a conveyance to his ancestor and descent to him. Alongside this bill, however, there survives another bill concerning the same alleged right to the same land. This second bill names as defendants the steward of the manor and one John Colcock. It is alleged that the steward refused to enter the conveyance to the complainant's ancestor on the court rolls, because Colcock claimed a joint-tenancy with the surrenderor at that time. Colcock is said to support his claim by a certain document made at the time of the original grant, but according to the complainant his name does not appear on the court rolls or copy. Nevertheless, the lord "is advised to make livery of the said . . . land to the said Colcock and not to the said suppliants." It is requested that Colcock and the steward be examined about the truth of the matter, and that the steward be required to bring the court rolls with him.

Unfortunately, no further pleadings survive. Interpretation of the case depends upon the relation between the two bills. Savine suggests that the lord probably justified himself, whereupon the complainant tried another approach. This is possible, but there are certain difficulties in the way. If the claim in the second bill is reasonable at all, the lord must have justified himself by showing that Colcock was entitled. If he pleaded this, the truth of Colcock's claim should have been determined in the trial of the first suit. Alternatively, the lord might have interpleaded Colcock. In either event, there would seem to be no need for a second suit to find out whether the lord was right in preferring Colcock. It seems more probable, therefore, that the first bill was either withdrawn as unpromising or defeated on demurrer, after which the complainant resorted to the second. If this is what happened, the two documents together are evidence that lords were not liable to their copyholders in 1437–38, when these bills were brought. The second bill, like those discussed above, might state a good cause of action despite the copyholder's impotence against the lord. It is essentially an evidentiary bill. The main point is to set the court rolls straight, and the Chancellor might be willing to help men repair this sort of evidence as well as any other.

The next case[9] is much more acceptable evidence of equitable protection for copyholders in the fifteenth century. The defendant, Gybon, is the lord. The bill says that the father of Kyngesden, complainant, was seised of a copyhold in fee and died seised. Kyngesden should have inherited, but "because your beseecher was in the field with our sovereign liege lord, the King that now is, at Shirborn in helmet, and it was noised . . . that your said beseecher was slain there, one Amy, pretending to be daughter and heir to the said John, entered into the said mease." Kyngesden then returned and sued his sister Amy and her husband in the manorial court. The homage found that Kyngesden was son and heir. Kyngesden then paid his fine for admittance, as well as arrears of rent. Nevertheless, Gybon has refused to give judgment on the verdict, "supposing wrongfully to have the said mease to his own use."

To this bill, which plainly seeks to hold the lord to observance of customary rights, Gybon answers. He says that his only personal claim is to take the profits during the litigation between Kyngesden and Amy, as the custom permits. No judgment has been given because the verdict is defective, the homage having found that Kyngesden was son and heir to his father, but not that the father died seised of the tenement in dispute. If the homage will present the latter fact, the complainant shall have what "right and justice requiren."

For replication, Kyngesden says that Gybon has impliedly admitted that his father died seised, so that it does not matter whether the homage presented this. But he adds that the fact of his dying seised was presented.

Gybon's rejoinder is partly illegible, but its purport is clear. Various details of the suit between Kyngesden and Amy are added. It is said that Amy's husband, who was codefendant, died in the course of the litigation, so that according to the custom Kyngesden should have started a new suit, which he has not done. Secondly, Amy claimed that her father had conveyed the land to her and her husband in fee. The homagers said they had no knowledge of this conveyance and prayed a respite until they could look into the matter. Apparently they had not come to any determination, for Gybon prays that the Chancellor examine those in whose presence the disputed conveyance was purportedly made, "so that the very truth to this court may be known." Finally, Gybon alleges that a majority of the homage presented that Kyngesden's father had forfeited the tenement. This, Gybon now says, is the reason he first seized the land into his own hands. However, he apparently does not want to claim the land for himself by virtue of the forfeiture, for he says, "this notwithstanding, the said John Gybon is ready to do that [which] this court will award."

Gybon's pleadings perhaps reduce the value of the case as evidence of the Chancellor's willingness to enforce customary rights contrary to the will of the lord. They indicate that Gybon is ready to do whatever the custom demands, and that he has no desire to insist upon his possible right to a forfeiture. He gives the impression of being somewhat harassed by the complainant's involved lawsuit with his sister. He would apparently welcome the Chancellor's assistance to discover the truth about the disputed conveyance, of which his homage was ignorant. Perhaps, therefore, Gybon had no motive to resist the suit against him and considerable motive to plead the case to an issue which the Chancellor could investigate to Gybon's own convenience. If copyholders' suits were demurrable, Gybon was not the man to demur. Otherwise, the case is entirely in point.

About the remaining one of Savine's eleven cases[10] there is happily nothing to be said. It is a straightforward complaint that the defendant, lord of the manor, "against his own grant and court rolls hath put out the said beseechers." It comes from the relatively early date of 1440 or 1441, and no other pleadings survive.

None of the objections that can be made to Savine's cases is conclusive. It may be reasonably argued that most of these suits were brought on the assumption that the Chancellor would compel lords to observe customary rights, and that there are enough suits to justify believing that that assumption was correct. But the contrary may also be reasonably argued. It could be concluded with a good deal of justification that before the accession of the Tudors copyholders were given a hearing in Chancery only when they were able to avoid a direct challenge to the will of the lord. If there is any advantage in the hypothesis that the equitable protection of copyholders probably began in the atmosphere of official concern for the preservation of rural life under Henry VII, the early Chancery proceedings hardly stand in the way.

With a little more qualification, the same may be said of evidence outside the Chancery proceedings themselves. In a famous case of 1467,[11] about which more will be said when the history of the tenure in the common-law courts is taken up, mention was made of the copyholder's position in equity. In this case, Chief Justice Danby pronounced his well-known dictum that copyholders should be able to bring trespass against their lords. Justice Littleton, by way of objection to Danby's opinion, spoke as follows:

> Jeo veia un foitz un Sub pena port par tiel tenant envers son seignor, & fuit tenuz par toutz les justices que il ne recover rien par cel. Quar fuit tenuz que lentre le seignor fuit congeable sur lui entant que il est tenant a volunte . . .

To this, Danby replied:

> Le jugement en le Sub pena fuit a ma entent. Il fuit daver recoverie de franktenement, quar il ne puit aver nul auter brief pur recover le franktenement . . .

How is this exchange to be interpreted? Most obviously, it indicates that copyholders' suits in the Chancery were anything but commonplace. Littleton remembers one such suit and thinks it was unfavorable to the copyholder. The two judges have conflicting memories of it. Their interchange could hardly have taken place if, before 1467, intervention between lord and copyholder was an established practice, a familiar part of the Chancellor's jurisdiction.

Exactly what Danby and Littleton disagree about is not so clear. Since Littleton speaks of the opinion of all the justices, it would seem that the common-law judges were consulted as assistants in the Chancery case. The most straightforward reading of the report is to suppose that Littleton and Danby have flatly contradictory recollections of what the justices thought and accordingly of how the case was decided. But there is another possibility. The emphasis in Danby's remark may be put in either of two places. If he said "Le jugement en le Sub pena fuit a *ma* entent," he must have been contradicting Littleton absolutely. But suppose he said "Le *jugement* . . . fuit a ma entent." Then one might reconstruct what happened as follows: The judges were asked for an opinion and said that as far as they were concerned the copyholder is a mere tenant at will, and no special considerations entitle him to greater security than other such tenants. In view of this clear statement of the impotence of copyholders at common law, the Chancellor thereupon gave judgment in the copyholder's favor. On this construction, Danby meant that the Chancellor failed to follow the advice of the justices, holding, perhaps, that the legal impotence of the copyholder did not entail equitable impotence, or even that his legal weakness, attested to by the justices, was a reason for equitable assistance.

In either event, Danby's view of the Chancellor's position is supported by another scrap of evidence. Fitzherbert's *Abridgement* contains the following entry under 32 Henry VI (1453–1454):[12]

> Tenaunt a volunte par copy de court Rolle aver sub pena vers son seignour sil luy oust par Kyrbb et Pole en le Chauncery.

Perhaps this brief report refers to the same case that Danby and Littleton were debating about in 1467. There is no reliable way of telling whether it is a report of an actual holding or merely of a statement by counsel. There is no Kyrbb among the justices. Possibly the name could be a corruption of "Kirkeby," Thomas Kirkeby having been Master of the Rolls from 1447 to 1461. If Pole is the Ralph Pole who became a judge in the King's Bench in 1452,[13] the report might be taken as a decision of the Master of the Rolls and a Justice Assistant. If so, the report is of course significant.

Once again, there is enough evidence to enforce the supposition that by the middle of the fifteenth century copyholders' suits against their lords had been allowed in the Chancery. One might reasonably suggest that the earlier decisions were reaffirmed later, that with growing confidence in the availability of a remedy, suits became more frequent, and before the accession of Henry VII equity had taken an irreversible stand on the copyholder's rights. On the other hand, the evidence is so slight, one could justifiably conclude that before 1485 successful Chancery suits by copyholders were rare and isolated at best—so much so that prospective litigants and their lawyers probably hesitated to bring suit, especially if there was a chance of compromise. There was too little practice to establish a tradition, and in the absence of a tradition it is quite possible that some Chancellors refused to allow a remedy. Such a reconstruction is entirely plausible if one takes most of Savine's cases as, at best, weak evidence, at worst, evidence that a direct challenge to the lord's will was impossible; if one emphasizes the uncertainty of two judges in 1467 about how a copyholder's suit in Chancery had been handled and the clear implication of their words that such suits were by no means common; if one takes note of the doubtful nature of the report of 1452–53; and finally, if one observes that Littleton's *Tenures* says nothing about an equitable remedy for copyholders, unless his remark that "le seignour ne voet (in some versions 'poet') infreinder le custom que est reasonable en tielx cases" is taken as a reference to a restraint imposed by the Chancellor.[14]

By contrast, the evidence is strong that the Chancellor's intervention was routine by the end of Henry VII's reign. From 1486–1504, I have found eight cases directly in point.[15] Of these, six fall between 1493 and 1502.[16] The bills in all these cases seek to compel the lord, or someone whose right is as good as the lord's, to respect customary estates against his will. In the only case where pleadings beyond the bill are preserved, there is an answer to the merits.[17] I have found some sixty cases which can certainly or probably be assigned to Henry VIII's reign.[18] Though statistically these cases are a very small part of the preserved Chancery records, they are compelling evidence.

2

Although the records make it sufficiently clear that the Chancellor provided some sort of protection for copyholders in the early sixteenth century, they speak less clearly on the scope and nature of that protection and the reasons why it was bestowed. For the moment, let us leave the documents out of account and merely try to imagine how copyholders' claims would have looked to the ecclesiastical magnates who sat as Chancellors in the fifteenth and early sixteenth centuries.

There is a sense in which equitable protection almost had to come about, given the reluctance of the common law. If one is looking for motives arising from considerations of public policy, one need only point out that the Chancellors could hardly have avoided the anxiety over rural depopulation which prompted so much legislative and administrative activity and so much polemic. In addition, the sense that it was foolish to depress the merchantability of copyholds by perpetuating their legal nakedness may have figured as a motive. On the plane of casuistry and legal reasoning, it can be argued in several ways that the lord of a manor who evicts a copyholder violates duties appropriately enforced by a court of conscience. For one thing, he violates the duty of the strong to deal charitably toward the weak. For another, there is a fundamental unfairness about evicting a man to whom one has made a grant which, even though ambiguous, seems to assure him a certain estate, and from whom one has taken money plainly given in consideration of the expectation that such estate may be enjoyed. To treat such a grantee as an ordinary tenant at will is to pay heed to his technical classification while ignoring the understandings and assumptions of the parties to the grant. Finally, it is wrong to violate rights sanctioned by custom, even though the custom of the king's courts of common law will not permit them to be vindicated there.

Taken as a whole, the copyholder's case in equity seems a strong one, strong enough to permit the motives of national policy that may have weighed with the Chancellor to be easily implemented. Longstanding habits of leaving manorial affairs to landlords may have temporarily dissuaded the Chancellor from intervening. Among possible inhibiting factors one should also count such general principles of self-restraint as may have belonged to the traditions of the court. It is true that the Chancellor exercised a discretionary jurisdiction. The jurisprudence associated with the court is posited on general and far-reaching moral principles. On the other hand, one might expect the Chancery to share in the nature of law courts to the extent of becoming in some degree bound to its precedents and in some degree inclined to look for reasons against taking on new types of cases. There are many circumstances in which men could plausibly claim that the weaknesses of their legal positions and the legal privileges of their adversaries were contrary to good conscience. Some such claims were favored by the Chancellor. Those consistently favored form the familiar categories of English equity.[19] Other claims must have failed. It must sometimes have been decided that the interests of good conscience must be left to the consciences of individuals and the sanctions of community opinion. We do not know how many claims of some merit failed or how many anomalous claims, outside the familiar classes, succeeded. Nor do we know the criteria by which the obligations of conscience worthy of public enforcement were distinguished from those deemed unworthy.[20] Apart from any deliberate and abstractly conceived criteria, the court's inclination in practice may have been to follow the guide of precedents and disallow claims which did not at least resemble familiar types of complaint. It is not impossible that copyholders' claims, however good from a moral point of view, were for a time regarded as appropriately left to private conscience. Their distinctiveness may have caused them to be so regarded. Their ultimate acceptance may have come about because lawyers persuaded the Chancellor that they resembled in a significant way claims already acceptable to the court.

It is not sufficient, in any case, to explain the Chancellor's reception of copyholders' claims by pointing to their equitable strength in general. The very fact that that strength has several elements creates a problem. It must be asked whether one of the equitable arguments which might have been used was in practice urged upon the Chancellor with particular emphasis, with the result that it came to be regarded as the basis for copyholders' standing in the court and the theory on which complainants should draw their bills. This question is important because the scope of protection afforded might well depend on what the accepted basis for claims was.

Two of the arguments for the copyholder seem likely candidates to provide a clear and exclusive theory, if there was such a theory. Let us distinguish them as (i) the argument from the character of the transaction between lord and copyholder, and (ii) the argument from customary rights.

(i) The first argument says that in granting by copy, and accepting a fine as consideration, the lord has given an assurance that the manorial estate conveyed will be respected. The lord's action has induced the grantee to rely on being allowed to enjoy the land for the duration of that estate. It is therefore inequitable for the lord to take advantage of his common-law privilege to put the tenant out at will.

It would not be surprising, in the light of the general character of equitable remedies, for the Chancellor to find this argument particularly persuasive. Although it is no doubt true that the obligations of conscience enforced by equity contain several casuistical strains, equity was perhaps more than anything else concerned with preventing men from enjoying the legally uncontrollable fruits of deceitful and misleading behavior. It was largely concerned with protecting those who, with some color of reason, trust that those with whom they deal will act in accord with what is naturally understood when they deal together and not seek to exploit the strict legal rights which a sharp diligence might discover.

If we assume that the assurance implied in the grant and the reliance inevitably induced formed the crux of the lord's equitable duty to respect copyhold estates, several inferences may be drawn, and several questions must be asked:

(1) It would seem that anyone who grants any piece of land by the standard copyhold formula in a sense assures the grantee that he may enjoy a life-estate, fee, or whatever; any such grant is likely to induce reliance. This is so even if the land in question is not customary land, or even if it does not lie within a manor. Does it follow that the grantor of such land is as much obliged to permit the enjoyment of a fee or life estate as the grantor of proper customary land? Although the case raises a problem, I do not think the consequence is necessary. It may be argued principally that the grantee in such case may not rely with sufficient color of reason on what the grant seems to assure. If the land does not lie in a manor at all, it may be further argued that the grant is meaningless except as it conveys an estate at will. For if the grant is to X and his heirs according to the custom of the manor of Dale, and there is no such manor, it is impossible to say precisely what estate has been assured him. Some specific manorial custom is necessary to define the incidents of the estate. It seems possible, therefore, that the lord's obligation could arise from the character of the transaction and the custom still be relevant in equity.

Suppose, however, that X claims to have been evicted from a copyhold duly granted him and the defendant answers that the land is not customary. Let us grant that in itself this is a good defensive plea. It remains a question what the defendant has to show to sustain it. Suppose that the evidence shows (a) that the land lies within the manor of Vale, (b) that for the past forty years it has been held by copyhold tenants, and (c) that earlier than forty years ago the tenement was not within the customary lands of the manor, but was held by a succession of freehold or leasehold tenants. By the standards which the common law was to apply to the validation of copyholders' claims, the complainant here has no case. The land is not customary because it has not always been customary; it is not affected by a special law capable of raising rights because, as far as this tenement is concerned, such special law does not stretch back beyond legal memory. In equity, however, on the assumption that the lord's duty arises from the nature of the transaction but that the custom is relevant, the complainant might have a good case. The land has been held under copyhold grants long enough to give it the reputation of customary land. It is a reasonable supposition that the complainant and his grantor proceeded under the impression that a proper customary title was conveyed. The tenant relied with color of reason. The manorial rules governing proper customary land may be taken to define the incidents of the estate assured to the tenant.

(2) If the lord's obligation originates from the nature of the transaction, it has the personal quality of pure equitable duties. The question then arises whether or not the duty incumbent on a particular grantor would be capable of passing to another person. This question occurs in two forms.

(a) Suppose the lord of a manor grants to X by copy and dies. Is the lord's heir bound to respect X's manorial estate? If A is lord of the manor for life and grants a copy and dies, is the reversioner bound? If B is lord and enfeoffs C of the entire manor, is C bound? Does it matter whether C had express knowledge that his feoffor's conscience was bound? Would accession to the entire manor and its court rolls be taken as presumptive notice of outstanding copyholds? Or would C's right to receive the copyholders' rent take the place of notice?

(b) Suppose the lord grants a copyhold to X and then grants the same tenement, but not the entire manor, to Y, either by copy or by common-law conveyance. Is Y bound to stay off the land and bear the loss? Or does Y's liability depend on whether or not he is a *bona fide* purchaser for value, that is, on whether or not he had notice of X's equity? To all these questions one is probably inclined to answer that the equitable duties of the grantor would pass to subsequent purchasers, whether of the manor or the particular tenement, but that they would so pass only if such subsequent purchaser had notice, actual or presumptive, of the prior copyhold. This solution is in keeping with the principle of equitable jurisprudence that when A is bound in conscience to refrain from exercising his full legal rights over a piece of property, subsequent purchasers are likewise bound if they knew about the circumstances from which A's obligation arose. Good conscience requires that one who takes title to property knowing that the prior owner was subject to equitable duties shall observe the same duties.

(3) The question also arises whether the lord's duty would extend to anyone except the person to whom he made the copyhold grant. Suppose a copyhold is granted to X and his heirs, and X dies. Is the lord obliged in conscience to admit the person whom the custom designates as heir? On the one hand, it seems that the grantor gave an assurance that X and his heirs might enjoy the equivalent of a fee. On the other hand, because fines for copyholds usually fell due on each change of tenant, it is arguable that under normal circumstances X would not have given consideration for more than a life-estate. Similarly, is the lord obliged to admit someone to whose use X has surrendered his tenement? It might be argued here that a further act on the lord's part, acceptance of the surrender, begets a further duty. It remains questionable whether any duty is owed to the surrenderee, with whom the lord has had no direct transaction and from whom he has taken no money.

(4) If the assurance which the lord gives and the reliance he induces generate his obligation, there is a question as to how the obligation must be discharged. Must the lord suffer his grantee to occupy the land for the duration of the manorial estate? Or might he

clear his conscience by making good any actual loss incurred by the tenant, that is, by refunding the fine and compensating the tenant for any expenses undertaken in the expectation that he would be allowed to enjoy the full estate?

(5) Finally, a point of procedure arises as to how a copyholder should draw his bill in the Chancery. Is it sufficient to allege a grant and the payment of a fine, without making an elaborate claim to the effect that the land has been demised by copy from time out of mind and continuously enjoyed by customary tenants (leaving it to the defense to invoke the custom insofar as that is relevant)? Is it requisite, on the other hand, to allege actual, or even substantial, loss incurred by relying on the grant?

(ii) The second argument, from customary rights, says that the copyholder has in essence legal title to his tenement. By virtue of its immemorial history, the custom of the manor has the status of law. For as long as memory extends, the custom has put certain lands of the manor in a special category. It has permitted those lands to be granted by copy in such and such estate, and it has regarded the duly admitted tenants of those lands as owners within whatever precise meaning it gives to ownership. Such rights of ownership have been upheld and defined by the manorial court. The common law, because of its own traditions, allows no actions to the copyholder expelled or excluded from a tenement which the custom designates as his. The normal remedy of a copyholder whose manorial ownership has been interfered with is in the manorial court. If, however, such interference comes from the lord, the manorial court, where he or his agent presides, cannot be expected to give the tenant effective protection in fact and perhaps will not be procedurally equipped to do so. In such cases, it is appropriate for the Chancellor to invoke his extraordinary jurisdiction and see that the copyholder enjoys such rights as the custom gives him.

Such use of the Chancellor's powers would not be surprising, even though it is different from his enforcement of obligations of conscience which were not obligations of law. It was very common for the Chancery to enforce rights capable as a matter of law of being vindicated in the king's courts of common law but incapable as a matter of fact of being so vindicated. Corrupted jurors and the excessive local influence or intimidating conduct of one of the parties were the common factual impediments to justice which drove men to the Chancery. Vindication of manorial rights insofar as the manorial court is incapable of enforcing them is analogous to vindication of common-law rights which the common-law courts could not enforce. If the Chancellor was persuaded by this line of argument, his position would have contradicted that taken by the contemporary common-law courts only insofar as the latter disputed that the rights arising under manorial custom were in fact immemorial. Insofar as the common law was merely prevented by its own traditions from allowing copyholders a remedy, the Chancellor would not be contradicting it.

If we assume that the Chancellor was persuaded to protect copyholds as "legal" interests practically and procedurally unprotectable elsewhere, the inferences to be drawn are quite different from those drawn on the alternative assumption discussed above:

(1) A complainant's right to recover would be as good, and only as good, as the right which in other circumstances the manorial court would defend. A showing that the land in question had not continuously figured among the manor's customary lands, or that it was not demisable by copy in the estate claimed, would defeat his case. There is no way of knowing precisely what proof would be held sufficient to show that land was customary, or whether evidence to the contrary would be held incompetent if it was too old. These questions were to give the common law trouble in the future. But in principle it would be necessary to prove that the land had been affected by an immemorial manorial law.

(2a) The normal custom was that any rightful *dominus pro tempore* might grant copies binding on all those subsequently seised of the manor, whether by descent, purchase, or accrual of an estate in reversion or remainder.[21] Under this custom, a claimant would have as good a case against his grantor's successors as against the grantor himself.

(2b) If the defendant was not the lord, but someone to whom the particular tenement had been conveyed after the complainant took his copyhold estate, the case could only reach the Chancery if the manorial court could not or would not provide a remedy. (If the subsequent purchaser was a copyholder, the manorial court would of course have jurisdiction. It could only fail to provide a remedy as a matter of fact, because of bias on the lord's part or some disturbance of the process of justice by other persons comparable to the interferences which drove many common-law cases into the Chancery. If, however, the subsequent purchaser was a common-law lessee or a feoffee, there would seem to be some question about the manorial court's jurisdiction over him.) Having reached the Chancery, such a case should be settled precisely as it would be settled in the manorial court, granted that the manorial court had jurisdiction: whoever had the better manorial title should win. It would be irrelevant whether the subsequent purchaser took in good faith, without notice.

(3) The lord should be obliged to admit heirs and surrenderees insofar as the custom could be construed as bestowing the equivalent of ownership in fee and the right to alienate freely, subject to fines and forms. The lord's obligation to admit surrenderees might, however, be conceived differently. If it is granted that the copyholder has a property interest in the tenement under manorial law, a surrender to the use of another could be taken as a conveyance in trust. The lord would be bound in conscience to admit the beneficiary, just as a feoffee to uses was obliged to make estate. The common law was subsequently to hold that surrenders are not actual conveyances to the lord, but there is no reason why the Chancellor should have taken this position.

(4) If the copyholder's right is "legal," it is a right to occupy the land. The remedy would almost certainly be a decree enjoining the defendant from interfering with the complainant's possession.

(5) Bills drawn under the second theory should take some trouble to plead the custom. It should not be necessary to allege actual loss: under this theory, either the land is the complainant's by the appropriate property law, or it is not.

Although the two theories just discussed are alternatives, it is possible that they could be combined in the following way: Let us assume that the Chancellor was persuaded by the argument from customary rights and that copyholders ordinarily brought their bills on the theory that their rights were "legal" in nature. It does not follow that a person who lacked a good claim under this theory could not recover under the other one. The Chancellor may have been persuaded *both* that the duly admitted tenants of true customary land are in the nature of legal owners and entitled to whatever extraordinary assistance is necessary to maintain their prescriptive rights *and* that the transaction between grantor by copy and grantee raises a merely equitable right. It would then be possible for a grantee of land not strictly customary to recover under appropriate circumstances. It would also be possible for a claimant to choose to assert the equitable right generated by his transaction with the lord and thereby avoid the hazards and difficulties of proving the custom. Finally, under the relatively informal pleading rules of the Chancery, it would be possible for a complaint to incorporate claims based on both theories.

I do not believe that the Chancery pleadings will prove that the court was persuaded by one or the other of the two theories, or that they will give certain indications of the scope of protection. The pleadings do, however, contain some features which point to one of the two approaches, some which point to the other. The best procedure for examining the evidence will be to classify it according as it reveals different features of possible significance for understanding the rationale and practical character of equitable protection.

(i) One feature that is conspicuous in numerous bills suggests the first theory, namely, that the Chancellor regarded copyholders' rights as arising from the nature of their transaction with the lord, rather than from the custom as such. It is common, though not universal, for complainants to allege that they have paid a fine and to specify the amount. It is also frequently alleged that expenses have been incurred for building and other improvements.[22] Little can be made of the fines. If the essence of the claim were customary title as such, it might still be necessary to show that the title was matured and forfeiture avoided by payment of the customary fine, and there is no reason why the exact amount should not be made part of the record. But the expenses are another matter. If the complainant had only to make out a good customary title, why should it make any difference whether he had spent money on improvements or not? Either the land is his under the special law of the manor or it is not, whatever he has done with it.

The allegation of expenses, and perhaps also the care complainants take to show just how much money they have paid for a fine, seem to me to admit of two explanations, assuming that these features of the bills are not surplusage. If no other evidence stood in the way, they would perhaps point to the first theory. They would suggest that the Chancellor was not satisfied with a showing of customary title, that he was still ready to protect copyholders from what amounts to fraudulent dealing, but that he would do so only upon proof that the complainant had parted with value in consideration of the lord's implied assurance. It would seem, however, that the allegation of a fine, without regard to expenses, would be sufficient to fulfill this requirement, unless a small fine, amounting perhaps to a year's rent, were held to be too little consideration. The additional allegation of expenses would make better sense if the remedy were limited to monetary compensation, or at least if decrees gave the defendant the alternative of paying money or allowing the successful complainant to enjoy the land. There are a few cases in which petitioners apparently seek only pecuniary recompense.

The other possible explanation is that both the first and the second theories were used. A complainant who had a good customary title could recover on that, but in case one could not prove a custom, or did not want to incur the risk and trouble of doing so, one could rely on an equitable right to enjoy what had been granted for value and under such circumstances as to raise a reasonable expectation of enjoyment. Again, without customary right one perhaps could recover only damages and not the land itself. This explanation has the advantage of consistency with the evidence, to be considered shortly, which tends to contradict the other one.

(ii) One other feature of certain bills points to the first theory, whether or not the second was used jointly with it.[23] Some complainants seem to be assuming the applicability of the rule that purchasers in good faith without notice of outstanding equities are free from those obligations. For they take care to allege that the defendant—in such cases always a subsequent purchaser from the lord of the copyhold claimed by the petitioner—received his grant with knowledge of the complainant's interest. Such allegations can easily be explained if the first theory alone was operative, or if it could be invoked when a strict customary title could not be established. Indeed, there is one situation in which it may be doubtful whether such a strict title can ever be established. Suppose the lord, A, grants a copyhold to X and thereafter enfeoffs B of the same tenement apart from the manor as a whole. This transaction was said to sever the tenement from the manor. Consequently there is some difficulty in allowing X to invoke the custom of a manor from which his land is now detached. The common law was later to hold, probably largely on grounds of policy, that X's interest is unaffected by the severance and B cannot put him out.[24] It is conceivable that at an earlier time the Chancellor held that in this case X does not have a good customary title and is therefore at B's mercy unless he can show that B took his estate with notice of the copyhold already in being. B's obligation in that event woud be purely conscientious, but this would not prevent the lord's from being legal, in the sense of depending on immemorial custom.

(iii) There are a few cases in which the complainant plainly does not have a good customary title but seeks a remedy because of equitable circumstances in his favor.[25] The acceptability of such claims would obviously not imply that a copyholder having a good customary title could not recover on that alone. It means only what one would expect: that the Chancellor would not be bound by the customary, or "legal," rights of a case if they were contrary to good conscience. These cases may, however, have a bearing on the question of what would happen in the case of the copyholder who alleged a fine and expenses. On the whole, the equitable circumstances in these cases seem hardly stronger than the situation of the ordinary grantee by copy who had given a fine for his estate and perhaps invested still more money trusting in its durability, though this is certainly challengeable in particular cases. It may be argued that if a man plainly without customary title could sometimes claim the right to be treated as he should be treated in law if he and his predecessors really had enjoyed special privileges from time immemorial, then probably ordinary copyhold grantees could claim the right to be so treated without proof of strict customary title and even in the face of evidence rebutting such title. One might then go on to suggest that since equitable grounds for relief were available in the normal case—for after all practically every copyholder paid a fine—the Chancellor probably had no need to pass judgment on the "legal" situation of copyhold grantees or to develop a remedy for those who confined themselves to asserting a customary right. Such a conclusion would square with a good deal of the evidence, but unfortunately not with all of it.

(iv) Finally, there are several types of evidence that support the second theory, namely, that the Chancellor regarded copyholders' rights as customary in the strict sense, or "legal" in nature, though unenforceable at common law. At least this evidence does not lend countenance to the first theory. In the first place, there are some defensive pleadings which attack the complainant's customary title, alleging that the land is not customarily demisable by copy, or not so demisable in the estate claimed.[26] As is pointed out above, "custom" in an informal sense might be relevant to a purely equitable claim. Nevertheless, an answer which says that the complainant's estate is not duly sustained by the custom is best taken as a response to a "legal" claim. Such answers were probably drawn on the assumption that the adversary sought to assert in the Chancery, and could assert, such "legal" rights as he could claim within the manorial system of relationships. The question remains open whether or not such a defense would be good if, in addition to customary title, the petitioner adduced equitable considerations such as the payment of a substantial fine or the incurring of expenses. If the defendant showed that the supposed copyhold was not sustained by the custom, could he still be obliged to refrain from interference with the land? If not, was he nevertheless liable to refund the fine and make good the expenses, or would the loss fall on the grantee who by mistake put more money into a mere tenancy at will than he should have done? The evidence is not entirely unanimous on these questions, but it does suggest that the lord was at least liable to return the fine.

Secondly, bills for admittance brought by heirs, surrenderees, and claimants of customary widow's estates probably fit the second theory better than the first.[27] This is so because such complainants have normally not yet paid a fine. The fine paid by the original grantee or preceding tenant could hardly be taken as consideration for more than a life-estate, inasmuch as a new fine was ordinarily paid by each successive tenant. Only if the fine given by the original grantee greatly exceeded the amount of the fine customarily taken upon inheritance or alienation might this circumstance be altered, and I have found no cases in which this appears to have happened. If an heir, for example, alleged that his ancestor invested large sums in improvements on the tenement, there might be a strong equitable reason to compel the heir's admittance without reference to his strict customary right to it. However, I have found no cases in which petitioners for admittance try to rely on a predecessor's expenditures. There are enough bills for admittance to justify the conclusion that they were good. With one exception, however, all such bills that I have found must be assigned to the years of Wolsey's Chancellorship, 1515 to 1529, or later. This fact might encourage the hypothesis that copyholders originally obtained a Chancery remedy on the mere equitable strength of their position, and that only later, perhaps when common-law opinion about the tenure was changing, was strict customary right taken into account and bills for admittance allowed.

The next class of evidence should also be looked at chronologically. There are some simple complaints of expulsion which give no signs of reliance on any consideration other than customary rights as such.[28] There are also a few bills against disseisors in which the reason for applying to the Chancellor is the lord's unwillingness to do justice in the manorial court, and which give no exclusively equitable reason why the lord should not exercise his will by withholding justice according to the custom.[29] But these bills, of both types, are for the most part relatively late.

There are no cases in which, as far as appears, a copyholder seeks to maintain his estate against a lord who had the reversion or remainder of the manor at the time a temporary lord granted the copy. There is thus no evidence that the Chancellor enforced the usual custom that the *dominus pro tempore* may bind the fee. There are a few cases in which the defendant is a successor, apparently by conveyance or inheritance, of the lord who made the grant.[30] There is no doubt that such successors would be bound by the predecessor's grants if the Chancellor enforced custom. Complainants never take the trouble to allege that a new lord of the manor had notice of his predecessor's copyholds. But very likely a new lord, heir or purchaser, would be presumed to have such notice, since the court rolls come to him with the manor. Moreover, he will receive the copyholder's services, as a purchaser of the particular tenement apart from the whole manor probably would not, since the custom would seem to entitle only the lord to receive the services specified in copyhold grants which only he is entitled to make. In any event, emphasis on the fine is as common against new lords as against the grantor himself. The one bill against a new lord which says nothing about the fine and has the most distinctly "legal" ring, as far as the copyholder's right against his grantor is concerned, involves a special equitable circumstance which alone would entitle the petitioner against the new lord.

In sum, the evidence does not clearly support either theory. Perhaps the safest conclusion is that both were used. On the one hand, the Chancellor may have held that copyholders were entitled to treatment different from that of other tenants at will because they had always, from time immemorial, been so treated. This judgment may have been a direct contradiction of the judgment of common law. More likely, in view of the usual cooperation between the two systems of justice, it would have been a judgment to the effect that the inability of the king's courts to provide a remedy was merely procedural. That is to say, the common-law courts are bound by their own custom to restrict their remedies to certain classes of landholders, but this does not imply any repudiation by those courts of the basic point that the copyholder's privileges are immemorial and therefore of right. To arrive at a more confident guess on these matters, one would need to know just what the position of the common law in the late fifteenth and early sixteenth centuries was, and, as will appear, this is subject to many uncertainties. On the other hand, the Chancellor may have held that lords of manors may not always take advantage of their power to prove that the copyhold grantee's claim is not sustained by the custom. If the circumstances are such that the grant aroused reasonable expectations of security, the grantor must act as if the custom were sufficient.

Alternatively, it is possible that the theory and consequent scope of the Chancellor's remedy changed over the years. In the earlier period, the theory that copyholders, as distinct from villein tenants, had existed from remote times and that their privileges were immemorial, the theoretical basis for their future standing at common law, was perhaps not convincing. Another way of preventing injustice may have been found. Later, as the doctrine of immemorial continuance became fashionable and copyholders were using it in their arguments at common law, the Chancellor may have accepted it. As long as it is so uncertain just when the protection of copyholders in the Chancery became established, and just how the legal profession and the common-law judges were thinking about the copyholder's situation at any particular time, decision among possible interpretations must be suspended. One must be content to note that the Chancery proceedings are not neat evidence. They suggest that the attempt by lawyers, Chancellors, and probably judges sitting as assistants in the Chancery, to work out a solution to the problem presented by copyholders had its complications and its contradictions.

3

The Chancellor's role in copyhold matters was not confined to protecting the tenant in his manorial estate against the will of the lord. In addition, he continued to hear claims of the type to which, as we have seen, some of Savine's cases may be reduced: claims not adverse to the lord's will, and which might have been remediable even if the tenant had had no recourse against the lord. These cases do not call for extensive discussion. It will be enough to indicate the classes into which they fall and where they can be found among the records. In the first place, bills to compel trustees of copyhold land to carry out their fiduciary obligations continue to occur.[31] It should be noted in connection with these cases that the Statute of Uses did not apply to copyhold land, so that the rights of *cestui que use* of copyhold remained purely equitable. Secondly, there are bills to obtain possession of, and to repair, copyhold evidences.[32] Third, bills were brought complaining that the defendant, with whom the complainant had a dispute over copyhold, was in one way or another obstructing justice in the manorial court.[33] Claims of this class must be distinguished from those alleging that the lord's favor or maintenance of the defendant prevents the petitioner from asserting his manorial rights in the appropriate court. The latter challenge the will of the lord. The former contend that someone other than the lord himself—perhaps a manorial officer or the homage—has been corrupted, or that the defendant has employed trickery or violence. Finally, there are bills seeking to compel manorial officers to perform their offices conscientiously.[34]

Complaints against a defendant other than the lord, and not alleging that the lord has himself impeded the ordinary, "legal" workings of manorial justice, raise one problem of some interest. The doctrine is sometimes encountered that a lord within his own manor has equitable as well as legal jurisdiction, that with respect to his copyhold land he has the powers of a Chancellor.[35] It is obscure what practical consequences this doctrine had, either on the local level or in the eyes of central equity and common law. One might expect it to entail the rule that the Chancellor of England may not be petitioned until equitable resources within the manor have been exhausted. Some evidence points toward such a rule, but the evidence as a whole does not.[36] Some complaints against persons other than the lord himself allege that a vain attempt has been made to secure the lord's extraordinary intervention, in the nature of an equitable remedy. On the other hand, claims asserting such familiar equitable rights as those of *cestui que use* and the right to evidences are almost always addressed directly to the Chancellor of England, without any suggestion that something in the nature of equitable procedure had been pursued within the manor. Some complaints based on the obstruction of justice in the ordinary manorial court make no reference to attempts at equitable redress on a lower level. It seems probable that the lord's power as Chancellor within the manor was concurrent with the Lord Chancellor's broader power to enforce the obligations of conscience, rather than subordinate to it in a hierarchy of original and appellate jurisdictions.

Through the work of I. S. Leadam,[37] it is well known that the Court of Requests and the Star Chamber had a role in the legal protection of copyholders. I have found a good deal of material in the proceedings of those courts to confirm this. One must ask, however, whether that role was of decisive importance, whether the history of the tenure's legal position would have been much different if those courts had not existed. A certain answer to this question is impossible. But it seems probable that the two Conciliar courts merely supplemented and imitated the Chancery. The earliest records of these courts are from Henry VII's reign. Of the copyhold cases with which I am acquainted, only two Star Chamber cases (there are none from the Requests) can definitely be assigned to that reign, the rest of those that can be dated belonging to Heny VIII's. Even if one hesitates to date the beginning of intervention by the Chancellor before 1485, it seems likely that most early suits were brought in the Chancery, and that the initial decisions to allow a remedy were made there.

Requests bills by copyholders are indistinguishable from Chancery bills except in the form of address.[38] Some contain allegations which raise the same problems as similar contents of Chancery bills: fines, expenses, matter which seems capable of affecting the equities but unnecessary for a claim based on customary title. Other records suggest in one way or another that cases were tried on the issue of customary title. Whatever the solution to such problems, it is probable that the same law held whether a copyholder took his case to the Chancery or the Requests. If there was any criterion for choosing, it was presumably poverty, the Requests traditionally being a court for poor men's causes. It is unknown whether any strict test of poverty was applied and whether there were any significant differences of procedure between Chancery and Requests. As far as knowledge extends, similarities rather than differences stand out. It is possible that a litigant's choice between the two courts was wholly indifferent. It is probable that they administered a common body of equity, and that the traditions of the Chancery largely determined its substance.

Copyhold cases in the Star Chamber, on the other hand, are distinguishable from those brought in the Chancery and the Requests.[39] Practically all such cases, in common with Star Chambers claims generally, are grounded upon a complaint that unusual violence or riot has accompanied an infraction of the petitioner's rights. The language of bills clearly suggests that allegation of riot, or some other element of public liability, such as illegal enclosure, was necessary to establish the court's jurisdiction. It is unclear whether, if the allegation of riot was proved untrue upon trial, the court would retain jurisdiction to settle any residual private issue raised by the complaint. Be that as it may, the strictly private side of a Star Chamber claim might consist of a copyholder's contention that the lord had violated his manorial estate. There is no way of knowing whether the treatment of copyholders' claims in the Star Chamber differed from their treatment in the Chancery. Like similar claims in the Requests, they tend to show some of the same characteristics and raise some of the same problems as numerous Chancery complaints. The more important point is that copyhold cases in the Star Chamber are rather special, that a normal, comparatively peaceful dispute over customary land probably could not be litigated there but would be pursued in Chancery or the Requests. Under such circumstances, it is likely that the Councilors who sat in the Star Chamber followed the traditions of the Chancery when a copyhold matter arose among the civil issues in a case.

While it is not impossible that the Conciliar courts exerted an influence on the development of copyhold law in the Chancery, most influence probably flowed from the senior court to the junior ones. Despite all uncertainties, there is no reason to doubt that the first major step toward real legal security for copyholders belongs to the history of English equity as it developed in the Chancery, and that it had affinities with other currents in the main stream of equity. If extraordinary Conciliar jurisdiction had never flourished as it did under the early Tudors, the history of copyhold would probably have been much the same. The Conciliar courts, perhaps more responsive to considerations of mere policy than the Chancery, might have played a decisive part in the tenure's history if the Chancellor, perhaps weaving the two strands of policy and art into a solution to the problem posed by copyhold, had not already done the essential job.

The end of Henry VIII's reign only briefly precedes the end of the period when copyholders were protected in equity alone. After the common-law decision to intervene, equity played a concurrent role. The details of the relation between the two systems when both afforded copyholders a remedy is beyond the scope of this study. Probably the importance of equity diminished quickly. As a rule, disputes over copyhold property were probably taken to common law, the more so after the allowance of ejectment gave the copyholder a way to recover possession of the land. The Chancellor was left with the function of compelling lords to admit those entitled upon surrender or inheritance, for the common law refused to allow trespass on the case to persons wrongfully denied admittance.[40] In addition, he of course continued to enforce equity in copyhold matters when the strict custom which determined legal rights could not be taken advantage of without offending conscience. There are indications that he would give temporary protection to copyholders without clearly established customary titles, but it is very doubtful that in the later period a copyholder could be entitled in equity against his lord in the face of actual proof that the custom on which he relied was not continuous from time immemorial.[41] After the middle of the sixteenth century, the Chancery probably subsided to an ancillary position, rounding off the structure of legal protection worked out by the common law, and not seriously interfering with the cornerstone of that structure, the idea that copyholders' rights are sound only because they are immemorial. But it was the Chancellor mainly who saw copyholders through the heyday of enclosures and armed them to resist the effects of price inflation when, somewhat before the middle of the sixteenth century, they came to be felt. While the common law sat by, the Chancellor had to build his own edifice of protection, and the plan may not have been identical with the later one.

CHAPTER II

THE ACQUISITION OF COMMON-LAW REMEDIES

I

It is almost certain that in the late fifteenth century copyholders had no remedy against their lords at common law. Littleton says as much.[1] Before Henry VII's reign, the only known signs of a contrary opinion are the famous dicta of Chief Justice Danby in 1467[2] and Chief Justice Brian in 1482.[3] In editions of Littleton from 1534 and after, the opinions of Danby and Brian were added to the text as a counterweight to the statement of the law in the original.[4] Although Danby and Brian have been given credit for much more than isolated opinions probably at odds with prevalent views, it has been well recognized in modern times that they laid down dicta only and did not, as far as anyone knows, turn the course of the law.[5] This by no means removes the possibility that Danby and Brian were highly influential. The judges who finally decided to allow copyholders a remedy may have leaned heavily on these earlier opinions, without the slightest concern for whether they were dicta, decisions, or dissenting views.

Danby's opinion seems to be an *obiter dictum* in the strict sense that its connection with the case at hand is very loose. The case was trespass for taking a horse. The defendant pleaded that he was a lord of a certain manor, that the person through whom the plaintiff claimed title to the horse had died his copyhold tenant, and that in accordance with a manorial custom which permitted the lord to take as a heriot the best beast of every tenant who died seised of a copyhold in his manor, he had justifiably taken the horse. During the argument of this case, the question was put whether a copyholder has any remedy if his lord ousts him. The relevance of this question for the case is unclear. Possibly the plaintiff's counsel intended to argue that the custom relied on by the defense should be held invalid since copyhold tenure is not protected by the law, and it is unfair to allow the lord to take a heriot when there is no guarantee that the dead copyholder's heir will be permitted to enjoy his inheritance. Perhaps the defendant's counsel challenged the premise of this argument. In any event, Danby replies to the question as follows:

> Semble que il avera qar si le seignour luy ouste il fait a luy tort qar il est auxibien enherite pur aver cel terre a luy & a ses heires secundum consuetudinem manerii come ascun home est dez terres a le comen ley & il fait fyn quant il entre . . .

Justice Littleton challenges this opinion, citing first the decision in the Subpoena discussed above,[6] and then pointing out that "brief de faux iugement ne brief de droit il nauvera mye, qar nul franktenement est en luy eins le franktenement est en le seignour . . ." Danby then disputes Littleton's recollection of what happened in the Subpoena and goes on as follows:

> Et syr si le roy enter en ma terre ieo navera remedye mes mon peticyon &c. mes le roy est tenuz de droit de moy restorer issint est le seignor tenuz de restorer son tenant a volunte secundum consuetudinem . . .

Besides Danby and Littleton, no justices speak. But from the bar Catesby and Pygot challenge Danby's analogy with a trespass committed by the king:

> En vostre cas si le roy entre en ma terre uncore le franktenement est en moy et nemy en le roy qar il ne poit le aver sauns mater de recorde . . .

To which Danby says, "Ieo voil bien mes posito que il prist les profytes quel remedye &c.?" and Catesby and Pygot answer "Nul."

I shall come back later to the meaning of the arguments on both sides. For the moment it is enough to note that Danby apparently stands alone, that there is no report of how the case was decided, and that it is unclear whether the views of either side on the availability of trespass to copyholders would point to a resolution of the case.

Although it is correct to classify Brian's opinion as a dictum too, it is more closely related to the issue before the court. The action was trespass for breaking the plaintiff's close. The defendant pleaded that the land was customary and that it was let to him for life, "per force de quel il fuit seisi . . . come de franktenement solonque le custome de mesme le maner . . ." Then the defendant gave color to the plaintiff.

Two points should be noticed about the defensive plea. First, it raises squarely the converse of the question whether copyholders should have trespass, namely, the question of whether a copyholder does wrong to the lord if he occupies the tenement against his will. Second, by giving color the defendant obliges the plaintiff to plead again.[7] His reason for giving color is presumably that his affirmative plea in effect denies that the land is the plaintiff's. That being so, he can only avoid the objection that he ought to have pleaded the general issue by invoking the doctrine of fictitious color. With the help of the fiction, he can make a good plea in confession and avoidance, to which the plaintiff must either demur or reply.

He demurs, but to the form rather than to the substance of the plea, as I understand it. He does not say that the copyholder has no substantive rights against his lord, but that it is contrary to the defendant's estate to say that he is seised as of freehold. There is a verbal contradiction in saying that one is a copyholder, and hence a tenant at will, and then using the formula "seised in his demesne as of freehold," which is appropriate only to a common-law life-tenant. Brian rejects this argument on the plaintiff's part, saying in effect that the defendant has used the expression "seised as of freehold" by analogy only. As a life-tenant according to the custom of the manor, he is entitled to say that he is seised in his demesne as of freehold with the additional words "according to the custom." The court conceded Brian's point.

After this, Brigges, counsel for the plaintiff, says, "Si le seignour voit luy mister hors il nad remedy que prove quil est forsque tenant a volunte." It is not entirely clear why Brigges says this. Possibly he is still arguing for his original plea, despite the court's apparently unanimous rejection of it, hoping that by emphasizing the debility of copyhold estates he can still convince the court that it is absurd for a copyholder to say he is seised in his demesne as of freehold. Alternatively, Brigges may be starting a skirmish on the substantive point of the case, even though he has not entered a new plea. In either event, Brian contradicts him as follows:

> Ceo ne fuit unques mon opinion & come ieo croy unques sera, car donques tout le copy holde en Engleterre sera defete, pur que ieo entend que tout temps que le tenant paia le customes et service si le seignor luy mytt hors de possession il avera accion de trespass vers luy.

Catesby, now on the bench,[8] appears to agree with Brian's conclusion, though he is skeptical about some of his reasoning. He speaks as follows:

> Cest fort que le tenant prescribera vers le seignor, mes le pluis que moy move est, en tiel lieu ou terre est divisable que le testatour poit doner power a ces executors de vendre la terre nyent obstant que le heire est eins per discent, et lour vendication sera bon, mes cest per cause de custome.

Then Brian adds the following remarks in reply to Catesby:

> Issint est le custome del maner ou ils ont tiel estate come ilz ont allege. Et si le plaintiff ad tiel matter il poit monstrer coment le tenant ad faile de paiement de son service per que le plaintiff fuit seisi. Et coment il pur defaut de paiement de service enter et fuyt seisi tanques le defendant fist le trespass . . .

No other judge speaks. Were it not for one further circumstance, the report would justify the conclusion that this case was very likely a turning point. However, the report ends with a brief notation of the next step in the case:

> Et a auter iour le plaintiff weiva cest ple et demurra sur le ple le defendant pur ceo que il ne poit prescribe daver le terre vers son seignor, car cest contrary a son estate . . .

That is to say, Brigges dropped his formal objection to the defense and demurred to the substance. He finally rested on the fundamental point that a copyholder cannot set up a prescriptive title to be treated by the lord as if he had something better than an estate at will. He took this course knowing that Brian would not hold the demurrer good and with some reason to suppose that Catesby would concur with Brian. To have taken this risk, Brigges and his colleagues must have thought that the other two judges would reject Brian's opinion when they had to give judgment. They may have thought Catesby could be secured when the main issue was properly debated. To demur in these circumstances, they must have thought that the weight of opinion, including the opinion of the other bench, would oppose any change of the law in the copyholder's favor. Unfortunately, there is no report of later stages of the case.

In 1500 or 1501, some copyholders brought a bill in the Chancery complaining of expulsion.[9] After setting out the facts, the bill says, "Forasmuch as your said orators can have none action of Trespass nor other remedy at the common law against the said abbot because he is lord of the manor, they are without remedy in that behalf . . ." In general, Chancery bills are too vague to give a reliable indication of the attitude of the common law toward copyholders. The mere fact that a copyholder sues in equity or says that he has no remedy at common law need not mean that he could not maintain trespass and recover damages. It might mean only that the common law provided no way by which the land could be specifically recovered. As late as Coke's day, when ejectment as well as trespass was available to them, copyholders apparently had the option of suing at common law or in Chancery.[10] But this one bill is exceptional: it says flatly that trespass is not available.

This bit of evidence, together with the weakness of the two fifteenth century cases, gives the case of Tropnell v. Twynytho (1505–1506)[11] a good claim to be the first holding in the copyholder's favor. This case, brought in the Common Pleas, was an action of trespass for breaking the plaintiff's close. The defendants pleaded that the plaintiffs were seised of a manor; that the plaintiffs and all those whose estate they had in the manor had from time beyond memory demised the customary lands of the manor for years, for life, or in fee; that it was customary in the manor for such grantees by copy to enjoy the land so demised during the estate granted, so long as they rendered the services due and abided by the custom of the manor; that the land where the trespass was done was customary land; that it was demised to the defendants by copy; that they had rendered the services and done nothing against the custom; and that therefore the defendants entered and did the trespass, as well they might.

The plaintiffs demurred to this plea. Upon the first argument of the case, in Michaelmas, the report only tells us that Chief Justice Frowyck thought, "que le prescription est assets bon de lyer le Seignor que il ne poit ouster les customarie tenants." The reporter notes that the case was adjourned to Hilary term. He adds a "Quaere de cest matter." The report then goes on to give an account of further arguments in the case, not in Hilary, but in the next Michaelmas. Palmes argued for the plaintiff, upholding the demurrer. His arguments were rebutted from the bench by Justice Kingsmill, with whom Justice Fisher agreed. Kingsmill and Fisher said they had conferred with the other judges, who were of the same opinion. (Frowyck had died in the meantime, but it is noted again that the late Chief Justice was of the same opinion). The defendant accordingly made his plea certain, and the plaintiff was given a day to reply. The reporter adds another *Quaere*. I shall revert to the substance of the arguments in this important case when I take up the reasons for and against allowing copyholders standing at common law. For the moment, it is enough to notice that in 1506 one court held that a copyholder whose lands have been demisable by copy from time out of mind is no trespasser if he occupies the land against his lord's will. It is also important to note that in 1505 a lawyer would still risk demurring to a plea claiming a prescriptive title to customary land against the lord of the manor.

Although it is tempting to suppose that Tropnell v. Twynytho settled the copyholder's status at common law, I do not think it did. The evidence from the next half-century is inconclusive, but the weight of it indicates that Tropnell v. Twynytho was ignored, forgotten, or reversed until finally, probably shortly after the middle of the sixteenth century, the courts came around to the opinion already reached by the Common Pleas judges in 1506. A number of arguments may be made to this effect. In the first place, one should consider the frequency of copyholders' suits in the Chancery and the Conciliar courts throughout Henry VIII's reign.[12] Neither the mere occurrence of bills there nor anything in their contents is absolutely inconsistent with the simultaneous existence of a common-law remedy. It is nevertheless hard to believe that so many litigants, whose cases to all appearances would have been amenable to trespass, would have preferred equity to common law if they had had a choice. Admittedly specific recovery is a better remedy than damages, and the day when copyholders could recover possession at common law by action of ejectment still lay in the future. But such issues as whether or not a forfeiture had occurred could be tried as well at common law as in the Chancery. The equity bills themselves suggest that such issues were often the crux of copyhold litigation. In cases of forfeiture the lord was probably often willing enough to let the tenant continue to hold the land once he had paid a new fine or otherwise compounded for the forfeiture, or once a court gave judgment that no forfeiture had occurred. There is still less reason why suits against parties other than the lord himself should be brought in Chancery if they could be brought at law.

A more persuasive argument is the almost total absence of copyhold cases in the Yearbooks of Henry VII and Henry VIII. Once the courts allowed trespass, at least some copyholders would certainly have brought suit at common law. Such suits would inevitably have raised issues of law interesting enough to be reported. In Elizabeth's reign, the courts were confronted with a steady stream of copyhold cases involving difficult issues. These issues were debated, resolved, and reopened, as the leading questions of a new field of law naturally would be. Earlier authority is practically never cited in the Elizabethan cases.[13] Even allowing for a certain gap of time between the first decision recognizing copyholders' prescriptive rights and the occurrence of new cases presenting important legal problems, it is inconceivable that fifty years of copyhold practice lay behind the Elizabethan cases. Henry VIII's reign is less well reported than others, but there are quite enough Yearbooks to have caught at least some important copyhold cases if there were any.

As an adjunct to this argument, one should consider the character of the first systematic work on copyholds, Charles Calthrope's readings, given at Furnivall's Inn in 1574–1575.[14] Calthrope's lectures show all the signs of being a venture into a new field. He is apologetic and hesitant; he talks around copyholds, dealing with manors, prescription, and the like, without having much to say about copyhold law as that subject is conceived by Coke in *The Compleat Copy-holder,* for example; he plainly does not have a large body of case law to go on. Very little practice can be in the background of the Readings.

The one point to be made in favor of the supposition that copyholders could sue at common law in Henry VIII's reign is that the language of a few Chancery bills suggests the possibility.[15] This evidence is not very significant when weighed against the considerations above, and against the further evidence of two reports from Edward VI's reign. The first of these reports indicates that the copyholder's standing at common law was still in doubt in 1550. The second, from 1552–1553, may be an important holding that lords are not free to expel copyholders at will.

The case of 1550, as reported by Dalison, goes as follows.[16]

> *Saunders* demaund del Justices si tenant per Copie de Court Roule poet prescribe de scier bois sur le terre cressant. *Montague* La est tiel custome & issint use in the County de Middlesex Northampton & auters liewes. *Browne* Ad estre cy agree ore tarde que tenant per le custome poet prescriber de suffer le measons deschuer & destroyer lour meason auxi icy per que ceo est bon custome. *Montague* Jeo oy un fable que tenant per le custome poet seer in un parte de ses measons & comburer en lauter per le custome, mes en vostre case si voiles agreer que tenant per le custome avera le terre encountre le volunt de Seignior a luy & ses heires per le custome, per que donques ne poient ils per le custome succider le bois: *Saunders* Jeo voil agreer nul de vostre cases. *Montague* Certes en le Chancery il serra rule encounter vous sans doubt, & il est bon que un Acte de Parliament soit fait sur ceo.

This report presents certain problems of interpretation. In the first place, the grammar of Chief Justice Montague's remark about an act of Parliament poses a question. Inasmuch as no act of Parliament affecting copyholders generally was made or, so far as I know, considered, it seems likely that Montague means it *would* be a good thing if a statute *were* made. If this reading is correct, then about what should an act of Parliament be made—the power of a copyholder to prescribe to cut wood and the like, or to prescribe for the land itself? I think it must be the latter. Montague has just said that if copyholders may have the land against the lord's will they surely may prescribe to cut wood. His reasoning seems incontrovertible. Therefore Montague must be in doubt about the premise, that is, their power to prescribe for the land. A reluctance to legislate judicially on so important a matter would be natural, but a judge would hardly hesitate to hold prescription for trees permissible if the law were settled on the major point. When Saunders refuses to agree to any of Montague's cases, he surely includes the case which Montague has just invited him to agree to, namely, the proposition that the tenant shall have the land against the lord's will. Montague's reference to the Chancery probably has to do with the well-established security of copyholders in equity, not merely with how the Chancellor would deal with an alleged right to cut trees. The report is therefore clear evidence that in 1551 the Chief Justice of the Common Pleas was perhaps inclined to imitate the Chancery but felt the need of parliamentary sanction. Such an attitude is inconsistent with a tradition of fifty years' standing that copyholders may maintain trespass. Justice Browne seems to deal only with the validity of the particular custom in question. The holding he cites might not necessarily entail the copyholder's power to prescribe for the land, though it is arguable that it should. Without any knowledge of the case he cites—which might, of course, have been in the Chancery—nothing can be made of his remark.

The report from 1552–1553 is as follows:[17]

Nota per James Hales Justice que nul soit suffer ne oye a demaunder terres &c en briefe de droit ou auterment per lestatute de lymitacion de pluis temps que de 60 ans devant son briefe purchase que ore si terres ou tenements ou demesnes ount este lesses per copie de court roll per le space de 60 ans que cest bon prescripsion et bon copyhould terre. Et la fuit clerement agree per le dit Hales et Portman Justice de Benche le roye que le Seignor ne poet ouster son tenant per copy ou customary tenant quel est tout un per la ley cy longe temps que il fait son service et paie son rent due accordant al custome et son copy tenure. Et tout ceo fuit al

Serieants Inne eodem termino. Et ills agreeont la que lestatute de lymitacion quant al avowry ou demaunder des services de copyhould tenants per le Seignor nextenda al copyhouldes quant a cest purpose car lestatute ne serra entendue forsque de freehoulde enter verai Seignor et veray tenant.

The nature of the case to which this report pertains is not clear. It is possible that it does not relate to an actual case at all, but only to an extrajudicial discussion at Serjeants' Inn. On the other hand, the report may refer to a consultation among all the judges or an Exchequer Chamber proceeding concerning a case which arose in one or the other of the common-law courts. Such a case may be reconstructed along the following lines: A copyholder brought suit challenging the will of the lord. Evidence that the land was not demisable by copy was offered, but this evidence related to conditions more than sixty years before. The defense first argued that copyholders ought not to be permitted to set up a prescriptive title against their lords at all. This argument was rejected by Hales and Portman at least. Secondly, the defense relied on its purported proof that the land was not customary. Hales thought this proof ineffective, on the ground that the Statute of Limitations of 32 Henry 8. ca. 2 extends to copyholders' prescriptions, making sixty years of continuous demisability by copy sufficient to establish that land is customary and nullifying the effect of earlier evidence of non-user. The last part of the report, concerning the applicability of the Statute of Limitations to avowry for copyhold services, probably has nothing to do with the case. Having spoken on the application of the Statute of Limitations in one copyhold context, some of the judges probably spoke by the way on its applicability in another related one.

Whatever the occasion of the opinions reported, they are significant. Hales's opinion on the applicability of 32 Henry 8. ca. 2 to copyhold prescription was not followed.[18] But the opinion of Hales and Portman on the tenant's basic security may well be the first holding in the copyholder's favor which entered into a continuous tradition. Over the next twenty years, that opinion must have been affirmed in other cases, for the amount of copyhold litigation in the 1570's makes it certain that a remedy then existed. Brian and Danby were no doubt vouched as early precedents, and Tropnell v. Twynytho may have been relied on if it was known. But the judgment of Hales and Portman would have been in the climate of current opinion when the course of the law was irreversibly changed. Looking in the other direction, it is significant that the copyholder's rights against his lord were still disputable enough to be discussed in 1552–1553, and an opinion on the matter still striking enough to be reported.

In 1550, Chief Justice Montague was tempted to allow copyholders standing at common law, but still reluctant and hoping for parliamentary action. In 1552–1553, we find two justices free of such reluctance and willing to act without parliament. Insofar as it is permissible to project from the two reports, the weight of opinion can be seen shifting in the early fifties. In 1564, two judges of the Common Pleas indicated that they were probably ready to follow the new drift of opinion, but they regarded the copyholder's power to sue his lord in trespass as something less than obvious. The report is as follows:[19]

> Nota per Walshe & Dier sur lestatute de 31 H. 8 cap. 13 que si un feme ad widow estate dascun terre per Copy dount linheritance fuit a un Abbe si labbe voil faire leas in reversion de ceo que cest leas ne fuit bon per le statute auterment est dun leas a volunt per le Common Ley car si le copyholder poet aver action envers chescun estranger & le copihold serra done in issue & [que] prove le special interest & sont divers presidents que le Copyholder ad recover in trespas vers le seignor car come Brian & Danby disoient cy longment come ils fesoient lour duties & services ils ount auxi [auxibien] estate per lour Copy come auters al Common Ley.

Ten years later, one would not have had to suggest so timidly that "divers precedents" supported the allowance of a remedy.

Finally, in 1566,[20] "fuit agree que si le copieholder paya ses services et le seignor ousta luy il avera accion de trespass vers le seignor." The matter was still controversial enough to be discussed and reported. Thereafter, I have found nothing to indicate that the copyholder's standing at common law was any longer in doubt. The winning of his new position was probably a gradual process. The beginning of a shift in opinion is perhaps signalized by the insertion of Brian and Danby in Littleton in 1534; Edward VI's reign saw both a balance of conflicting opinions and the first stages of resolution; in Elizabeth's, the last doubts vanished.

The final stage in the evolution of common-law remedies for copyholders was the decision to allow them ejectment. With the acquisition of that action, the line between freehold and copyhold property was further blurred. The copyholder could recover actual possession of his land in the action which freeholders now almost always used instead of a real action. Originally the leaseholder's remedy, ejectment had been adapted and fictionalized for use by freehold tenants, but because of the roots of the action, it could not be brought unless the true plaintiff were able to create a leasehold. The writ served to recover a term of years, even though the suit actually tested freehold ownership. Consequently, the copyholder could not use the action unless his common-law lessee could maintain it, and about that there was some question. If a copyholder let his land by a common-law lease—as opposed to a surrender to the lessee's use for years—he would forfeit the land unless one of two conditions were fulfilled. First, custom sometimes sanctioned short-term leases without surrender. Second, the lord might license his copyholder to make a lease, thereby waiving his claim to the forfeiture. The question then arises whether, when a copyholder makes a lease warranted either by custom or by license, or when he makes an unwarranted lease, the lessee can maintain ejectment at common law.

I have found no authority on this question before 1572. In that year the power of the custom-warranted lessee to bring the action was questioned in court, but no decision is reported. The reporter says—either as his own opinion or the court's—that the licensed lessee is the stronger case and probably may maintain the action.[21] A report from 1573[22] says that the Queen's Bench was ready to allow ejectment on licensed leases, but that the better opinion of the Common Pleas was to the contrary. The Common Pleas view is said to depend on the argument that a copyholder's lessee may not be put in possession by *Habere facias seisinam,* an objection which seems as applicable to customary leases as to licensed ones. However, it was said in argument in Heydon's Case (1583) that in 15 Elizabeth the Common Pleas held that ejectment could be maintained on a lease warranted by custom.[23]

In the 1580's and 1590's, the action is frequently brought on copyholders' leases, and there is no doubt that the question was settled in favor of allowing it on any warranted demise. Its universal availability was assured when it was held that a custom warranting one-year leases without surrender is general to all manors in the realm and need not be specially proved.[24] There is even some authority that a totally unwarranted lease will support ejectment against strangers, though as to the lord it constitutes forfeiture.[25] Not long after the copyholder won trespass, his estate was further dignified by ejectment.

2

There is no shortage of motives to explain the change in the common law's position on copyholders and the attitudes of the precursors of that change. Whether in Edward IV's reign, or Henry VII's, or Edward VI's, the pressure of official anxiety over the fate of the small landholder was no doubt felt by the judges. Alongside the higher motives of social policy, one should place the more earthly instincts of commercial common sense. A great deal of land was virtually owned by copyholders.[26] Men from classes other than the small farmers who traditionally held copyholds must have wanted to buy customary land, a beautiful investment in an age when rents were rising and customary dues would stand still if law or morality enforced custom. Such men could not be satisfied with virtual ownership. That might be good enough for the subject and trustful tenants of a conscientious landlord, but anyone else would require certain, sufficient, and convenient legal protection, the insurance of merchantability. Perhaps the need for legal change was felt not so much because copyholders were in grave danger of exploitation as because they were in so little danger, because they were for the most part safe and respectable proprietors whose land was perversely withheld from the market by the antiquated condition of the law. These cross-currents of motivation are impossible to assess without a great deal of information about local, manorial realities and economic habits.

In addition to motives of policy and practicality, an ordinary sense of fairness probably had its role. Though justice according to conscience was in theory the Chancellor's province, and the common-law courts professed to administer the timeless custom of the realm, a sense of equity nevertheless could be the force behind legal rationalization. Because copyhold had come so far from being a true estate at will, genuinely understood to be dependent on the lord's grace, a counterpart of personal servility, it had become manifestly unfair to deny a remedy against a lord who tried to make use of his technical privileges. There is nothing unfair about an inferior tenure, subject to eviction at will, so long as the tenant really believes that is what he has. But probably those who granted and received copyholds usually did so in the fullest confidence that the grantee would enjoy a durable estate. The evicting lord was much more than uncharitable; he offended against equity in the deepest sense by offending against expectations nourished by usage and arising as if by natural instinct, by acting against "trust and confidence." By the time copyholders were held competent to prescribe at law, they probably had a prescriptive title in the philosophic sense to be treated like landowners.

The change in the common law was undoubtedly influenced by what had already happened in the Chancery. The equitable protection of copyholders was probably at once a result of benign development toward respectable ownership and the principal cause of the fruition of that process. Because the Chancellor had sheltered the later stages of its growth, copyhold had reached the point where the absurdity of turning away a copyholder who sued at common law was perhaps intuitively evident, even though legal reasoning might blur the immediate perception. In addition to altering the realities to which law is always in some degree responsive, the Chancellor may also have provoked the common-law judges to forthright competition. Like the expansion of assumpsit, the allowance of trespass and ejectment to copyholders may be an instance of the beneficent effect of tension between the two parallel systems of justice. Fees for the courts and the reputation of the common law could suffer if equity maintained a monopoly over too many classes of litigation. However, lest competition in the grosser sense be overemphasized, instances in which the catalytic rivalry failed to work should be remembered. Copyhold law provides an instance. Though urged to allow an action on the case against the lord by heirs and surrenderees wrongfully denied admittance, the common-law courts refused to do so and thereby left such complaints to the Chancellor. There were good technical reasons for this decision. The point is that those reasons prevailed.[27]

Although the position of the Chancery may itself have provided the common-law judges with a part of their motivation, it could equally well have hindered the play of motives which otherwise would have been more urgent. Without the Chancellor's protection, copyholders might have lived under the threat of enclosure and extortion, and their holdings might have lain unmerchantable. But since the Chancellor did the essential job, the common law could allow itself the luxury of scruples. When all is said that can be said about possible motives, it remains probable that reason itself was the strongest motive. The common law probably changed mainly because the judges became convinced that the former stand of the law was logically indefensible, because arguments once effective to prevent change were eventually understood to be fallacious. Conversely, the change was slow because reason, abetted perhaps by motives with a contrary thrust, such as the instincts of men who themselves were lords of manors, inhibited the motives which would have redirected the law. Both authority and arguments of principle stood in the way, and the counterforce of better logic was necessary to push them aside.

In reconstructing the intellectual processes by which the common law changed its position on copyholders, one must rely mainly on speculation, assisted only by a few hints from the reports. Although certainty can hardly be approached, it is perhaps possible to think through the problem of how copyholders ought to be received in terms which would have been natural to lawyers and judges in the sixteenth century. First, the copyholder's contention that he can suffer wrong punishable in trespass at the lord's hand depends absolutely on the argument that the custom of the manor differentiates him from other tenants at will. He never claimed nor was held to have any greater common-law estate. A custom meant a practice of immemorial continuance. The idea that human habits can remain the same forever is of course fantastic to the historically minded. But to understand custom as a working legal concept one must escape from one's sense of history and make the assumption of an earlier age that, where there is no evidence of origin or intermission, things have been continuously the same for as long a time as men need concern themselves with.[28] Law is custom in those areas where natural reason and conscience do not control and human communities are free to choose their institutions. What has to all intents been done forever in a community is legally rightful; that which has been abstained from is wrongful. If within a certain manor the tenants at will of certain lands, having received grants in a certain form, and rendering certain services, have always been treated by their lessor and his successors as if they had the equivalent of freehold estates, then it is wrongful to treat them otherwise. Such is the copyholder's case.

Secondly, the jurisdiction of the king's courts of common law extends to the enforcement of all legal, or customary, rights. It is not confined to implementing one body of substantive rights, called the common law, to the exclusion of others. The term "common law" has three significances which are immediately relevant. It means legal jurisdiction, as opposed to equitable; that is to say, jurisdiction to remedy wrongs which are in essence violations of custom. Second, common law means the custom of the king's courts. Like other men, the royal judges are bound to go on doing what they have always done. Since, for example, assizes have always been confined to persons disseised of a freehold, the judges have no authority to extend the remedy to leaseholders or copyholders. Finally, common law signifies "the common custom of the realm." All this means is that in most places and among most groups of people in England certain practices are customary. Ordinarily, the customary rights enforced by the common-law courts are common, or general, ones. But the courts are not limited to enforcing these. If a litigant can show, bearing the burden of proof, that he lives in a place or belongs to a group of people where different practices are customary, he is entitled to the benefit of being treated as inhabitants of that place or members of that class have always been treated. He may prescribe to have the advantage of another law than common law, but one of equal dignity because of its equal antiquity. Violation of special custom is legally wrongful in exactly the same way as violation of general custom where that is applicable.

If these principles are correct, it follows that copyholders do no wrong if they enter on their tenements contrary to the will of the lord, and that the lord does wrong if he puts his copyholder out or otherwise interferes with his enjoyment. The common-law courts should refuse trespass to the lord and allow it to the copyholder. For the copyholder is in possession of land in a manor where from time out of mind the tenants at will *secundum consuetudinem* of that tenement have been treated like freeholders in comparable estate, provided they fulfill certain conditions. If a copyholder has a customary fee, for example, he and his predecessors have enjoyed, aliened, and inherited under innumerable successive lords. The tenement has never, as far as anyone knows, been conveyed by lease or feoffment, and therefore there are no grounds for inferring that the practice of treating its holders unlike ordinary tenants at will commenced at an ascertainable time, or that the land was ever severed from the manor, the locality whose custom is invoked. It is customary land, demised or demisable by copy of court roll from time out of mind.

The problem is to understand what obscured this view of the copyholder's position. If it was the view that prevailed and is correctly deduced from accepted principles, what arguments for a time diverted the judges from its logic? Two objections are suggested by the reports. The first involves a conflict between two of the senses of "common law." On the one hand, if indeed it is customary for lords of manors to abstain from exercising their wills against copyholders, it is wrongful for them to do so. On the other hand, it is customary for the king's courts to remedy trespasses committed in respect of land only when the injured person is possessed of a term of years or better (except, perhaps, when the trespasser is a stranger to any rightful interest in the land). A tenant at will cannot be injured by the lessor or one who enters at the lessor's will, and whatever else is true the copyholder remains a tenant at will. Since a lord who breaks the custom is a wrongdoer, it is perhaps appropriate for the Chancellor to restrain him, but there is no customary warrant for the common law to extend the action of trespass to a tenant at will, or to withhold it from the person regularly entitled to it, that is, a lessor at will whose tenant refuses to vacate at request.

This argument is answerable in two ways. It would not hold if there were evidence that copyholders had ever enjoyed common-law protection. As will be seen, some Elizabethan lawyers thought there was such evidence, and therefore that any refusals on the part of the courts to intervene were departures from the older and better custom. The role of this argument, which is largely based on a misinterpretation of the medieval books, in the earlier and decisive cases cannot be ascertained. Probably it was an afterthought. A second, and probably more important, argument is that the custom of the common-law courts in matters of tort is to remedy any wrong which consists in the violation of custom. Evidence that no tenant with less than a term of years has ever recovered against his lessor is not evidence that the court customarily withholds personal remedies from any class of person. General acceptance of the theory that law is custom and the king's courts enforce custom is sufficient evidence that the courts habitually act on that theory. Something more decisive—such as the existence of writs for the real actions which are restrictive in language—is necessary to prove that the courts have habitually limited themselves to helping particular classes of landholders. Probably this is what Chief Justice Danby meant when, in the face of objections that the common law is helpless so long as copyholders are merely tenants at will, he insisted that nevertheless a lord who violates custom "fait a luy tort." [29] An injured person is one who is not treated as he is accustomed to be. It is irrelevant how the common-law courts are wont to classify his estate in the land. However, this reasoning was not evident to others in Danby's time. It must have become so before the common law changed its course.

A further difficulty in the way of allowing trespass to copyholders was perhaps even more serious. This objection appears to have been the center of debate in Tropnell v. Twynytho, and signs of it can be seen in the case of 1482. In Tropnell v. Twynytho, the following argument is made: A tenant at will, copyholder or otherwise, in Blackacre, may not prescribe in his own name to have common of pasture or some other incorporeal hereditament in Whiteacre. Rather, the prescription must be in the name of the lord of Blackacre, for himself and his tenants at will. Therefore, a tenant at will of the manor of Blackacre may not prescribe against the lord of Blackacre for security in his copyhold estate. The logic of this argument is hard to understand, but an attempt must be made to grasp its plausibility, for it was made seriously in Tropnell v. Twynytho, and it is at least closely related to the basis for the substantial demurrer in the case of 1482.

Suppose that a tenement in the manor of Blackacre is let to X by copy. X pastures beasts in the wastes of the adjacent manor of Whiteacre and on that account becomes involved in litigation with the owner of Whiteacre. X claims that the common of pasture is rightfully his, because from time out of mind he and his ancestors and those whose estate he has, tenants in fee of the said tenement at the will of the lord after the custom of the manor of Blackacre, have used to pasture their beasts there. It is clear that X's claim will fail on the pleadings: a copyholder cannot prescribe against strangers in his own name.

This need not mean that he cannot prescribe against his own lord for his copyhold unless the reason for his impotence against the owner of Whiteacre extends to the other case. Let us therefore analyze the result in the case of the common of pasture. At first sight, it does not seem to be a reasonable result. There seems to be no reason why all the following things cannot be true: (1) The tenement in question has been demised by copy in fee from time out of mind. (2) From time immemorial it has been enjoyed, aliened, and inherited as if it were a fee. (3) The present tenant and all his predecessors in estate have continually pastured beasts in Whiteacre. If they are all true, X's use of the common ought, on principle, to be rightful.

One of three conclusions must therefore be drawn. The result in the case of the common might of course be wrong. If it is right, it might be a consequence of a more or less arbitrary custom of the king's courts that they will not listen to claims against common right unless such claims are made by or in the name of freehold tenants (indeed, by tenants in fee).[30] Finally, it is possible that the result would never have been arrived at were there not substantial objections to a copyholder's claiming that he and his predecessors have used the common from time out of mind. In other words, the custom of the king's courts is not arbitrary, but is itself evidence of conditions of great antiquity. It is evidence that in the indefinitely remote past, when the custom of the king's courts took form, a copyholder's claim to be entitled to common in a stranger's land was recognizable as absurd *prima facie.*

Disallowing the first possibility, the second and third have serious implications as to the copyholder's power to claim a right to security against his lord. The second goes only as far as procedure. It amounts to saying that it violates the accustomed practice of the common-law courts to listen to the claims of a tenant at will against common right, but the right claimed—whether the common or security in his manorial estate—exists nonetheless and may be asserted in the Chancery. However, this argument is rather easily answered. If the only problem to get around is an accidental custom of the court, this can be done by showing that a copyholder's claim to security against his lord is distinguishable from his claim to common. Whereas the latter, conceived as a right belonging to the copyholder himself and not as derivative from the lord, can only be claimed as a right of the claimant and his predecessors in estate, the former can be claimed as a right which exists because such security has always been enjoyed by the grantees in such form of certain lands within the manor of Blackacre. The claim to common in Whiteacre is personal; the claim to security in one's copyhold estate is local. It lies in custom, the custom running throughout the locality called the manor of Blackacre.[31] The restriction of the right to prescribe to freeholders covers only the personal type of claim.

In Tropnell v. Twynytho, Kingsmill clearly distinguishes personal from local prescription.[32] It seems also to be the point of Catesby's opinion, which Brian is willing to accept, in the case of 1482.[33] (In the latter case, the copyholder's lack of power to prescribe against strangers is not, so far as appears, relied on, but only the more obvious point that there is a contradiction in a man's saying that he holds land of another in less than fee and also that he and his predecessors in estate have infringed some common right of the overlord from time immemorial. Such a claim is absurd because any estate in less than fee must have sprung out of the fee at an ascertainable time in the past and cannot have existed forever, let alone enjoyed some exceptional privilege. This argument is also answerable by the pointing out that it can only touch personal prescription.) Because of the nature of the rebuttal made by Kingsmill, one would be justified in concluding that the argument from the copyholder's incapacity to prescribe against strangers never went deeper than procedure and was fairly easily disposed of with the help of the distinction already stated by Catesby. There is no evidence to the contrary, and if one hesitates it is only because the argument taken in that way does not seem a sufficient explanation of the inhibitions which apparently still stood in the way of legal change.

Without belaboring the point unduly, the third possibility above should perhaps still be considered. Is it possible that the judges saw a difficulty in the simultaneous existence of a rule that copyholders may not prescribe against strangers and a rule that they may claim security in their manorial estates against their lords by virtue of time? And is it possible that this difficulty was too fundamental to be removed by distinguishing personal and local prescriptive claims? It seems to me at least plausible to reason that the rule forbidding prescription against strangers would not be a part of the ancient custom of the king's courts if there were not something suspect about the copyholder's claims to an exceptional status from time immemorial. If they had secure estates, fees to all intents, in centuries past, the tenants of such estates probably had incorporeal rights in others' land, and the law would hardly have made it impossible to assert them. The fact that copyholders have customarily been put in exactly the same position as ordinary tenants at will when it comes to claiming commons and the like at common law—neither can prescribe for himself; the user of either counts only as evidence that the lord has the rights for himself and his tenants at will—probably means that copyholders were once ordinary tenants at will. After all, this inference is in a sense correct. As will appear, there was little historical sense of the realities, neither of how old copyhold as such was, nor how much like copyhold villenage had been. Evidence of antiquity on the modest scale of a hundred years or less was more likely than not to inspire presumptions of antiquity on a vast scale. The change in the copyholder's legal position owed much to illusion, and perhaps its slowness in coming about owed something to an inference from legal rules which reduced the fruitfulness of illusion.

If the remodeling of the law to make room for copyholders' claims was held back by some rules already part of the law, it was perhaps pushed on by another. In his chapter on copyholds, Littleton says that if the heir to a copyhold of inheritance enters immediately after the ancestor's death, without admittance, he is no trespasser against the lord, "pour ceo que le custome de la maner en ascun cas luy puit aider de barer son seignor in accion de trespass." [34] No cases establishing this rule are known, but there probably were such cases. The rule itself is common sense directed against the evident unfairness of making a man liable to punishment for asserting his hereditary claim in the natural way to what he understands to be his own. It probably stood peaceably for a time alongside the rule that admitted copyholders cannot insist on their manorial rights at common law. But it is also likely that when the copyholder's position was scrutinized more closely, and his case at common law urged more sharply, the incompatibility of the two rules was pointed out. It is hard to distinguish the heir's prescriptive right to enter assuming that his ancestor's holding will be regranted to him from the admitted copyholder's right to occupy the land against the will of the lord. Both prescriptions must be good or both bad. There is one holding from the early sixteenth century at variance with Littleton's statement.[35] Perhaps the first solution was to find consistency by rejecting both prescriptions, but as Littleton gained authority with age it perhaps became harder to doubt him and more convenient to achieve harmony in the opposite way, by accepting both prescriptions.

3

Shortly after the middle of the sixteenth century, objections to the copyholder's case had been cleared away. It was generally agreed that this special class of tenants at will had always enjoyed exceptional privileges and that they were therefore entitled to the benefits of trespass at common law. So far, we have not considered whether or not the judges were worried about the actual historical fidelity of the premise. We have assumed that they were willing to say that no evidence of commencement is evidence of perpetuity. We have considered objections that could be made even if this were granted—objections which, at their weakest, say that though the copyholder has rights he is procedurally impotent to enforce them, and which at their strongest deduce from certain common-law rules that copyhold privileges cannot be immemorial. It is now time to ask whether the historical facts themselves were taken into account; whether it was suspected that a short time previously copyholders had not existed except as villein tenants, and that no land had forever been granted to hold at the will of the lord *secundum consuetudinem manerii* without the imposition of labor services and the connotations of servility.

There is scarcely any evidence on this matter before Elizabeth's reign. In that reign and the following one, attempts were made to deal with copyhold historically. For the most part, they were attempts to prove that copyhold was ancient enough to be immemorial and had always been distinct from villenage. Arguments to this effect perhaps betray a certain nervousness, as if it were vaguely apprehended that the abstract possibility that copyholds as such could be very ancient did not quite square with reality. It was a matter of urgency to interpret medieval sources in such a way that the myth of the law's eternity would be saved. Some commentators, however, did not concur with those who maintained the historical probability of immemorial copyhold customs. To some, the accomplished fact of the copyholders' legal security was acceptable without antiquarian apology.

The main sources for the view that copyholders had existed from the earliest times are Calthrope's readings and Coke's *Commentary upon Littleton*. (When he wrote *The Compleat Copy-holder,* Coke to some extent changed his tune.) The arguments in both books are on the whole the same, though Coke is more copious and more cautious. The following is the historical passage near the beginning of Calthrope's readings:[36]

And concerninge their antiquity it appeareth by a certeyne booke intituled de Priscis Anglorum Regibus translated oute of the Saxon tongue by William Lambert of Lincolnes Inne that copiholdes weare long before the conquest and then called by the name of folklandes Chartre landes then called by the name of Bookelandes as you may see in the begininge of the book in his treatyse de rerum et verborum explicone and by Mr. Bracton an auncient wryter yf the lawes of England in his book whearin he vouchethe divers precidents and Recordes of R. Henry 3 therin is that made of allowance of copiholders or customarye tenants as doing their services due, the lord ought not to compell [sic] them accordinge to the Justices opinions. Sithens in the time of E. 4 & R. 2 as appearethe by Fitzh. his abridgemente they weare the[n] allowed & preferred by a speciall wrytt for that purpose and the lord theirby compelled to do right and in the tyme of H. 4 tenants by the veirg which ar in the same nature that copiholders weare then allowed by the name of Sockmen in franktenure and in the tyme of H. 7 weare allowed ayde of the kynge for defence of their estates and so in lyke sorte have copiholders in their nature hadd their allowaunce in everye kyng's time sithence untill this daye whearin the Justices seeme nowe to be of that opynion of the said Mr. Bracton and the said Justices in the tyme of E. 4 weare before. And thus mutche havinge shewed of their antiquitye and allowance in former tyme I will farder proceede in some particuler proofes theirof by the lawes and Statuts of the Realme

And because I fynde none that seemethe so mutche to deface the estimation of copiholdes as Mr. Fitz. dothe in his Na. bre. in his wrytt de recto clauso: I will first sett downe his wordes and iudgment in the same place and after prove the good estimacon of copiholders by other auctorytyes. Mr. Fitz. saithe that this terme copiholders or tenants by copye of courte Rolle is but a terme newlye founde and that in auncient tyme they weare called tenants in villenage or of base tenure and saithe he dothe appeare by tholde tenures for that no copiholders weare spoken of their and yeat their weare at that tyme sutche tenants but then they weare as he saithe called tenants in villenadge or base tenure and saith also as appearethe in 14 E 4 that tenants by copye of courte rolle if false iudgment be geven against them in the lordes Courte they shall have no wrytt de falso iudicio but to sue to their lord by way of petition because to hold by copye of courte rolle which is called as he saithe base tenure is to holde in villenadge which said opinion of Mr. Fitz. hathe been by dyvers wrested and taken to make no difference betweene tenure in villenadge and tenure by copye of courte Rolle or base tenure. Whearin what interpretacon soever may be made of Mr. Fiz: meaning it is verye evident to be seene that not only his owne auctoryte which he vouchethe of the olde tenures is otherwyse to be understood but also dyvrs & yea as I suppose other authorityes in the lawe do make an apparent division betweene those tenures. I meane betweene tenants by copye and tenants by villenage touching the natures of their tenures. And first touching thauctorityes of the olde tenures it is verye playne that that booke makethe distinction betweene tenure in villenage and tenure in fee base which is understood this tenure by copye at the lordes will and callethe it a fee although but a base fee and maketh divers distinctions betweene them and saithe that the tenants in villenage must do all sutche services as the lord will commande them. But otherwise he saithe it is of tenants in fee base & Thus it seemethe the said booke of the olde tenures by Mr. Fitz: misrecyted which I am bold to affirme yeildinge nevertheles great reverence to his great learninge because Mr. Thornton a man deeplye learned in his late readinge at Lyncolnes Inne uppon a newe statute of forgers takinge occasion one daye of readinge to intreate some whate of forgers of court Rolls did their reade and affirme playnlye that Mr. Fitz. did in this poynt mutche mistake the said booke of olde tenures & besides for the farder credit of copiholdes it is to be noted that the great auctorytie of Mr. Litt. who amonge the rest of his tenures doth make a devided chapter hearof differinge from his tenants in villenage sheweing their the sutes

& assurances of copiholdes affirminge farder that they have an inheritance accordinge to the custome of the mannor & although he saithe that they have an estate but at the lordes will accordinge to the common law & that if the lord put them oute it is said the[y] have no remedye but by peticon and yeat he wryteth not that of his owne opinion, but that it is said of an unknowne opinion. But Brian cheefe Justice in 21 of E. 4 saithe that his opinion ever was & ever shalbe that if sutche tenant at will payinge his service be put oute by the lord he shall maynteyne an action of trespas against the lord and so seemethe the judges opinion at this daye so is Danbye cheef Justice opinion in 7 E. 4 that tenant by the custom is aswell inherytable by the custome as he that hath freeholde by the comon lawe according to which reasons the said opinion of Mr. Bracton with the precedents of H. 3 & the wrytt used in the time of R 2 be ageeable besides other reasons & Rulles at the common law provinge the same as things by use & contynuaunce may chaunge their first & original nature as the comen service of soccage tenure was in the beginninge as Mr. Litt. saithe to till the lordes land & do sutch lyke bond service & yeat nowe by former consent of the lordes & contynewaunce of tyme chaunged into monye & a more easye service & so it may be said of copiholders so longe as the tenants themselves be free althoughe their tenures weare never so bond in the beginninge yeat by contynewaunce of tyme they may growe to somme more freedome & libertye another reason and rule their is at the common lawe to this intent that some things there be which at the beginninge weare but voluntarye & yeat after by contynewaunce of time growe compulsarye as appeareth by 27 Ass. and Mr. Brooke's abridgment in the title of prescription that a man which at the beginninge did but of his owne meere good will & assertion without any consideration or tenure mende a common bridge or repaire an high way after by contynewall usinge of it was compelled to do it wheather he would or no and so it may be said of theise copiholders that though in the beginninge it was the lordes only wil when what and how to grant them yeat nowe when theise grants have continewed tyme oute of mynd the copiholders doinge their sutes and services to their lordes and behavinge themselves as copiholders should do the[y] ought to enioye their copihold wheather the lord will or no. And thus mutch for the reasons allowinge copiholdes by the common lawe.

Calthrope's first argument is as impressive as it is erroneous. Lambarde's definition of folkland and bookland, as quoted without comment in the section on copyholds in Coke on Littleton,[37] goes as follows:

> Terra ex scripto Saxonice Bockland. Fundum veteres aut ex scripto qui Bockland, i. bookland, aut sine scripto qui Folkland dicebatur, possidebant. Quae fuit ex scripto possessio commodiore erat possessione, libera, atque immunis. Fundus sine scripto censum pensitabat annuum, atque officiorum servitute quadam est obligatus. Priorem viri plerumque nobiles atque ingenui, posteriorem rustici ferre et pagani possidebant.

It is no wonder that Calthrope and Coke, with the help of the presumption against major change common to their times, should suppose that bookland and folkland were older names for freehold and copyhold land, totally wrong as this is. The mere existence of a tenure other than freehold before the Conquest does not, of course, prove that the owner or holder of folkland enjoyed customary privileges like those of copyholders. Unless Calthrope was ready (as he might well be) to assume that the degrading institutions of personal serfdom and insecure villein tenure could not have existed before freeborn Englishmen were subjugated, holders of folkland might as well have been at their lords' mercy.

Bracton, however, is taken to prove that this was not the case as early as Henry III's reign. The reader of Bracton could hardly fail to know that there was villenage and villein tenure in the thirteenth century. But according to Calthrope's interpretation, there were also copyholders. Calthrope does not say what passages in Bracton he is relying on. Coke makes this clear, saying "*Bracton* calleth copiholders *villanos sockmannos,* not because they were bond, but because they hold by base tenure, by doing of villein services."[38] Coke then cites two passages (Lib. 2, cap. 8, fol 26, and Lib. 4, cap. 28, fol 209). I think there is no doubt that Calthrope had the same passages in mind. Once again, he makes a serious, but understandable, misinterpretation.

The villein socman in Bracton is actually the ancestor of the later tenant in ancient demesne. In the thirteenth century, this class of ancient demesne tenant conveyed by surrender and held by relatively menial agricultural services. He was protected in his estate by the king's writ of right close, or "little writ of right," directed to the bailiff of the manor and commanding him to do justice in the manorial court according to the custom. The freehold was held to reside in the lord. It is true, therefore, that the villein socman was a good deal like a copyholder, with the important qualification that he had the "little writ." Subsequently, villein socmen experienced different fates. Some came to convey by deed. The courts then invented the "conveyancing test" to determine who was entitled to the little writ, holding—unhistorically—that this privilege belonged only to those who conveyed by deed. Those who did not pass the conveyancing test, with a few exceptions, sank to the remediless condition of villein tenants and like others of that class re-emerged as copyholders.[39]

Perhaps Calthrope and Coke ought to have suspected that that is what happened. A third passage in Bracton, not cited by Coke, shows that the little writ belongs to tenants who seem to meet the description of villein socmen, though there they are called *glebae ascripticii*.[40] In the passages which are cited, it is reasonably clear, though not explicit, that he is talking about ancient demesne manors and not others. If tenants in ancient demesne existed in Henry III's time, as they were no doubt assumed to have done, it is hard to identify them with any class of tenants discussed by Bracton except villein socmen. Bracton's discussion of villenage shows that it too had some points in common with copyhold.[41]

On the other hand, copyholders were also presumed to have existed on general principles and "known" to have existed before the Conquest. They were a more important class of tenant than tenants in ancient demesne. Villein socmen, as Bracton describes them, look like copyholders in that they convey by surrender and lack the freehold, while the sixteenth-century beneficiary of the little writ conveyed by deed and had the freehold. Even if it were inferred—and inference from Bracton's text is required—that villein socmen are associated with ancient demesne, there is no particular reason why they could not exist elsewhere as well. To identify them with copyholders was hasty, but not outrageous.

Once the identification was made, Bracton seemed to supply an excellent argument that copyholders should be protected at common law. For he says the lord may not expel them so long as they pay their services, and this must mean that the courts would not permit expulsions contrary to the custom. Since this restraint on the lord was not interpreted as a peculiarity of ancient demesne manors and identified with the little writ, the views of Henry III's judges could be considered identical with those of Brian and Danby and the Elizabethan courts. To state it another way, in keeping with the theory of copyhold rights, in Henry III's day the custom of the courts was to regard the special privileges of copyholders as immemorial, and that is a good reason to banish any doubt that they actually are. If one missed the point that the little writ was the principal procedural device for protecting villein socmen, one could easily conclude that they successfully brought trespass against their lords when Bracton wrote.

To show the continuity of the legal protection of copyholders, Calthrope cites precedents from Richard II and Henry IV. Coke's specific citation makes it clear what case from Richard II Calthrope had in mind. This is Philipott v. Wade (1390),[42] an entirely relevant case, for it is evidence that at least once a writ in the nature of mandamus was issued requiring a lord to do justice toward a copyholder in his manorial court. If such a restraint was ever placed on the lord's will, it probably follows that he should also be liable in trespass for entering upon a copyholder contrary to the custom. The case is anomalous, and there is no evidence that it was followed, but that matters little for Calthrope's purposes. The important point for him is that the case proves not only that copyholders existed in the late fourteenth century, but also that their privileges were then held at least by some to be immemorial. Any holding in favor of copyholders must be evidence of the timelessness of the tenure, so long as one assumes that the courts could not have favored them on any other basis. In fact, Richard II's judges might have allowed a "special writ" to copyholders without illusions about the newness of the tenure in their day and its relation to villenage.

Having laid out his case, Calthrope undertakes to correct Fitzherbert's reading of the *Old Tenures*.[43] Here there is right on both sides. Fitzherbert did fail to say that the *Old Tenures* contains a heading "Fee base." On the other hand, he says that at the time that book was compiled copyholders were known either as tenants in villenage or in base tenure. "Base tenure" may refer to "fee base." The term "copyholder" does not occur, and all Fitzherbert claims is that the word is new, not the tenure. Calthrope rightly enough attaches importance to the fact that a base tenure could nevertheless be a kind of fee, but Fitzherbert does not deny this. The definitions of "fee base" and "villenage" in the *Old Tenures* do not lend much support to Calthrope's view that copyholders were anciently a distinct class and a legally protected one. Fee base is defined simply as "a tenir a la volunte le seignour." Of villenage, the *Old Tenures* says, "Tenir en pure villenage est a faire tout ceo, que le seignour luy voit commaunder. La descriptio de villenage est villeyn de sank et de tenure. Et il est de que son seignour prent redemption de sa file marier ou sou mesmes en franchese. Et cest que le seignour puit oustre des terres ou tenementz a sa volunte." Perhaps the most reasonable interpretation is that tenurially there is no difference between the two except in the nature of the services. Calthrope's assumption, however, is clearly that villein tenants could not have had customary fees and special privileges from time out of mind, and granting this he is justified in citing the *Old Tenures* as authority that special tenants at will who did not hold in villenage existed in the late fourteenth century.

Calthrope's arguments from Littleton are reasonable as far as they go. As Fitzherbert obviously knew, Littleton does have separate chapters on villenage and copyhold. His rather perfunctory discussion of villenage[44] is such that one might easily conclude that this tenure was not very common in his day, that it was only distinguishable from copyhold by the nature of the services, and therefore that copyhold had probably split off from villenage with a latter-day commutation of services. But if one is convinced of the antiquity of the distinction, Littleton need not interfere. The second argument, that Littleton seems to avoid associating himself with the view that copyholders have no common-law remedy, is strained if plausible. It is no wonder that Littleton expressed himself with a note of uncertainty, inasmuch as some of his contemporaries certainly wanted to allow a remedy, but Calthrope and Coke are a little wishful when they interpret his caution as a sign of disapproval of what was still probably the majority position. They should have noticed that Littleton in his cacapity of a judge seemed to disagree with Danby's opinion.

The last part of Calthrope's historical introduction does not seem altogether consistent with what goes before. After saying that copyholders existed before the Conquest and suggesting that their privileges were considered immemorial enough in Henry III's reign to merit legal protection, he then concedes that there may have been a time when they were subject to arbitrary treatment. However, this time is not specified. The effect of the last sentences is merely to state the principle of prescription upon which the copyholder's case in any event depends. If there was a time when copyholders knew all the insecurity of villein tenure, it was beyond memory. All the historical evidence, as Calthrope reads it, supports the legal inference of immemorial continuance.

Next to Calthrope, the earliest historical observations on copyholds were made by John Kitchin in his *Court Leete et Court Baron,* first published in 1579.[45] Kitchin's account is practically the same as Calthrope's. He repeats the identification of folkland and copyhold, quotes Bracton to the same purpose as Calthrope, and cites Fitzherbert with the comment that even if copyholders once held in villenage "ceo ne fayt eux villeines," as if their personal status were the point. Like Calthrope, Kitchin concedes that there may have been a time when copyholders were really tenants at will, but he is no more concerned than Calthrope with a possibility so remote in time. On the whole, Kitchin does not seem especially troubled by the problem of historical justification, as befits the author of a practitioner's manual.

Although in the *Commentary upon Littleton*[46] Coke seems to be in general agreement with Calthrope, he is more cautious and less explicit. For example, he confines his dispute with Fitzherbert to terminology, citing unexceptionable evidence that names other than villenage and base tenure were applied to the tenure quite early and that the term "copyholder" itself can be found in a Yearbook from Henry V's reign. He quotes Lambarde without forcing any conclusion as to the identity of folkland and copyhold. A few words suggest that Coke did not reject the possibility that copyhold had developed out of villein tenure, provided the distinction between the tenure and the personal status of villenage is kept in mind. Coke does not insist that Bracton is evidence of copyholders' legal security, but only of their existence under the name of villein socmen. On the other hand, he cites Britton's description of villein socmen as virtually an anticipation of Brian and Danby.[47] This is perhaps more egregious than Calthrope's use of Bracton, for Britton, as well as *Fleta,* which Coke also cites,[48] makes the association between villein socmen and ancient demesne and the little writ much clearer than Bracton does. Because of his use of Britton in this way, it seems safe to conclude that Coke's views do not differ materially from Calthrope's.

The most novel feature of Coke's account is his citation of the chapter on murder in the *Dialogue of the Exchequer* as a mention of copyholders. After a discussion in that chapter of whether it is murder for a Norman to kill an Englishman, the following digression occurs:[49]

Discipulus: Miror singularis excellentiae Principem [William I] & accerimae virtutis hominem, in subactam & sibi suspectam Anglorum gentem hac usum misericordia, ut non solum Colonos per quos agricultura posset exerceri indempnes servaret; verum ipsis Regni majoribus fundos suos & amplas possessiones relinqueret.

Magister: Licet haec ad suscepta negotia quibus debitor factus sum non attinent, tamen quae super hiis ab ipsis indigenis accepi, gratis exponam. Post Regni conquisitionem, post justam Rebellium subversionem, cum Rex ipse Regisque proceres loca nova perlustrarent, facta est inquisitio diligens, qui fuerunt qui contra Regem in bello dimicantes per fugam se salvaverunt. His omnibus & item haeredibus eorum qui in bello occubuerunt, spes omnis terrarum & fundorum atque reditum quos ante possederant, praeclusa est: magnum namque reputabant frui vitae beneficio sub inimicis. Verum qui vocati ad bellum nec dum convenerant, vel familiaribus vel quibuslibet necessariis occupati negotiis non interfuerant, cum tractu temporis devotis obsequiis gratiam dominorum possedissent sine spe successionis filii tantum pro voluptate tamen dominorum possidere coeperunt. Succedente vero tempore cum Dominis suis odiosi passim a possessionibus pellerentur, nec esset qui ablata restitueret communis Indigenarum ad Regem pervenit querimonia, quasi sic omnibus exosi & rebus spoliati ad alienigenas transire cogerentur. Communicato tandem super his consilio, decretum est, ut quod a dominis suis exigentibus meritis interveniente pactione legitima poterant obtinere, illis inviolabilis jure concederentur: caeterum autem nomine successionis a temporibus subactae gentis nihil sibi vendicarant. Quod quidem quam discreta consideratione cautum sit manifestum est, praesertim cum sic modis omnibus ut sibi consulerent, de caetero studere tenerentur devotis obsequiis Dominorum suorum gratiam emercari. Sic igitur quisquis de gente subacta fundos vel aliquid hujusmodi possidet, non quod ratione successione deberi sibi videbatur, adaptus est; sed quod solummodo meritis suis exigentibus, vel aliqua pactione interveniente obtinuit.

It is now evident how Coke reconstructed the history of copyhold tenure. Before the Conquest all small agricultural holdings were in effect copyholds. After that upheaval, many Englishmen were depressed into villenage. The more fortunate remained personally free and obtained estates at will. At a very early date, the king intervened to guarantee estates of inheritance to these tenants at will. They became legally protected copyholders. When Bracton describes, as villein socmen, a class of legally protected tenants who are still not freeholders, he must be referring to these favored Englishmen. The thread of villein socmen runs on through *Fleta* and Britton and may be spliced with the first Yearbook references to "tenant by roll" in the late fourteenth century and "copietenants" in the early fifteenth. The *Dialogue* is a valuable additional source. Though Coke has hardly pondered all the difficulties raised by his evidence, his interpretation is not fantastic.

The historical passages in Coke's *Compleat Copy-holder*[50] seem to reflect more systematic and careful consideration than the brief notes and citations in the *Commentary upon Littleton*. They present a very different picture of the tenure's history. Again Coke starts with a firm conviction that Anglo-Saxon folkland was identical with copyhold land. He admits his uncertainty about the security of folkland holders, but conjectures that they were literally dependent on the lord's will and in fact frequently victims of arbitrary expulsion.

His reason for surmising that this was true before the Conquest is that it was certainly true afterwards. Generally speaking, the small landholder and agricultural worker under the Normans was a villein and a villein tenant. Bracton's characterization of tenants in villenage is quoted as a description of the unhappy condition of the copyholder's ancestors. Villein socmen are clearly distinguished from the true villeins who later became copyholders. Their particular connection with ancient demesne still does not seem to be clearly understood. But, strangely enough, on Bracton's authority they are classified as freeholders. They are taken as ordinary socage tenants who were once called villein socmen only because they did agricultural services, not because of any of the material disadvantages of villenage or even of copyhold.

Coke's admission that copyhold originated in villenage, together with his belief that villenage was an utterly insecure and unprivileged tenure, undermines the convenient case that copyholders' rights are historically as well as legally immemorial. Coke seems content to face this fact. It is enough to know that a long time ago, if not in the indefinitely remote past, most villein tenants acquired a new name and became accustomed to better treatment, and that in due course the courts took notice of these changes, the Chancery leading the way. The present position of the law is an accomplished fact. It cannot be neatly and confidently justified by the historian.

An anonymous early seventeenth-century commentator on Littleton[51] takes an approach similar to Coke's in the *Compleat Copyholder,* but markedly different from Calthrope and Coke's other account. He gives what is in many ways the soberest and least speculative of the early histories of copyhold. Nothing is said of folkland or Bracton. Fitzherbert's statement that copyhold was once villenage is confirmed in an interesting way. The commentator points out that copyhold is rare in Kent because villenage was not known there. Alone among his contemporaries, this writer refers to the evidence of ancient copies, "where such copyholders are named tenants in villenage, and in Latin *nativi tenentes,* and this term or word, namely, tenants by copy of court roll, is not mentioned or named." No attempt is made to prove that Littleton agreed with

Danby and Brian, but the problem of whether he wrote "poet" or "voet" is noted. It is pointed out that it was Littleton himself who challenged Danby in 1467. The commentator seems to assume what after all is most likely, that Littleton and most of his brethren were probably not ready to give copyholders a remedy.

Common-law protection, like the privileges of copyholders themselves, is therefore relatively new. How can it be justified? The anonymous commentator says simply that "after long custom and continuance of time had fixed such estates, then the common law did take notice of them and of the said custom, reputing them to be more than tenants at will only (*scil.*) to be tenants at will according to the custom . . ." He then makes a striking comparison between the law's attitude toward uses and its attitude toward copyholds:

> . . . for uses, at the first invention and creation of them, were but trust and confidence between the parties, no ways issuing out of the land, but collateral, annexed in privity of estate, and unto the persons touching the land; for he that had a use has *ius neque in re neque ad rem,* yet in long time those uses and confidences came to be reputed in some respects as chattels, and they were devisable, and in some respects they were reputed hereditaments, of which there might be *possessio fratris;* though in judgment of law and truth before the statute 27 H8 cap. 10 they were neither chattels nor hereditaments; for they were not assets unto the executors nor unto the heir.

The source of this comparison might be Francis Bacon's readings on the Statute of Uses of 1600, where the following passage occurs:[52]

> I have sought likewise whether there be any thing which maketh with them [uses] in our law; and I find that Periam, Chief Baron, in the argument of Chudleigh's case compareth them to copyholders. And aptly for many respects: First, because as an use seemeth to be an hereditament in the court of chancery, so the copyhold seemeth to be an hereditament in the lord's court: Secondly, this conceit of imitation hath been troublesome in copyholds, as well as in uses; for it hath been of late days questioned, whether there should be dower, tenancy by the courtesy, intails, discontinuances and recoveries of copyholds, in the nature of inheritances at the common law; and still the judgments have weighed, that you must have particular customs in copyholds, as well as particular reasons of conscience in use, and the imitation rejected; And thirdly, because they

both grew to strength and credit by degrees; for the copyhold at first had no remedy at all against the lord, but was a mere tenancy at will; afterwards it grew to have remedy in chancery, and afterwards against the lords by trespass at the common law; and now lastly the law is taken by some, that they have remedy by *ejectione firmae,* without a special custom of leasing. So no doubt in uses, at the first the chancery made question to give remedy, until uses grew more general, and in the chancery more eminent; and then they grew to have remedy in conscience; but they might never maintain any manner of remedy at the common law, neither against the feoffee nor against strangers; but the remedy against the feoffee was left to the *subpoena,* and the remedy against strangers to the feoffee.

Bacon, like the anonymous commentator, has no illusions about the antiquity of copyhold or its legal position. Whether or not Bacon is the source, they may be considered together.

Is the comparison with uses more than a nice conceit? At first sight it seems to be little more. Uses developed and changed, both in the layman's eyes and in the Chancellor's; the popular attitude and the legal attitude toward copyholds altered with time. So far the two cases are parallel. But does the parallel point to any principle by which the legal protection of copyholds can be explained and justified? The basic position of Bacon and the anonymous commentator seems to be that although the special privileges of copyholders have no claim to historical eternity, the courts were nevertheless entitled to take notice of manorial reality. For a long time—so long that evidence of commencement is absent—estates at will have been granted in special terms. It is notorious that the parties to these grants expect them to confer something more than estates at will. Copyholds have been regarded by the manorial courts as analogous to freeholds. Under these circumstances, the royal courts, whether of equity or of common law, ought to determine legal right and wrong by the criterion of lay expectations and intentions. The timeless custom of the realm or of particular localities is not the sole source of rights even at common law. A custom old enough to raise expectations can be legally significant even though it is not really immemorial; what is reputed as custom is sometimes more important than what actually is.

Now, perhaps, a meaning can be seen in the parallel with uses. Bacon and the anonymous commentator make the reasonable assumption that it took time for the Chancellor to decide to apply some of the rules of real and personal property to uses. They are perhaps suggesting that the decisions by which changes in the equitable rules on uses came about reflected changes in lay attitudes, reflected "custom" in the loose sense of ordinary habits of thought. According to this theory, there was perhaps a time when the Chancellor required land held to the use of a man and his heirs to be conveyed to the heirs after his death, notwithstanding his attempt to devise it to someone else. The fact that this rule was abandoned can best be explained by supposing that the Chancellor gradually realized that the creators of uses intended them to be devisable, that a conveyance to the use of A and his heirs is no more intended to convey an equitable interest to the heirs by purchase than a feoffment to a man and his heirs is intended to give the heirs a legal interest. From the actual practice of men it came to be inferred that those who had uses thought they had something which would as a rule behave like the corresponding common-law estate—barring "special matter of conscience," such as the very consideration that a "use in fee" is hardly intended to be undevisable like a legal estate in fee. So it may be inferred that those who give and take copyholds think that the part of the grant which confers the customary estate, rather than the part which conveys a tenancy at will, defines the nature of the interest transmitted.

Objections to this parallel can easily be made. It may be argued that it is an excellent justification for the equitable protection of copyholders, but not for their standing at common law. Equity must refer to the intentions and expectations of men, and thence to "custom" in the looser sense. Common law is custom in the stricter sense. A copyholder prescribes, and this means he pretends to rights of unlimited antiquity. Since the common law permits copyholders to prescribe, the courts must believe that the pretense corresponds to facts, either because there is historical evidence that this is so, or because the historical evidence is so obscure that it has to be discounted and a legal inference made from the absence of evidence of commencement. The common-law courts ought not, and probably would not, permit copyholders to prescribe if there were any certainty that copyhold customs could not be immemorial.

To this, Bacon and the anonymous commentator could make two replies. On the one hand, they might question whether the common-law courts ought to insist that rights enforced there must arise from timeless custom. They might argue that even if the protection of copyholders was the product of an historical illusion, it is still entirely justifiable. On the other hand, they might contend that in fact the common law had not always been governed by the theory that immemorial custom alone is the source of legal rights. It is possible that the decision to allow copyholders trespass was made for reasons of simple justice and practicality, with reference only to the looser type of custom. The line between equity and common law may not always have been so firm as dogma would have it. In either case, Bacon and the anonymous commentator, and perhaps Coke in *The Compleat Copy-holder,* sound a more modern note than such writers as Calthrope. In terms of jurisprudence, their analysis points to a theory of rights which is much less dependent on historical make-believe. In terms of legal history, they perceived correctly that the law had expanded its scope by many different devices, including some which savor of equity, and had not always struggled so hard to maintain the myth of timelessness.

Nevertheless, one may doubt whether those who had the clearest understanding of the history of copyhold also had the best appreciation of the history of the common-law decision to allow copyholders protection. It is possible that Calthrope, writing at a time when the change in the common law's position was new and probably still in dispute, conveys the flavor of professional thinking at the time of the change. There is no evidence whether an array of historical proofs was ever drawn up in court to persuade the judges that at least as early as Henry III's reign copyholds existed under protection of law. In two cases, of 1595 and 1597, Justice Walmesley of the Common Pleas cited Bracton to prove that copyholders must convey by surrender.[53] Walmesley probably, therefore, accepted the identification of villein socmen with copyholders. Other judges, however, seem to recognize that copyhold had evolved out of villenage and had only recently been recognized in law.[54] On the whole, it seems likely that Calthrope's views enjoyed a certain currency. The judges probably wanted to be satisfied that the copyholder's prescription does not pretend to be historically incredible, and an historical proof was ready for the purpose. Misinterpretation wedded to a curious but tenacious jurisprudence produced fruitful results. The disturbing authority of Fitzherbert was explained away. Taking a much darker view than necessary of the realities of villein tenure, lawyers satisfied themselves that copyholders had never held in villenage and had consequently enjoyed their customs time out of mind.

CHAPTER III

THE ELIZABETHAN COURTS AND THE COMMON LAW OF COPYHOLD

Around the middle of the sixteenth century, the common-law courts probably decided that the copyholder's claim to trespass was justified. For upwards of a decade after the possibly decisive case of 1552–1553, the reports give little evidence of litigation involving copyholds. Very likely copyholders' lawyers were for a while unsure that the judges would persist in their favorable judgment and therefore preferred to sue in the Chancery. But in the 1570's a stream of copyhold cases begins to flow strongly. The right of copyholders to have their customary estates protected by royal justice was established once and for all, and many cases came before the courts, bringing with them a host of delicate problems. The courts had to turn to working out the common law of copyholds.

In a way, "the common law of copyholds" is a contradiction. Essentially, a copyholder has such rights as the particular custom of the manor gives him. Unless the custom of all manors is the same on some point, the general custom of the realm can hardly contain rules affecting copyholds. In fact, the courts held that some manorial customs were all but universal and therefore would be held applicable unless an exceptional custom were pleaded and proved. That is one sense of "the common law of copyholds." Moreover, issues could arise which were covered by no special custom as far as appeared in evidence. The courts had to decide whether the appropriate common-law rule of property could justifiably be applied. Moreover, special customs established in evidence sometimes required interpretation. Furthermore, it was sometimes argued that a statute applied or did not apply to customary tenants, and only the common-law courts could decide this. Finally, there were a few problems which custom could not solve, which could not be solved by invoking or refusing to invoke a well-known common-law property rule, and which therefore called for particular originality and command of principle. To arrive at settled answers to many specific problems arising under these heads was to create a common law of copyholds.

Settled answers were not easy to come by. One need not study the Elizabethan copyhold cases very long to realize how far one is from *stare decisis*. Decisions and opinions contradict one another on all sides. The judges are usually ready to re-examine issues and debate them on principle. One gets the impression that they were much concerned with settling a new field of law, but by no means willing to sacrifice sound principle to swift agreement. As time goes on, issues to which a superficial solution had been given at first seem to have been thought through more deeply. But a deeper analysis in the jurisprudential terms of the sixteenth century need not produce more practical solutions. Owners of copyholds in Elizabeth's reign deserve a measure of pity. Surely simple rules, and above all agreement on any set of rules, would have been in their interest, whether or not lawyerly consciences were satisfied.

These impressions are greatly reinforced if one consults unprinted reports of cases. The legal tradition preserved by the accident of having been printed is more coherent. But the accident is probably a happy one, for it must have helped bring about a true settlement in the earlier seventeenth century. A later generation of lawyers could overlook a good deal of past confusion if they considered mainly what appeared in the printed books. The magisterial Coke, both in his reports and in *The Compleat Copy-holder,* laid down the law of copyholds, not always with the strictest respect for what the courts had actually decided or failed to decide. The classic positions of the common law of copyholds, the rules which later found their way into the standard treatises, took form.

I

The simplest type of problem raised in the copyhold cases is whether to apply the appropriate common-law property rule when no special custom is available. The relevant legal values are apparent. From a practical point of view, there would seem to be some advantage in having strictly analogous rules for freehold and copyhold property, barring interference from some special manorial custom. Predictions of the legal consequences of acts involving copyhold could be made by referring to well-established and well-known rules. On the other hand, the relevant common-law rules were often antiquated and useless vestiges of feudalism. Willingness on the judges' part to desert them whenever possible in favor of common sense would bespeak a significant lack of reverence for every jot and tittle of the law. These two conflicting practical values must be weighed against the values of legal logic. Behind the common-law rule some fundamental principle might lie. It might be one which for technical reasons ought to be applied to copyhold, but it might be so closely connected with the very nature of freehold as to be inapplicable elsewhere. If any tendency can be discerned in the Elizabethan cases, it is toward the opinion that certain common-law rules at first applied to copyhold ought not to have been, had their rationale and essential character been rightly understood.

Let us start with the most useless of the common-law rules, those concerned with discontinuance, descents cast, and tortious fees. There was a great deal of debate about the applicability of these rules, especially the one on discontinuance. That rule is as follows: If A is seised of lands in tail, and wrongfully enfeoffs B (that is, in fee, in tail, or for the life of anyone except A himself) and dies, the heir in tail, remainderman, or reversioner may not enter on the feoffee, but must sue for the land by action of formedon. Likewise, if C is seised of land in the right of his wife and conveys more than an estate for his own life and dies, the wife or her heir may not enter upon the feoffee, but must sue by action of *Cui in vita.* The feoffments by A or C are said to discontinue the estate tail or the wife's estate and put the entitled parties to their action. Suppose, then, that X is a copyholder in tail, or a man in possession of a copyhold in the right of his wife. X surrenders the tenement into the lord's hands to the use of Y and his heirs, and Y is admitted accordingly. X dies, and his heir in tail, or his wife, enters upon Y. Y sues in trespass at common law. No special custom covering the situation is alleged. Is the heir or wife a wrongdoer for entering instead of pursuing a manorial plaint in the nature of formedon or *Cui in vita*? In its first form, this case obviously can arise only if customary land can be held in tail. That vexed and complex question is discussed later. For the moment, it may be assumed that copyhold can be entailed. In the second form, the case could not arise if the Statute of 32 Henry VIII, ca. 28, applied to copyhold, for that act abolished the rule of discontinuance as far as estates held in the right of a wife are concerned. However, the statute was clearly held inapplicable.[1]

All the earlier Elizabethan authority holds that copyholds may be discontinued.[2] The courts took the natural course and invoked the common-law rule. One argument against doing so was advanced and rejected. It was pointed out that if a freehold tenant in tail surrenders his estate to the reversioner, instead of enfeoffing a stranger, no discontinuance occurs, since he does not purport to convey more than he rightfully may. It was then urged that a copyholder's surrender into the lord's hands is in effect a conveyance to one with a reversionary interest. The court was quick to detect the fallacy in this argument. It was pointed out that a copyholder's surrender to uses is not a conveyance to the lord at all. The lord is merely an instrument to effect the transfer from surrenderor to surrenderee. The latter comes in *per* the surrenderor, and the lord does not enter the chain of copyhold titles. This principle was established clearly in several contexts and on the whole not seriously challenged.[3] The court was therefore right in repudiating the first argument made against discontinuability.

None of these early holdings was printed. However, one equally early printed report was later cited as authority that copyholds may not be discontinued. Although it may be used for that purpose with some color of justification, it is not a clear holding and indeed has very little meaning.[4] In any event, the tide turned against applying the common-low rule. Bullen v. Grant (1589),[5] and especially Bullocke v. Dilbye (1594),[6] both Queen's Bench cases, clearly hold that copyholds may not be discontinued without a special custom. A lost case, Foxlie v. Colson, was cited as authority. The reasoning seems to have been as follows: Granting that a surrender to uses passes nothing to the lord, nevertheless a copyholder cannot make a tortious conveyance. Though a copyholder in tail or in the right of his wife purports to convey a fee, by surrendering to the use of a man and his heirs, the surrenderee in fact, and notwithstanding the form of his admittance, gets nothing more than could rightfully be given, an estate for the surrenderor's life. A copyhold surrender cannot convey a tortious estate because there is no livery of seisin, and at common law a conveyance by a particular tenant without livery—for example, a surrender to the reversioner—will not confer a tortious fee.

Oldcot v. Levell, a printed Queen's Bench case of 1603, confirms the judgment that copyholds may not be discontinued.[7] But the unprinted Elbridge v. Norris and Gurrey v. Sanderson[8] (1602) reverse Bullocke v. Dilbye at least as far as discontinuances by copyholders in tail are concerned. The reasoning was as follows: Littleton says that plaints in the nature of formedon will lie in manorial courts. It is a rule at common law that formedon will never lie except against someone seised by virtue of a tortious feoffment. Thus, if a tenant in tail conveys a rightful estate for his own life and dies, and the grantee persists in occupying the land, he is a simple disseisor, and formedon is not the proper action to bring against him. The same must be true of plaints in the nature of formedon. Therefore a copyholder must be able to convey a tortious estate. Since he can only do so by surrendering in greater estate than he has, such a surrender must serve the purpose of livery of seisin.

In 1604, the Common Pleas decided 4 to 1 that a copyholder in tail may discontinue.[9] The court expressly refused to follow Bullocke v. Dilbye and vouched judgments to the contrary. Livery of the verge by a copyholder was said to be "auxy fort come livery del terre de freehold." But this case is also unprinted. Though the two benches at the beginning of the seventeenth century appear to have agreed that at least a copyholder in tail may discontinue (and if he can convey a tortious estate presumably a copyholder in the right of his wife can too), this fact was probably lost sight of and the printed cases followed. Coke's opinion against discontinuance was probably more influential than the solution actually reached by the courts.[10] Later treatises do not touch on this obscure point of law.

Moving on to a second rule, if a common-law tenant for life enfeoffs someone in fee, his estate is forfeited and the reversioner or remainderman may enter. The feoffment is wrongful, the estate conveyed a tortious fee. If a copyholder in tail may discontinue, a copyholder for life ought to forfeit by surrendering to the use of a man and his heirs. Either the lord or a copyholder in reversion or remainder should be entitled to enter. There are, however, no holdings that such a surrender will work a forfeiture, and a little evidence to the contrary.[11] This is indirect confirmation of Bullocke v. Dilbye.

The authority on a third common-law rule is again conflicting. At common law, if A disseises B and dies, and A's heir enters, B may not enter upon the heir, but is required to bring a writ of entry to recover the land. "The descent cast tolls the entry." In Gravenor's Case (1593), in the Queen's Bench, Gawdy and Popham said that descent of a copyhold will toll the disseisee's right of entry. A Syon's Case of 9 Elizabeth is cited as so adjudged.[12] In Joiner v. Lumberd (1604) the same court *per* Popham held that a descent cast will not toll the entry.[13] In 1610 the King's Bench was divided on the question.[14]

2

Practically speaking, it could make little difference whether the rules on discontinuance, tortious fees, and descents cast were applied to copyholds or not. The applicability of certain rules on future interests is much more important. The value of conformity with the law governing freehold property is pitted against the value of escaping from feudal rules which are notorious in legal history for defeating men's real purposes.

The simplest type of future interest is the remainder. A remainder is an estate limited to take effect immediately upon the cessation of a prior "particular estate" for life or in tail. If, for example, A makes a feoffment to B for life, or to B and the heirs of his body, and then to C and his heirs, C's interest is a remainder in fee. Estates in remainder can also be for life or in tail. A multiplicity of remainders may be limited to take effect successively. If no remainder at all, or no remainder in fee, is limited upon a particular estate, the feoffor retains a reversion. If a remainder is limited unconditionally to a person *in esse* and ascertained at the time of the conveyance, it is known as a vested remainder. If a remainder is limited to a person not *in esse* (as to the eldest son of A, when A has no son), or unascertained (as to the right heirs of A, when A is a living person and it is therefore uncertain who his heir will be), or if a remainder is limited to depend upon a condition (as to A if he shall have attained the age of twenty-one when B dies), the remainder is known as contingent. It is a rule of law that a contingent remainder must vest before termination of the particular estate or be destroyed. Thus, if A enfeoffs B for life, remainder to the right heirs of C, and B's estate ends, either by death or forfeiture, during C's life, A will have the land as of his reversion, and C's heir will never be entitled to the land.

With respect to this type of future interest, conformity between freehold and copyhold property was achieved with relatively little dispute. There was some doubt as to whether a grantor or surrenderor could create remainders without the warrant of a special custom, but it was held that a custom authorizing copyholds in fee is to be interpreted as including the right to limit the fee or part of it by way of remainder.[15]

It was a little harder to establish that remainders in copyhold are always transferable interests, like vested remainders in freehold. Suppose a copyhold is surrendered to the use of X for life, and then to the use of Y and his heirs. X is admitted tenant, but Y is not admitted to any estate. Does Y have a vested interest which he can surrender to another's use? Or does he have what should probably be called a mere "possibility" of an interest, nothing more than a right, enforceable only in equity, to secure admittance after X's life-estate ends? A preponderance of early opinion holds that the admittance of the particular tenant vests all remainders.[16] Remaindermen do not need to seek admittance when the preceding estate ends, but only to pay a fine if one is customarily due. This rule undoubtedly became a permanent part of the law. It directly imitates the common-law rule that livery of seisin to a particular tenant serves the remainders.

Executory interests raise more complex problems. The creation of executory interests in common-law land was made possible by the Statutes of Uses and Wills. Neither act applied to copyhold.[17] Therefore, the only way to permit copyholders to create the same range of future interests as contemporary holders of common-law land would have been to find reasons against applying the rules which forbade creation of executory interests except by virtue of the statutes.

An executory interest is perhaps best defined as a legal future interest which is clearly not a remainder. That is to say, it will not accrue to its holder immediately upon the normal ending of a prior particular estate. "Normal ending" includes death of a life-tenant, forfeiture of a life-estate by virtue of an unwarranted conveyance, and failure of issue under an entail. Executory interests are usually classified as "springing" and "shifting." A shifting interest is an estate reserved to someone other than the feoffor to take effect upon the breach or performance of a condition: for example, A enfeoffs B and his heirs, but if C pay B ten pounds before Michaelmas, then to C and his heirs. By the common law, this feoffment is wholly ineffectual to give C any interest. By a conveyance to uses and the effect of the Statute of Uses, however, C can be given a legal interest as follows: A enfeoffs D to the use of B and his heirs, but if C pay B ten pounds before Michaelmas, then to the use of C and his heirs. Because the statute translates the equitable estates into legal estates, C gets an executory interest of the shifting variety.

A springing interest is any legal future interest which is neither a remainder nor a shifting interest. Two varieties may be given as examples: (1) a future freehold interest without any particular estate, as if A enfeoffs B and his heirs from Michaelmas next; (2) a future freehold interest which cannot take effect until an interval expires after the ending of the particular estate, as if A enfeoffs B for life, and then, one year after the death of B, the land to go to C.

By the common law, B, in the first example, and C, in the second, take no legal interest under these feoffments. They could not be given the sort of legal interests the feoffments purport to create until after the Statutes of Uses and Wills.

With respect to copyholds, the issue is whether a surrender—for example, to the use of X and his heirs, but if Y pay X ten pounds before Michaelmas, then to Y and his heirs—is effective to give Y an interest; or whether a surrender—for example, to the use of X for life and then, one year after the death of X, to the use of Y and his heirs—gives Y any interest. An inclination to follow the common law in these cases, and hold the purported shifting and springing uses void, would bespeak strong adherence to the view that parallelism between customary and common-law land should be favored. Such parallelism could be secured in these cases only by violating the surrenderors' obvious intentions. Given the existence of the Statute of Uses, it is hard to say that the common-law rule against executory interests expressed a policy still relevant in the sixteenth century. The rule was simply part of the law's inheritance. If one looks back to the time when the common-law rule against executory interests in fact made them impossible, a policy can be discerned behind it. It seems questionable, however, whether even that policy would be served by holding surrenders of copyhold to executory uses invalid.

The common-law policy was to prevent proliferation of interests unlikely to be notorious because too dissociated from actual seisin and from livery of seisin. In general, the world has a right to expect that one to whom land has been openly and formally delivered has taken the freehold in a straightforward sense and is therefore answerable for the land. In general, livery speaks for itself. The effect of livery must of course to some extent be defined by the feoffor's words. He must say if he is giving up all he has, that is, conveying a fee simple. He must say if he intends a gift to the feoffee and the heirs of his body, in which case he necessarily retains something to himself. He must say if he intends that the feoffee's estate be conditional and liable to revert to him, the feoffor, upon breach of the condition. Otherwise, the act of livery will mean only that he is conveying his possession "as of freehold," in other words, creating an unconditional life-estate and retaining the fee to himself as a reversion. Thus the livery has one of four meanings. So much anyone with notice of the act knows. It is certain that only the person now seised, by virtue of the livery, and the person who was seised before and who made the livery, can be interested in the land. Recognition of remainders as legitimate interests greatly complicates, perhaps for practical purposes destroys, the straightforwardness of livery and seisin. The feoffor's words can now create any number of interests besides what the actual recipient of livery takes and what the feoffor himself retains. It has ceased to be notorious who is interested in Blackacre. But there is perhaps some point in respecting the original policy that livery should have a simple and informative meaning by drawing a line somewhere. Both the rule on the destructibility of contingent remainders and the rule against shifting and springing interests draw this line. It is at least still clear that no one except the giver and receiver of livery will be involved with the land, unless there are vested remainders when the immediate feoffee's estate terminates.

In the case of copyholds, it seems doubtful whether even a far-fetched inconvenience would accrue from upholding surrenders to executory uses. The terms of surrenders were as notorious as the fact of surrender. Unlike the terms of private charters of feoffment, they were testified in court and entered on the roll. There would seem to be little danger of confusion over the state of manorial ownership, little likelihood that at a given moment it would be unclear who was answerable for the land.

The validity of surrenders to executory uses was not debated in many Elizabethan cases. In later times, it was thought that copyhold surrenders, unlike freehold conveyances before the Statutes of Uses and Wills, can create executory interests.[18] This opinion does not seem to be very firmly posited on early authority, though that authority is not decisive. Clampe's Case (1584, Queen's Bench)[19] involved an attempt to create a springing interest by surrender. Coke was of counsel and argued that it is impossible to do so. His side won, but there was a pleading point in his favor which may have decided the case. Nevertheless, in Simpson v. Southerne (1610, Common Pleas) Clampe's Case was cited as authority that surrenders to executory uses are invalid.[20] Justice Dodderidge expressed regret that the intent of the parties should be defeated by such a rule, but he felt bound by Clampe's Case and therefore concurred with the rest of the court in following it. In the unprinted Palmer v. Peacocke (1610), Justice Williams of the King's Bench upheld the rule urged by Coke in Clampe's Case.[21] A man was seised of a copyhold jointly with his wife for their lives, remainder to the husband in fee. He attempted to surrender his remainder, and it was unanimously held invalid. Having a joint estate for life and a remainder in fee, he is to be treated as if he were a tenant in fee, and a tenant in fee cannot convey a future interest without limiting a particular estate. An earlier decision in the Common Pleas by Wray and Manwood was vouched as authority, and the losing side's purported authority was rebuffed as a mere opinion of counsel.

In Palmer v. Peacocke, Justice Williams was reminded from the bar that a short time before he had expressed an opinion inconsistent with his views in that case. He took the reminder in rather bad grace, but the advocate was quite right. In Middleton v. Holmes,[22] also of 1610, the issue was the validity of a surrender to the use of one's elder son in tail, on condition that he pay ten pounds to the younger son by a certain day, and if he fail to pay, then to the use of the younger son. Justice Yelverton thought this attempt to reserve a condition to a stranger was invalid. Williams, however, argued that surrenders, like uses and wills, should be taken according to the intent of the party. Since there appears to be no difference in principle between the shifting interest in this case and the springing interest in Palmer v. Peacocke, Williams had apparently changed his mind in the later case. Middleton v. Holmes was compromised without decision, and no judges except Yelverton and Williams gave opinions. An earlier dictum, by Justice Beaumond in the Common Pleas in 1594, accords with Williams' opinion on shifting interests in Middleton v. Holmes.[23]

Simpson v. Southerne and Palmer v. Peacocke are the strongest cases, and they hold that executory interests cannot be created by surrender. The best conclusion is that in the early seventeenth century the courts were inclined, despite misgivings, to make copyholds imitate the common law in this respect, unsound as this may have been in the eyes of later commentators.

I have found no cases directly concerned with the applicability of the Rule in Shelley's Case to copyholds. Its applicability was affirmed by dicta, however. This rule serves to prevent evasion of feudal dues and the restriction of alienability. It is best explained by an example which illustrates its normal operation without introducing certain complications. Suppose A conveys to B for life, and then to the right heirs of B. The Rule in Shelley's Case says that this conveyance will be treated as if A had simply conveyed to B and his heirs. B is at once seised in fee simple, and there is no contingent remainder in his heirs. As a result, B can alienate in any estate he likes. If B dies seised, his heir will come to the land by descent and will be liable to such feudal incidents as wardship. If the heir could come to the land by way of remainder (as a purchaser, to use the term of art) he would not be so liable. It was probably never doubted that a surrender to the use of X for life, and then to the use of the right heirs of X, gives X the copyhold in fee.[24] The reasons behind the Rule in Shelley's Case seem to hold for customary land. If the rule were not applied, X's power of alienation would be restricted. An opportunity for defrauding the lord of the fine due on inheritance might be afforded, though whether this would actually be true depends on the doubtful question of whether remaindermen were liable for new fines in the same way as heirs. The interest of various persons in customary wardships might also be injured if the rule were not applied.

There was more debate over whether to apply another rule affecting future interests. Suppose X is seised of a copyhold in fee and surrenders to the use of Y for life, and then to the use of the right heirs of X. Does this create a contingent remainder in the right heirs of X and cause them to take by purchase? Or does it leave X with his old reversion, which he can transfer to another? If X makes no such transfer, will his right heirs take the reversion by descent? At common law, a feoffment for life, with remainder to the right heirs of the feoffor, did not create a contingent remainder and had no effect except to convey a life-estate. After the Statute of Uses, a conveyance of freehold to the use of A for life, and then to the use of the right heirs of the feoffor, likewise failed to create a contingent remainder. The failure of the Statute of Uses to alter the practical effect of the common law in this instance may be explained as follows: If A enfeoffs B and his heirs to the use of C for life, but declares no further uses, he will be understood as if he had limited the use in fee to himself. The unspecified use "results" to A. By effect of the Statute of Uses, this might be thought to give C a legal life-estate and A a remainder in fee. But since A originally had the legal and equitable fee, he will be considered to be in possession of his old use and estate, rather than of ones newly created. We are now ready to proceed to the case at hand. Suppose A enfeoffs B and his heirs to the use of C for life, and then to the use of the right heirs of A. The use in fee will result to A, owing to the possibility that C will die before A, and hence before A's heir is an ascertained person. The Statute of Uses will execute a legal life-estate to C, but the policy of preferring the old use and estate will leave A in the same position he occupied before any conveyance was made. The effect is the same as if, without respect to the Statute of Uses, A had enfeoffed C for life, with remainder to his own right heirs; that is, C has a life estate and A has a reversion in fee.[25] If, therefore, copyholders were allowed to create contingent remainders in their own right heirs by surrender, they would be able to do something that no freeholder could do. A man might wish to create such a remainder, however, because by doing so he could remove his own capacity to alien the land and assure his heir's succession. Such is the presumptive intent of one who surrenders to the use of a stranger for life, then to the use of his own right heirs. The value of allowing the party's intentions to take effect is counterbalanced by the value of keeping land as readily alienable as possible.

The earliest case I have found on this point is from the Common Pleas in 1573.[26] The report gives the opinions of two judges only, and these are sharply opposed. Justice Manwood says that a surrender to the use of one for life, and then to the use of the right heirs of the surrenderor creates a good remainder, and Justice Monson takes the contrary position. If Manwood's argument is expanded somewhat beyond his bare words so as to bring out the implications of his position, his opinion seems to me to be based on two premises. First, a surrender is a conveyance of the surrenderor's whole interest to the lord. Secondly, insofar as a surrenderor fails to designate the whole use, the surrender is to be taken as if it were to the lord's use. (Thus, if a copyholder in fee surrenders to the use of one for life and says nothing more, the lord will have the land to his own use after the end of the life-estate.) If these premises are conceded, Manwood's conclusion certainly follows. The surrenderor divests himself of all interest. If the life estate should end before the surrenderor's death, and hence before his heir is ascertained, the lord would be fully entitled to the land. The contingent remainder limited to the right heirs would be destroyed. Whether that limitation could take effect as a legal executory interest after vesting is another question. If the life tenant outlived the surrenderor, the right heir would of course take as a purchaser.

Monson, it seems to me, challenges both premises. As to the first, he says that surrenders pass nothing to the lord, who is merely an instrument to effect the transmission from surrenderor to surrenderee. In upholding this theory of surrender he was to have the weight of opinion on his side.[27] From the proposition that the lord takes nothing by a surrender to uses, it follows unmistakably that the right heirs cannot be purchasers. Conceived as a conveyance direct to the surrenderee, the surrender does not dispose of the surrenderor's whole interest. He retains a reversion, and his right heir can therefore only come to the land as of the reversion by descent, for that is the older and better title.

In addition, Monson upholds his conclusion by an argument which in effect concedes the first of Manwood's premises but denies the second. Even granting that after the surrender the entire estate is in the lord's hands, uses not expressly designated result to the surrenderor. Under no circumstances, unless such an intention is made explicit by the surrenderor, should a surrender be taken to give the lord himself the right to enjoy the land. Thus, after the surrender in this case, and before admittance, there is a use for life in the surrenderee for life, a contingent use in the right heirs, and a use in fee in the surrenderor. Admittance, in whatever form, will only translate these uses into legal interests.[28] The surrenderor will accordingly have the fee, which will be regarded as his old fee. His right heirs can only take by descent of this fee to them, so there is no remainder.

It would be futile for Manwood to argue with Monson on the first point, for the two theories of surrender are flatly contradictory. On the second point, Manwood has a reply, and this may be what is implied by his words in the latter part of the report. Monson perhaps adheres too closely to the analogy of a feoffment made after the Statute of Uses to the use of A for life, then to the use of the right heirs of the feoffor. In that case, because the Statute must at once execute all the uses it can, the fee must be executed to the feoffor. (Likewise, under the Statute of Wills, if land is devised to A for life and then to the right heirs of the devisor, the right heir, who of course is ascertained at the moment the devise can take effect, will be held to take by descent because that is the better title.)[29] But is it necessary that admittance to a copyhold be construed as instantly executing all the uses limited on the surrender? If it is conceded that the lord takes an interest by the surrender, what is wrong with holding that admittance is to the life tenant only, the residue of the fee remaining in the lord, though subject in equity to the contingent use in the right heirs? Then, if the surrenderor were to die before the life tenant, the ascertained heir could demand admittance to an estate in remainder and take as a purchaser. If, on the other hand, the life tenant died first, perhap the surrenderor could rightfully go to the Chancellor and demand admittance for life (on the assumption that there is no intention for the lord to have the enjoyment of the land at any time). But this would leave the reversion in the lord, subject perhaps to the equitable obligation to admit the surrenderor's right heir after his death.

The next Michaelmas, still in 1573, the effect of a surrender to the use of one for life, and then to the use of the right heirs of the surrenderor, was again discussed in the Common Pleas.[30] Chief

Justice Dyer remarked that this would "make a question," but he announced no opinion one way or the other. In Sere v. Baker (1583), the Common Pleas was again confronted with that question.[31] On the first argument of the case, the court is reported to have resolved that the transaction creates a good contingent remainder. On the second argument, this is given as the opinion of Justices Anderson and Periam, with Justice Meade dissenting and nothing said about the other two judges. Anderson and Periam thought that a surrender to such uses would operate as a conveyance to the lord. Meade denied this. To reinforce his opinion, Meade puts the case of a surrender by X to the use of Y on condition. In such case, there is no doubt that X may enter if the condition is broken. This implies that the lord took no interest, for if he did, and admittance were therefore a grant from him, a condition would be reserved to a stranger, which cannot be. Anderson and Periam answer this argument by saying that a surrender to a use upon condition should be taken as a conditional conveyance to the lord, subject to the use. That is to say, X conveys his whole interest to the lord on condition; the lord makes a grant to Y, who is of course subject to the same condition as his grantor; if the condition is broken, of course X may enter. Finally, Meade makes a concession. He grants that a copyholder might surrender in such a way that he could cause his own heirs to take by purchase. If he were to surrender to the lord to the intent that he regrant the land to one for life, remainder to his own right heirs, there is a clear conveyance to the lord, and the heirs would take by purchase. Meade simply insists that an ordinary surrender to uses must not be taken as a conveyance to the lord.

Sere v. Baker and the two reports of 1573 are all unprinted. The only printed case dealing with the same point is Allen v. Palmer (1588) in the Queen's Bench.[32] The report of Allen v. Palmer gives no decision, but only Coke's argument from the bar. Coke says essentially what Anderson and Periam say in Sere v. Baker: that the surrender passes the surrenderor's whole estate to the lord. The eighteenth-century writer Fearne was scandalized by Coke's argument and wrote a learned refutation of it.[33] Though Fearne was right in saying that later opinion was to the contrary, Coke cannot be accused of inventing an outrageous argument in his client's cause. The unprinted Elizabethan cases prove that there was a distinct current of opinion running in Coke's direction. It is, to be sure, hard to reconcile the opinion of Manwood, Anderson, Periam, and Coke with the standard view that a surrender is not a conveyance to the lord. But it seems to me quite reasonable to interpret *some* surrenders as transmissions of interest to the lord, when that is necessary to preserve the intent of the parties. As Meade conceded, a copyholder could give his surrender that effect by choosing the right words to show his intent. Why could the nature of the uses not be an equally good sign of intent that the surrender operate in an exceptional way?

3

So far, we have been concerned with cases where the question was whether or not to apply a common-law rule of property to copyhold by analogy. The much debated issue of whether copyholds can be entailed involves that question and several others as well. In the ordinary manor—excepting those where custom warranted only life-estates—copyholds could be granted and surrendered in fee. The courts held that a custom which authorizes copies to a man and his heirs authorizes by inclusion any lesser estate, as for years or life.[34] Suppose then that a duly warranted copyhold is granted to X and his heirs. Later, X surrenders the tenement to the use of Y and the heirs of his body. Without question, X may make such a limitation, for if he is entitled to surrender to the use of a man and his heirs generally, he may surrender to a man and his heirs of a restricted class.

But what estate does Y have? There are only two practical alternatives: a fee simple conditional or an estate tail. If the statute *De Donis* (Statute of Westminster II, ca. 1) applies to copyhold land, he has an estate tail. With respect to common-law land, *De Donis* made entails possible by giving the action of formedon to the issue of persons granted land to themselves and the heirs of their bodies. By this action, the issue could recover from those to whom previous holders under the gift had made conveyances. Before the statute, if A gave land to B and the heirs of his body, and B enfeoffed C and died, B's issue had no recovery. Even before the statute, if B in this case had died without ever having had issue, A could recover the land by action of formedon. But the statute, by a further provision, altered the circumstances under which a reversioner could recover by the action. After the statute, A could recover if B died without issue living, regardless of whether he had had issue at some time. An analogous writ was framed, subsequent to the enactment of *De Donis,* whereby remaindermen under gifts in tail could recover from alienees. In the end, therefore, there were three varieties of formedon, "in the descender," "in the reverter," and "in the remainder."

If *De Donis* does not apply to copyhold, what Y in the above case has depends on the custom of the manor. If no special custom defining the effect of such a surrender to one and the heirs of his body exists, and if, in the absence of a special custom, it is appropriate to apply the common law, Y has a fee simple conditional. That is the name of the estate conferred by a conveyance of freehold to a man and the heirs of his body before *De Donis.* (As indicated above, a fee simple conditional could be conveyed away as a fee simple absolute if issue were born to the donee, regardless of whether they survived him. But if the donee retained the land in his own possession and died without living issue, the land would revert to the donor, regardless of whether issue had been born to the donee. If the donee conveyed away and died without ever having had issue, the land would also revert to the donor.) A special custom having the same effect as *De Donis* would have to be pleaded and proved in a common-law suit. This could be a hazardous business, for there was a good deal of disagreement as to what was sufficient evidence for that purpose.

The main general point to be made about the Elizabethan cases on entails is that despite much disagreement the courts were more inclined than later authorities to think that *De Donis* applied to copyholds. Historically absurd though this view is, it bespeaks a liberal disposition to assimilate the ownership of copyhold land to ordinary common-law ownership. The most efficient way to assure that copyholders could create the same estates as freeholders, and to prevent people who assumed they had entails from suddenly discovering that they had fee simple conditionals (the hoariest of relics in the sixteenth century), was to hold that the equity, if not the words, of the statute covered customary land. There are indications that copyholds were frequently conveyed with the intention of creating entails.

The earliest Elizabethan report on the matter of entails, from 1571 in the Common Pleas,[35] goes as follows:

> Auxi loppinion del Seignor Dyer fuit a auter temps cel terme que si Coppihoulder in taile in tiel mannor lou per le Custome Coppihoulders poient estre intailes surrender al Seignor al ops dun estranger et devi lissue poet aver son pleynt en nature dun formdon in discender et purge le discontinuance et issint que le Statute de Donis conditionalibus extend a cest base tenure sibien come al ffranktenure et charter tenure vide accordant Litt. fo. 16 Plowden 233 et Brooke 15 H 8 ti. tenant per coppie et alibi 26 quaere tamen si la ne soit nul president en le Court Rolls lou tiel accion ad este ust si poet estre mainteyne ieo nient obstant semble en reason il poet pur ceo que nul negative prescripcon doit prevaile contra un Statute que est un loy positive et poet estoier enconter le comen ley car comen ley mesme en effect nest auter que un auncient usage et custome per tout le realme et pur ceo un privy custome in lieu certeyne lou il est accustome poet encounter ove un generall custome bien mes nemy issint nest un statute quere tamen.

Dyer's opinion is apparently that the statute extends to copyholds, but that it has no effect except in those manors where there may customarily be copyholders in tail. What does this mean? It seems to me that there are three possible interpretations. First, it may mean that the statute extends to copyhold, but it is possible to prescribe against the statute. The heir in tail may not bring formedon in the descender if the evidence shows that the manorial court has continuously ignored the statute. As the reporter says, however, such an opinion would be in conflict with the well-known principle that there is no prescription against a statute.[36] Secondly, the meaning may be that the statute extends to copyhold and may not be prescribed against, but can obviously affect only those manors where the custom warrants grants to a man and the heirs of his body (or to a man and his heirs, if it is held that the broader custom contains the narrower). In a manor where only life-estates are customary, if the lord grants a copyhold to a man and the heirs of his body, and the grantee aliens, the heir in tail is not given a plaint in the nature of formedon. But this is in no sense prescription against the statute, for the grant contrary to the custom could in any event only convey a life-estate. Finally, Dyer's opinion might mean that the statute gives an action—the plaint in the nature of formedon—but does not give the rights asserted in that action. If, by a duly warranted grant, a copyhold is given to a man and the heirs of his body, and he aliens, the heir in tail may sue by plaint in the nature of formedon, provided that before *De Donis* the custom gave him some other way of recovering the land, as by entry or by plaint in the nature of *mort d'ancestor*.

The citations in the report of 1571[37] do not entirely clarify Dyer's opinion. Littleton says simply that plaints in the nature of formedon may be brought in manorial courts. His words seem to me to imply the applicability of *De Donis* so as to turn fee simple conditionals into estates tail only if customary estates tail could not exist independently of the statute and plaints in the nature of formedon could not have been brought before the writ of formedon was invented by parliament. (As will be seen, some lawyers thought that the imitative plaint, or the equivalent, could not have preceded the statutory writ, and therefore that entails of copyhold must exist by virtue of the statute or not at all.) The citation to Plowden refers to Manxel's Case. Plowden, of counsel, was arguing that *De Donis* applies to uses. Along the way, he said that copyholds are within the equity of *De Donis* and cited Littleton to this effect.

The second, and perhaps the first, of these citations, do tend to support the direct applicability of the statute to copyhold. They suggest that the second interpretation of Dyer's opinion given above is correct. The third authority, the case in Brooke, seems to have a different meaning. The opinion of the justices reported there appears to be an answer to the argument that plaints in the nature of formedon cannot have been brought from time out of mind. The justices agreed that this was not a good argument against the possibility of customary estates tail. Their assumption seems to have been that the statute does not apply. For if it does—even in the limited third sense above—there is no point in arguing whether plaints in the nature of formedon could antedate the statute and hence be immemorial.

Although Dyer's opinion of 1571 is hard to interpret, it seems likely that it upholds the forthright applicability of *De Donis* to customary land. The only real objection to taking it this way is the citation from Brooke, which is probably merely a mistake. If Dyer is so taken, his views are possibly against the weight of opinion in the 1570's. In 1573, the Common Pleas was directly confronted with the question of whether a plaint in the nature of formedon in remainder will lie.[38] The three judges whose opinions are reported (Harper, Monson, and Manwood) agreed that copyhold is not within *De Donis*. They proceeded to say that customary estates tail are possible and that there is no objection to presuming that plaints in the nature of formedon or the equivalent have been brought from time out of mind. (Nothing is said about what evidence of a custom of entailing is sufficient to raise the presumption.) Littleton is interpreted to mean that in some manors plaints in the nature of formedon are immemorial. In a Chancery case of 1575,[39] Chief Justices Wray and Dyer gave an opinion as assistants to the Lord Keeper in which they said ". . . if by the custome of the Mannor it been usuall to entaile copiehold lands lying within the said Mannor where the said entayle is made then the Intaile may bee good. If now [no] such custome be in the Mannor where the said entayle is made it is not good for that the Statute in that case provided doth not so far extend." This opinion may be taken either as a flat denial that the statute affects customary land in any way or as a repetition of the opinion given by Dyer in 1571. It does not, after all, say that the statute does not extend to copyhold at all, but only that it does not extend so far as to define the consequences of a grant to a man and the heirs of his body in every manor, regardless of the custom. The presumption must be that Dyer still adhered to his earlier opinion in one of its possible senses. In the manuscript report of the Chancery case, Haselrigge v. Grey in the Duchy Chamber (1579) is noted as a holding to the same effect as the opinion of Wray and Dyer. In a later case, it was cited as authority that *De Donis* extends to copyhold.[40] This is further evidence that Wray and Dyer meant to hold that the statute can affect copyhold under some circumstances.

In Heydon's Case in the Exchequer (1583),[41] Chief Baron Manwood commented incidentally on the applicability of *De Donis* to copyhold. After giving a well-reasoned statement of why parliament in all likelihood did not intend the act to cover customary land, he goes on to say that copyhold may be entailed by "the custom cooperating with the statute." What does this expression, which was to be repeated in the future, signify? It would seem that the only way the statute can contribute is to authorize plaints in the nature of formedon, so named. Either the statute gives formedon in descender to heirs in tail against their ancestor's alienee in such manors where before the statute the heir could enter upon the alienee; or else it permits the equivalent action to be named formedon, on the assumption that before *De Donis* the heir had a right of action but not a right of entry.

The first reported Queen's Bench case is Hill v. Morse (1585).[42] In this case, two customs were alleged: first, that land in the manor could be entailed, and second, that it could be disentailed by a simple surrender by the tenant in tail. Coke, of counsel, argued that the second custom is invalid. Citing Manxel's Case and Haselrigge v. Grey, he maintained that *De Donis* applies to copyhold. If this is so, then the alleged custom is a prescription against the statute and invalid. The court said only that without such a custom there may not be entails of copyhold, which seems to be a clear repudiation of Coke's premise.

In Bullen v. Grant (1589) the Queen's Bench was again confronted with the problem of interpreting a copyhold grant to a man and the heirs of his body.[43] This case seems to have been argued on the assumption that the custom can and must support estates tail, for the issue was what evidence will prove that a grant to a man and the heirs of his body gives an estate tail. Coke argued that such a grantee must have aliened, and that the issue, reversioner, or remainderman must have avoided the alienation. Chief Justice Wray, to judge by Leonard's report, or the whole court, to judge by Croke's, rejected this argument and said that the grant would be intended a tail unless the contrary were shown.

In Gravenor's Case (1593),[44] the Queen's Bench was evenly divided on the applicability of the statute in the absence of any custom defining the effect of a grant to a man and the heirs of his body. (There could be no such custom in this case, for it was expressly found that land in the manor had never before been granted to a person and the heirs of his body.) Justices Gawdy and Clench gave textual and historical arguments against extending the statute and held that the grantee had a fee simple conditional. Chief Justice Popham and Justice Fenner said that the act applies. Popham made a number of arguments in favor of applying it. He pointed out that *De Donis* had a history of liberal construction, having, for example, been extended to uses. Then he argued that since the Statute of Westminster II, ca. 3, was interpreted to have created a plaint in the nature of *Cui in vita* as well as the writ of that name which it expressly creates, the first chapter of the same act might as well be interpreted as giving both the writs of formedon and the imitative plaints. Finally, Popham argues that unless copyholds can be entailed by force of the statute they cannot be entailed at all. The reason for this appears to be that since there was no formedon before the statute there could not have been plaints in the nature of formedon, and unless a copyholder could recover by plaint in the nature of formedon he was not a tenant in tail. Why the plaint, or an equivalent action with another name, could not have existed before the statutory writ is not clear: Popham simply refuses to believe in that possibility, sensibly enough from an historical point of view. In Gravenor's case itself, the verdict of course ruled out the possibility that the manor had a customary equivalent of formedon. Behind Popham's opinion there is probably the feeling that any decision which eliminated purported entails of copyhold would be an unfortunate defeat for many people's expectations and intentions.

Fenner's somewhat obscure opinion does not seem to accept Popham's last argument. Though he agrees with Popham on the applicability of the statute, he seems to believe in the possibility of customary entails. Gawdy and Clench see no objection to estates tail of copyhold by prescription. Gravenor's case was finally decided on another issue.

In Stanton v. Barnes (1594),[45] Justice Gawdy mentioned the split in the court over the application of *De Donis*. The division of opinion reappears in Dell v. Higden (1595).[46] In the latter case, it was expressly found by the verdict that customary land in the manor was demisable "en fee simple ou fee taile ou pur vie." The grant of a remainder to a man and the heirs of his body which was in issue was held, 3 to 1, to create a good tail. Popham repeated his opinion that *De Donis* applies and that customary entails are impossible. Fenner also thought that the statute applied, but said that even if it did not there was a good tail by the custom in this case. Gawdy held the statute inapplicable, but thought the verdict sufficient to establish that by the custom any grant in the manor to a man and the heirs of his body made a good tail, protectable by plaint in the nature of formedon. Clench alone dissented, holding at once that the statute does not extend to copyhold and that the verdict should be construed as establishing only that copyholds are customarily demisable to a man and the heirs of his body. To establish that the grant made a good tail, Clench thought, an additional finding that heirs in tail had customarily recovered by plaints in the nature of formedon would be required. He therefore held that the estate in this case was a fee simple conditional.

After Dell v. Higden, the Queen's Bench seems to have swung toward the position that the statute extends to customary land. In February 1602, Justice Clench retired from the bench and was replaced by Sir Christopher Yelverton.[47] In two cases from Easter term of that year, Gurrey v. Sanderson and Elbridge v. Norris,[48] it is reported as held that a copyhold grant to a man and the heirs of his body makes an estate tail "deins lestatute de donis condicionalibus sans ascun speciall custome de garrant ceo." In Rooke v. Wharton (1603),[49] the applicability of the statute was upheld by all four judges. They said that Littleton proves its applicability, because he says that plaints in the nature of formedon may be brought, and this could not be true if the act does not apply. Justice Gawdy, who was still on the court, must have changed his mind.

These last three cases are unprinted. Only a misreported Dell v. Higden survived in print as a firm holding that the statute applies. Except for Dyer's early opinions, there is no evidence that the common-pleas judges were inclined to extend *De Donis* to copyholds. The seventeenth-century courts had few precedents to trouble them when they held that custom alone—or perhaps custom cooperating with the statute—can make an entail of copyhold. In the *Compleat Copy-holder,* Coke preferred not to throw his authority either way; in the *Commentary upon Littleton,* he says that the custom cooperating with the statute will make entails; his reports perhaps contributed to the impression that Elizabethan precedents were predominantly against applying *De Donis*. The opinion against extending the act no doubt represents the sounder statutory construction. Indulgent evidentiary requirements for proving customs of entailing compensated for the practical advantage lost by restricting the scope of the statute.[50]

In Heydon's Case, one of Manwood's reasons against extending the statute was his fear that estates tail of copyhold could not be disentailed. There are other signs as well that this problem complicated the issue of whether copyholds could be entailed. If there were no means of disentailing, copyholds in tail would be "perpetuities" in the old sense of that term. A great deal of legal ingenuity was devoted, in the sixteenth century, to the invention of "perpetuities" in the sense of unbarrable entails, and a great deal of judicial energy was devoted to their successful prevention. The normal means of disentailing, with respect to common-law land, was to suffer a common recovery upon a feigned title. In its simplest form, the common recovery worked as follows: A is tenant in tail and wishes to convey a fee simple to B. B then sues A in a collusive proprietary action to recover the land. Upon being sued, A vouches C, who is also involved in the collusion, to warranty. That is to say, C is called in to defend A's title on the fictitious supposition that

C had conveyed the land to A with warranty. C loses the suit by default, whereupon B has judgment to recover the land, and A has judgment to recover from C lands equivalent in value to those lost. B now has the land in fee, as claimed under his feigned title. The recompense in value awarded to the tenant in tail from his warrantor was held adequate to bar the issue, remainders, and reversion, despite the collusive nature of the action, and despite the fact that care was taken to make sure that the warrantor, or "common vouchee," actually had no land to serve as recompense.

Assuming that either custom or *De Donis* warrants estates tail in customary land, can the copyholder in tail be sued in the manorial court upon a feigned title, vouch a "common vouchee," who suffers judgment to go against him, and then have judgment to recover from the vouchee lands equivalent in value to those lost? If he goes through this procedure, will the estate tail be perpetually barred? These questions might arise in two forms. First, it might be alleged that from time out of mind procedures analogous to the common recovery had been pursued in the manorial court and customarily had the effect of barring the entail. Is there any reason why this should not be held a good custom? Secondly, there might be no evidence that proceedings in the nature of a common recovery had ever before been brought in the manor. Is there any reason not to imitate the common law and hold that the first copyholder in tail to recover in value from a warrantor has successfully disentailed?

Except for Manwood's dictum, Dell v. Higden[51] is the only Elizabethan authority on the effect of a manorial common recovery. In that case, it was expressly found by verdict that no common recoveries had been suffered in the manor before the one in question. The printed report of Dell v. Higden says that it was held that the entail is barred by the recovery, but a much more complete manuscript report shows that this is not what really happened. According to the latter, only three judges gave opinions on the point. Justice Clench did not need to because he did not think there was an estate tail to be disentailed. Justice Gawdy thought that the recovery was ineffective, while Popham and Fenner thought it a good bar.

Gawdy said that the recovery would be good if a custom had been specially found, but that without one there is no basis for holding that a copyhold estate can be warranted. Consequently, there is no basis for upholding the voucher to warranty and recovery in value in the manorial court. Gawdy's reason for this is that copyholders have only estates at will, and at common law it is a good counter-plea to a voucher to say that the feoffor had only an estate at will. This reasoning seems dubious. The question is whether a rule analogous to the common-law rule will be applied to copyhold, not whether the common-law rule is itself directly applicable to an estate at will. This objection to Gawdy's reasoning is probably implied in the opinions of Fenner and Popham. On the other hand, it may be said in defense of Gawdy that the courts had never established a clear policy of always when possible applying the common-law rule by analogy. The opinions of Popham and Fenner answer two other arguments against allowing the recovery. First, it was argued that a warranty attached to a surrender cannot be good because a surrender is a conveyance to the lord. It is as if A were to convey land to B to the use of C and attempt to warrant the estate which C might take from B by a subsequent conveyance without warranting B's estate. At least before the Statute of Uses, this would have been impossible. The copyholder who surrenders cannot warrant an estate to the lord, who has a paramount interest. (If A enfeoffed B for life, and B surrendered to A with warranty, A could not vouch B because the title which B could defend would only be A's title.) In answer to this, Popham restates the familiar principle that a surrender is not a conveyance to the lord. Secondly, it was argued that the recompense in value which the copyholder received from his warrantor must consist of copyhold lands within the manor, and that such recompense is inadequate to bar the entail. Popham replies that when common recoveries are had in ancient demesne, the recompense consists of other ancient demesne lands in the same manor, and yet the entail is barred.

In the seventeenth century and later, the view that common recoveries of copyhold are good bars was no more favorably received than the view that *De Donis* applies. On the other hand, customs permitting copyholds in tail to be disentailed by a simple surrender in fee were liberally allowed. This, combined with the opinion that evidence of successful plaints in the nature of formedon is not necessary to establish a custom of entailing, meant that as a rule a surrender of copyhold to a man and the heirs of his body gave an estate which would revert upon failure of issue before alienation and could have remainders limited upon it. But it could not be discontinued or recovered in formedon. It was in fact *sui generis,* neither proper estate tail nor proper fee simple conditional. From a practical point of view, this result was perhaps as satisfactory as the bolder course of extending both *De Donis* and the rules of warranty on which common recoveries depended.[52]

4

Besides the problem of what rules to apply within the manorial system of property, the Elizabethan courts were concerned with what may be called the coordination of that system with the common-law web of relationships. Here again, settlement was not an easy or straightforward process, and there are once more signs of a deepening command of principle, sometimes at the expense of practical convenience.

There are several situations in which one man's customary interest and another man's common-law interest could come into conflict. Suppose, for example, that a copyhold escheats or is surrendered to the lord's use, and that the lord then encumbers the entire manor. Perhaps he grants a rent charge out of the manor, or enters into a Statute Staple or Statute Merchant. (Statutes Staple and Merchant were special bonds secured by the obligee's land. If the debt was not paid, the creditor could sue execution and recover a special quasi-freehold interest in the land for as long as it took him to collect the debt from the profits. A rent charge is technically a real property interest. In effect, it is the right to collect an annuity from a landowner secured by the right to distrain beasts on specified land out of which the rent is granted to issue.) Then suppose the lord grants the escheated or surrendered land by copy again. May the person having the rent distrain on this copyhold? May the obligee on the Statute have the copyhold in execution and avoid the grant? Or suppose the lord marries between the escheat and the new grant. If his widow is assigned the copyhold as part of her dower, may she avoid the customary estate? Finally, suppose that after the escheat the lord conveys the manor to A, excepting the timber trees, which he reserves to himself. A makes a grant by copy and the copyholder cuts timber trees, in keeping with a custom which permits copyholders of the manor to cut trees for the purpose of repairing their houses. Is this copyholder a wrongdoer toward the former lord who reserved the trees?

One's immediate instinct is probably to say that the interest created first should be preferred. In the cases stated above, the person with the rent should be able to distrain, the obligee on the Statute should have the land in execution, the dowager should be able to avoid the copyhold, and the copyholder should have no right to cut trees which did not belong to his lord when the copyholder took his estate. This seems to have been the first reaction of the Elizabethan courts too. But on further consideration, in later cases, there was an about-face with respect to all the situations above. It was held, in effect, that the rent charge and other interests are only apparently, not actually, prior to the copyhold. Before any of those common-law interests were created, the lord of the manor *pro tempore* had a customary power to grant copies. Therefore the recipients of those interests took them subject to that power, which is exercisable at any time.

The basis for this latter opinion seems to be the rule that the lord of the manor for the time being, regardless of the quantity of his estate, and provided only that he be in rightful possession of the manor, may grant copies in any estate warranted by the custom. A tenant of the manor by a one-year lease may grant copyholds in fee if the opportunity presents itself, though he must not reserve less than the accustomed services. The reversioner or freehold owner is bound as if he had made the grant himself. This rule was regarded as part of the common law because it was the custom of practically all manors in England. Like any such rule, it could be prescribed against.[53] The rule implies that copyholds are not derived out of the grantor's estate. In other words, any copyhold estate is paramount to the estate which any particular person has in the manor, and consequently to any encumbrance on the manor created at an ascertainable time. The fee itself is liable to be bound by the exercise of the lord's power at whatever time it is exercised, and thus anything carved out of the fee—a rent charge, security for a debt, title of dower, a particular interest in trees apart from the soil—is equally liable to be bound by the exercise of that power. The lord does not convey his own, but "executes the custom." Before any grant within the time of memory was actually made, the custom was there as a thing executory, ready to be executed at any time.

These far-reaching implications were not immediately seen. The first relevant report, from 1566, relates to dower.[54] A man devised that J. D. and S. C. might grant copies for the payment of his debts, which they did. The testator's widow then brought a writ of dower and was assigned the copyhold. Justices Dyer and Welch said that the copies were in any case invalid because the grantors were not lords of the manor. But they added that even if the husband had granted the copies himself after marriage, the dowager could avoid them because her title of dower antedated the copies.

A similar case arose in the Common Pleas the next term,[55] different only in that the manor was devised for years, so that the grantors undoubtedly were entitled to grant copies, and in that the entire manor, rather than the copyholds separately, was assigned as dower. This time, it was reportedly held that the dowager could not avoid the copies. Another undated early report from the Common Pleas may refer to the same case.[56] The latter gives only the opinions of Justices Browne and Weston, who held that the wife may not defeat the copyhold estates. The power of the *dominus pro tempore* to bind reversioners is cited as a reason, with the curious and certainly mistaken addition that even a disseisor may bind the rightful owners by his grants. Grantors are said to do what they do as "officers to execute a custom," and the copyholders to be in *per* the custom and not *per* their grantors. Certain common-law precedents are vouched—for example, when a church appurtenant to a manor falls vacant after the husband's death and before assignment of dower, and the husband's heir enters and presents, the dowager shall not avoid the presentment. The language used is so general that it seems unlikely that the opinion of the two judges depends on the fact that the dowager received the entire manor and was therefore herself lady of the manor for life and entitled to receive the services and grant copies herself if the opportunity occurred. Though the dowager who does not receive the entire manor may be in a weaker position,[57] the theory that the custom and customary estates are paramount seems to apply to her case as well. The Common Pleas was apparently divided on the issue of priority between copyholds and title of dower in the 1560's. Nothing is heard from the Queen's Bench until 1584, when Coke reports it was held that copyholds granted after accrual of title of dower may not be avoided.[58]

In 1570, the Common Pleas was presented with the following case:[59] A manor was given to a man and his wife, and to the heirs of the husband. The husband granted the stewardship of the manor for successive lives, and granted the stewards forty pounds' rent issuing out of the manor for their lives as payment for executing the office. The husband died, and the wife, being seised for life by survivorship, granted a copyhold. The rent being in arrears, the steward distrained on this copyhold. It was held that he could maintain the distraint. The wife admittedly was not charged, since her interest as a joint tenant was older than the rent charge. However, the court reasoned that the copyholder was not in *per* the wife, but "eins dels intier inheritance que fuit charge." This implies that if the husband had been sole seised in fee when he granted the rent, any copyholds subsequently granted would be charged, which is contrary to the later rule. The doctrine that copyholders do not come in *per* their grantor was invoked, but not carried so far as it was to be carried in another case. It should be noted that Weston and Welsh said that the result would be the opposite if the wife had only admitted upon surrender instead of making a new grant, inasmuch as the surrender is not a conveyance through the lord, which Bendloes denied.

Also in 1570 the Common Pleas is reported to have held, with respect to Statutes Staple and Merchant, that the encumbrance affects copyholds granted after the lord entered into the obligation.[60] Arguing in Heydon's Case (1583, Exchequer),[61] Egerton was seeking to establish that copyholds are a sufficiently durable interest to come within the Statute of Monasteries. In order to suggest that copyholds are to most intents as solid as common-law estates, he says that they will figure, as it were, in the common-law scale of priorities, a later copyhold being postponed to an earlier rent charge and vice versa. No one is reported to have denied this.

In 1594 a case involving an exception of timber arose in the Queen's Bench.[62] Lord Paget leased the manor of Marlowe, Buckinghamshire, to his brother Thomas for sixty years, excepting all timber trees. It was customary for copyholders to cut trees growing on their own tenements for repairing their houses without assignment, and, upon assignment by the lord or his bailiff, to cut trees growing anywhere on the demesnes of the manor for that purpose. A copyholder was assigned trees by the lessee's bailiff, cut them to repair his house, and was sued in trespass by Lord Paget's heir, now owner of the freehold. Only Justices Gawdy and Fenner were present to give opinions. They said that "the better opinion" (as if to suggest that the matter was disputable) was that the custom was insufficient to sustain a plea of not guilty, "car les defendants nont ascun interest in larbers." It seems certain therefore, though this is not explicit in the report, that the copyholder took his interest, or was presumed to have taken it, after the exception of the trees was made.

In conclusion, though the Elizabethan precedents are not strong, they are on the whole in favor of arranging copyholds alongside common-law interests in the order of priorities and against the rule that any copyhold, whenever granted, is paramount to any common-law interest. Swaine v. Beckett (1609 in the Common Pleas),[63] the leading case for establishing the later rule, is possibly contrary to the weight of earlier opinion. That case was substantially the same as the Queen's Bench case of 1594 above. It was held that copyholders who take their estates after an exception of timber may continue to cut such trees as the custom permits them to. Dicta in Swaine v. Beckett say that later copyholds take priority over earlier titles of dower, rents, and encumbrances imposed to secure debts entered into by Statutes Staple or Merchant. The theory that the grantor of copies merely executes the custom, or exercises a power on behalf of the entire fee, is relied upon.

In Sammer v. Force (1610),[64] the King's Bench decided to follow Swaine v. Beckett, Fenner alone dissenting, in accord with his earlier opinion. That case held directly that a later copyhold is not charged with a prior rent, and affirmed the same law for Statutes, Recognizances, and dower. Although he was one of the majority in Sammer v. Force, Coke gave what may be a hint of misgivings, for he said that if the lord were to grant a rent out of a particular copyhold instead of the whole manor, and named the tenant of the copyhold, and then the copyhold escheated and was granted anew, the new copyholder would hold charged. Whether Coke's view is sound might be questioned. Does it not seem to convert a fundamental principle for determining the priority of interests into a mere rule of construction, to the effect that a rent granted out of the whole manor is meant to be subject to the lord's power to grant by copy? In any event, Coke's dictum suggests a feeling that the rule in Swaine v. Beckett is inconvenient. The rougher approach of preferring interests, whether freehold or copyhold, according to the time of their actual creation was perhaps more sensible and more in line with everyday expectations and intentions than the more elegant rule which became a permanent part of the law.[65]

5

Another problem arising from the simultaneity of common-law and customary interests in the same land is that of severance, of the consequences a common-law conveyance of copyhold land apart from the manor as a whole will have. Suppose that X is a copyholder in fee; A, the owner of the manor where X's land lies, enfeoffs B in fee of just the tenement held by X. Are X's interests affected in any way? Does B take over the powers and rights of lordship which belonged to A? If one has no compelling obligation to logic and the theory of customary rights, it is easy enough to propose a fair and convenient solution. Surely it is just to rule that X will lose nothing by his lord's act: he should enjoy the land during his life;

his heir should be able to inherit it; he should be as free as before to alien his land. On the other hand, there seems to be no reason why X and his successors should not be subject to the same rent, fines, and forfeitures as before. Incomes from the lordship over X's copyhold should go to B. It is difficult to find any reason for them to go to A while the copyhold estate lasts, both because he has divested himself of all interest in the land and because, in practice, the understanding of the parties would probably be that A intended to grant B something of immediate value, the right to the dues of a signory, like a common-law lessor who alienates the freehold during the term. Suppose, however, that X's copyhold escheats, or is forfeited or surrendered to B absolutely. Then, on practical grounds alone, it might be sensible to hold that B has no power to make a new grant of the land by copy. Having been taken into the family of interests protected by the common law, copyhold ought perhaps to have been recognized for the complicating nuisance it was. As venerable manors melted away, the chunks of customary land that broke off should perhaps have been allowed to dissolve into the sea of ordinary common-law land.

Insofar as this solution merely provides that X will not lose his land, it is almost beyond challenge. But in general it encounters serious intellectual difficulties, and even the duty to show elementary fairness to the copyholder must assert itself in the face of some theoretical objection. The difficulties arise from the consideration that before the severance X's rights exist vis-à-vis such person as is lord of A's manor; the power to grant and admit by which X's rights are created is vested by the custom in that person, as are the counterrights to rent and other incomes which transactions between the lord and his copyholders bring into being. B does not answer the description which a statement of the custom gives—lords of such a manor. It is hard to see how B can exercise any of the powers or enjoy any of the ensuing rights with which the custom has invested only those who answer that description. It is of course legitimate to ask why the lordship of the manor could not be fractionated, why it is impossible to say that A and B now have partitioned shares of a power which the custom does not literally restrict to one person.

This escape is cut off, however, by a general proposition of law: manors are not divisible by the act of the party, though they may be divided by act of law, as by partition among coparceners or assignment of dower. This rule has wider reference than to copyhold matters and is supported by the best authority.[66] It rests on the idea that a manor is a prescriptive unit.

These considerations as they stand need not be fatal to the protection of X's enjoyment of the land, at least as long as he lives. His personal right to possession existed before any change in the common-law ownership and might as well continue. However, the above reasoning does seem to insist that B cannot have a right to the rent. Since it is difficult to urge that A should continue to receive it, the conclusion seems to be that X's obligation to pay rent is extinct. But this would mean a windfall for X. It may then be argued that the fairest thing is to cancel all rights and obligations and hold X's estate extinguished too.

Then the severance would seem to affect the alienability and inheritability of X's estate. Both the conveyance of copyhold and its hereditary transference require admittance by the lord, and it seems that B has no power to admit. Granting that X's estate survives during his own life, there is perhaps a way to assure his heir's succession. The heir to a copyhold was entitled to enter without admittance,[67] though he was required to obtain it and pay his fine within a certain time. If there is no one able to admit him and receive the fine, it seems he can never fail in his duty and thereby give B the right to defeat the possession which he has established by entry. Surrender is another matter, since the surrenderee has nothing before admittance. It seems that either severed copyholds must become inalienable, or else the strong objections to letting B stand in A's place must be ignored. If the latter course were taken, there would perhaps be no reason why B should not make totally new copyhold grants. If, however, it were decided to steer a policy-minded course along the lines of the model solution above, the standard device for distinguishing admittance from grant is available: in admitting, the lord is merely an instrument to effect a transference, and he does not enter the chain of titles.[68]

A further complexity is introduced when the many connections between copyhold ownership and manorial courts are considered. In the case as stated above, B can hardly hold a court for litigative purposes, even if it is conceded that X is his tenant, and the objection that he has no manor and no prescriptive right to hold court is overlooked. B has only one copyholder; there is no homage to find facts and present the custom; X can neither implead an intruder by plaint for his land nor be impleaded by one having better right. Aside from litigation, routine dealings with copyhold often customarily required the cooperation of an homage. Deaths of tenants, the identity of their heirs, the facts of surrenders and forfeitures commonly had to be presented in court. If there is no homage, how can such customs be observed?[69] On the other hand, unless A retains the right to rent and fines, it is hard to say that A's court still has jurisdiction over X's tenement.[70]

These problems become less acute if the case is changed. Suppose that A had enfeoffed B of ten of the twenty copyholds in his manor. Then, from a merely practical point of view, B has enough copyholders to hold court. Only the theoretical objection that B has no manor and no court whose law and jurisdiction rest on immemorial usage stands in the way. The force of this fundamental point is mitigated only if the case is again changed to say that B received all twenty copyholds apart from the rest of A's manor. Then it is possible to argue that although B does not appear to have received a whole manor—and has not, in the classical sense of demesnes and services, freeholders, and copyholders—he has actually received an entire "copyhold manor," all the land affected by a definite segment of the special law of the larger manor, all the homage. The situation is the same, it may be claimed, as if A's manor had consisted exclusively of twenty copyholds, a type of manor which might exist.[71]

The difficulties and arguments which become evident in analyzing the problem of severance abstractly are reflected in one aspect or another in the Elizabethan cases. The many interrelated facets of the problem were not, however, aired together in a single reported case. It is possible to say something of the judges' approach and inclinations from the piecemeal evidence of particular cases, but the most important conclusion is that the matter was not settled in a convincing way. The solution ultimately incorporated into the law, which may be largely Coke's work, was a triumph for principle over practicality, for though existing copyholds were not held to be destroyed by severance, it was held that they become inalienable. This unfortunate rule is not pointed to decisively by Elizabethan opinion, though it was accepted by a few judges. Once again, there are indications of a shift which may be interpreted as deepening command of principle or as growing pedantry.

The earliest report bearing on severance is probably from 1576–1577 in the Common Pleas.[72] It was agreed, with Justice Monson doubting, that copyholds "remain" after severance. This probably means only that estates in being survive and implies nothing about their alienability. In 1583, in the same court, it was said by counsel that alienation of the freehold of a copyhold will not impair the copyholder's interest.[73] The court conceded this "en manner," but Chief Justice Anderson said that no court could be held or court roll made. Anderson's opinion probably implies that the alienee has no power to admit or grant *de novo*. Sir Christopher Hatton's Case was cited by counsel as authority that the alienation will not impair the copyholder's estate. This case, of which no report survives to my knowledge, is often cited in other cases. From the ways it is used, it is not clear exactly what it decided, and indeed it seems likely that the decision was open to different interpretations.[74]

In Beale v. Langley (1587),[75] it was argued before the Common Pleas that severance destroys even existing copyholds because services and forfeitures are extinguished. In accord with the indications given in the earlier reports, the court rejected the conclusion, agreeing that copyholds in being will survive. This opinion was grounded on the consideration that it is unfair to allow lords to subvert their copyholders' estates at will. As to whether the services and forfeitures become extinct, the judges were in disagreement.

The facts of Jackson v. Neale (1594–1595, Common Pleas)[76] vary somewhat from report to report. Following a manuscript report, it appears that the lord of a manor leased all the copyholds in his manor for 1000 years, and the power of the lessees to make copies was in question. Justices Anderson, Walmesley, and Beaumond thought the lessees may not hold court, but Justice Owen said that this opinion was contrary to Hatton's Case. On further argument, all the judges agreed that the lessees could hold court for the sole purpose of admitting (hence not for making new grants). This opinion was put on the ground that otherwise lords could "destroy" their copyholders' estates—i.e., presumably, make them inalienable and perhaps even uninheritable. If it is true, as other reports of the case do not confirm, that all the copyholds were severed in this case, Jackson v. Neale is not strictly authority that customary tenements remain alienable when only one or several are severed, but the reason extends to that case, and the court gave no countenance to the notion of a "copyhold manor."

In Bright v. Fort (1595, Common Pleas),[77] a severed portion of a manor including copyholds for life descended to the Countess of Derby, and she and her husband granted copies. Although it is not entirely clear, it seems probable that the severed portion did not include all the copyholds of the old manor. The grants in question seem clearly to have been new grants. The judges, Owen absent, agreed that the grants were void. In a dictum, Chief Justice Anderson said, and Justice Beaumond agreed, that if a copyhold of inheritance is severed the copyholder and his heirs will have the land, but that it becomes inalienable. This opinion does not seem consistent with the position taken by these two judges in Jackson v. Neale, unless their earlier position either depends on the fact that all the copyholds were separated from their original manor or extends only to admittance upon inheritance.

In the Queen's Bench, the leading case on severance, and the earliest one I know about, is Melwich v. Luther (or Luter or Lutter), from 1588.[78] In this case, three copyholds for life were severed and the alienee granted a copy. The issue was essentially the power of the new owner to make original grants, despite the fact that the tenement had been surrendered by the copyholder, for this surrender was absolute, not to a use. (When the case was before the Exchequer Chamber, counsel brought up the argument that a severed copyhold for life may be regranted upon absolute surrender for as long as the copyholder at the time of severance lives, even though an escheated copyhold of inheritance, for example, is not regrantable. There is no sign that this argument had any effect. The conveyance was apparently treated like any other new grant.) The side arguing against the validity of the grant conceded both that copyholds in being survive severance and, on the authority of Hatton's Case, that the alienee here could have held court for the purpose of admitting upon surrender. The Queen's Bench held unanimously that the grant in question was good, contrary to the predominant opinion of the Common Pleas. It was argued that Hatton's Case extended even to new grants, and although it is not certain, it is probable, in the light of later cases, that the court accepted this interpretation.

Ewans for the losing side then brought a writ of error in the Exchequer Chamber. Unfortunately the case did not come to judgment there, but Croke reports that the majority of the judges were minded to reverse the Queen's Bench. In Bright v. Forte, a "Constantine's Case," which appears to be Melwich v. Luther under a different name, was discussed.[79] It was claimed that the Queen's Bench judgment was entered secretly without the order of the court. It was also said, and confirmed by Chief Justice Anderson, that all the judges thought that judgment wrong. In a not altogether satisfactory way, therefore, Melwich v. Luther as a whole is unfavorable to new grants after severance, at least when only part of the copyholds are removed from their old manor. It should be observed, however, that the case involved additional facts which may have affected the opinion of the judges. The grant in question was made in the court of another manor owned by the grantor, in a county other than where the copyhold lay. The grant was to hold according to the custom of the manor *ibidem,* and it was argued that the *ibidem* referred to the manor in whose court the grant was made. This interpretation of the *ibidem* was naturally disputed. Obviously the land could not be held according to the custom of a manor of which it had never been a part, and the grant so interpreted would clearly be void.

In Murrell v. Smith (1591),[80] Justice Fenner gave what Croke reports as an unsupported dictum that a severed copyhold becomes both inalienable and incapable of being granted anew. Coke, who himself agreed with Fenner on this point, reports the case simply as a holding that a single severed copyhold is inalienable. In the unprinted Moysier v. Walker (1595),[81] however, three Queen's Bench judges, including Fenner, agreed that a lessee of severed copyhold may hold court to take surrenders or grant copies, citing Hatton's Case. The words "ou graunt copies" are most naturally taken as extending to new grants. An anonymous and unprinted report of 1596[82] shows Fenner and Popham favorable at least to the alienee's power to make copies upon surrender to uses. Popham speaks of a quasi-manor consisting only of copyholds. It is not certain whether he means that such a manor exists in any event, or only when all the copyholds are severed together. In Gaye v. Kaye (1599),[83] one third of a manor was assigned as dower and the widow granted copies, by original grant as far as appears. The reports of this case are mainly concerned with another point, but at the end Chief Justice Popham says that copyhold grants—including, presumably, new ones—may be made after severance. It is significant that he speaks generally, rather than to the particular circumstances of this case, for it may be possible to distinguish the case of a widow receiving copyholds as part of her dower, by act of the law, from that of an ordinary severance by act of the party. Again, Hatton's Case is relied on.

The best conclusion from this evidence is that most Elizabethan judges, especially on the Queen's Bench, did not favor the rule that severance makes copyholds inalienable, a rule which is practically foolish and unfair, but which the theory of copyholders' rights does recommend. There was considerable opinion in favor of allowing even new grants after severance. Although to allow them may have some practical disadvantages, doing so would have been a useful device for achieving the general position that severance changes no material part of the copyholder's rights. For if the new common-law owner can make original grants he can clearly admit, and if he comes that close to standing in the old lord's place, there is no reason why he should not receive rents and fines and the benefit of forfeitures. Although it is not consistently interpreted, Hatton's Case seems to have checked such inclination as the judges may have had to think through the problem of severance theoretically, a role which decided cases did not always play. On the other hand, there is no strong line of Elizabethan authority, especially in print. Coke had an almost open field to settle the law after his own judgment. His opinion was unfavorable both to new grants and to alienability, and that opinion passed into the tradition of the common law.[84]

6

In what ways are the histories of leading issues of copyhold law informative about the judicial process in the sixteenth and early seventeenth centuries? Although they will not by themselves establish generalizations, it may be useful to formulate certain general observations which they suggest.

In the first place, it is possible to distinguish two over-all conceptions of the problem that copyholds presented to the courts. One conception will perhaps seem correct to modern eyes; the other was probably more natural to the judges actually confronted with the problem. From a modern point of view, the judges faced with the issues discussed in this chapter seem on the whole to have been in such a position that their only choice was to *make* law. The case seems to call for judicial legislation, and hence for attention to the criteria by which legislative decisions should be evaluated. Properly speaking, this is only true of the first occasion on which a given issue, or type of issue, arose. Once a decision had been made, judges subsequently presented with a similar situation could have avoided the necessity to legislate, at least in the full sense of that term. Decided cases could have provided immediate authority in some circumstances, arguments and analogies in others. In the first instance, however, each issue, or type of issue, required an essentially legislative decision. The reason for this analysis is that the courts initially had no relevant materials which could enable them to fulfill a law-applying, as opposed to a law-making, role. Because copyholds had always been outside the ken of the common law, there were neither cases nor legal writings to provide direct guidance. Nor is it easy to think of principles well-established in other fields of law which are obviously qualified to take the place of a pre-existing body of directly relevant rules. The only helpful general principles are those which properly belong to a legislative context: to settle the law by making provisions which are convenient in a utilitarian sense, or are fair and reasonable.

An Elizabethan judge could hardly see the over-all problem presented by copyhold law in this light. There is no evidence that judicial legislation was consciously recognized as a fact. The intimation that it is commonly a fact and sometimes a necessity would probably have seemed improper. The assumption was that any issue presented to the courts admitted of adjudicative, as opposed to legislative, solution. It was probably taken for granted that rules to settle copyhold issues could be found somewhere in the large, inclusive tradition of the common law.

The histories discussed above suggest that the most obvious type of adjudicative source, from a modern point of view, the simplest device for escaping a legislative role, in fact carried little weight. That is to say, recent precedents immediately or closely in point were not regarded as binding, or so strongly authoritative as to be nearly binding. It is generally recognized that the modern view of the special authority or bindingness of judicial precedents was not established until much later than the period of these studies. The older view was that decisions are good arguments, but always rebuttable arguments. Judges were not regarded as obliged to follow decisions that seemed in any fundamental way mistaken. The criteria of mistakenness included not only such standards as inconvenience or unfairness, but also, and indeed primarily, nonconformity with principles of positive law gathered from a wide variety of judicial and extrajudicial sources. The early history of copyhold law confirms the truth of these generalities. Although at the start plainly relevant judicial precedents did not exist, they soon came to exist in sufficient quantity to provide guidance in new cases. But the early Elizabethan precedents were usually not allowed to count as more than rebuttable arguments. Subsequent cases were frequently debated anew, and the judges felt free to reverse decisions of which they did not approve.

Even those most committed to the rule of *stare decisis* will find it occasionally inapplicable. Sometimes the judicial authority alone, not to mention extrajudicial opinion of the sorts customarily given weight, is so confused and contradictory that it is a logical impossibility to follow the precedents. Some principle for discriminating among the authorities must be employed. On other occasions, the duty to stand by judicial precedents will conflict with the duty to settle the case at hand in a manner that seems just, sensible, and worthy of imitation. Although it is logically possible to prefer the former duty, it is morally difficult to do so in clear and extreme cases.

Because *stare decisis* is not a sufficient or absolute guide, it might be argued that the older jurisprudence was wise and realistic in denying it an explicit place. But the early history of copyhold law points up the weakness in such an argument. If the consciousness of being bound by prior decisions is sometimes confusing or confining, it can at other times prevent wasteful and impractical legal perfectionism. In copyhold matters, it seems to me, the Elizabethan courts were confronted with neither of the situations in which the rule of precedents is difficult or impossible to apply. The field was so new that there was no complicated mass of authority to disentangle. Moreover, the early decisions which formed the limited body of direct authority are rarely, it seems to me, subject to the criticism that they express or imply inconvenient or unfair principles of law. There was rarely a greater practical advantage to be gained by sacrificing the palpable advantage of swift settlement of the new field. In failing to adhere to the early decisions, the courts cast themselves adrift from the simplest and surest source of adjudication. They returned, unnecessarily, to their original condition: they were faced again with the problem of "finding" a law that cannot be said to exist elsewhere than in the small but useful body of early Elizabethan decisions.

It is implicit in their conduct that the Elizabethan judges would not accept the argument I have made. They would not concede that it would have been easy and advisable to rely on and follow the first wave of copyhold decisions. The discrepancy between their thinking and the line of reasoning I have taken may perhaps be explained as follows: I have gone on the assumption that the terms "inconvenient" and "unfair" should be applied to judicial decisions and legal principles only when one's intention is to criticize them from a utilitarian point of view, or from some other ethical point of view essentially external to the "mystery" of the law. I have assumed that judges have a right and a duty to amend the law discovered in authoritative sources only when they have stepped outside the confines of "art" and seen the law's inadequacies as a lay mind might see them. Sixteenth-century lawyers, by contrast, were probably unwilling, if not unable, to distinguish between "intra-professional" and "extra-professional" legal criticism as practiced by common lawyers themselves. The law, conceived as the timeless custom of the realm, was accorded a sacredness which, for some purposes and in some contexts, put it above criticism of a sort external to the habitual world of its professional guardians. Though courts of equity and the High Court of Parliament were granted the right and duty to criticize the law from the point of view of common reason, justice, and public policy and to amend it accordingly, common law judges were confined to applying a law which, they were on the whole convinced, no such external criticism could touch very deeply. On the other hand, common lawyers and judges permitted themselves extensive liberties, as masters of their art, to criticize the work of their brethren in the language of the "mystery" and by its own "artificial" standards. Sometimes, in the view of such lawyers, decided cases cannot be followed despite their practical and ethical sufficiency. They cannot be followed because they are wrong for graver reasons than insufficiency by the standards of fairness and convenience which laymen can employ. Sometimes the judges of the past have simply failed to practice the art as it should be practiced. By the same token, sixteenth-century jurisprudence would probably dispute my argument that copyhold law was a suitable area for strict application of *stare decisis* because of the absence of a lengthy and contradictory body of authority. My argument is valid only if one is thinking of the authority that could conceivably be relevant as a concrete and specific body quite obviously in point. It is invalid if authority is thought of loosely, as including the professional instincts of the law's living representatives, or if argument from the latest judicial decision seems no more properly argument from authority than the application of much more remotely relevant material warranted by books and tradition. The very absence of the modern rule of precedents suggests that older English lawyers conceived authority in such a loose and generous way: what was relevant was so multifarious that its counsel could hardly be decisive. In sum, the reasons I have given why the early copyhold decisions could well have been allowed to settle a number of issues are poor reasons from the point of view of the judges who had the choice of following or reversing those decisions.

One caveat should be added. The old system of reporting was so casual that the courts were often ignorant of what the judicial precedents were. If we could be sure that the courts which seem to disregard earlier decisions knew those decisions had been made, the point that precedents were taken lightly would be stronger. On the other hand, the failure of official or otherwise systematic reporting to develop, even after the introduction of printing, reflects lawyers' confidence in their right to argue and decide cases on their merits, without the sense of being bound by what previous judges had done.

Where, then, did the judges find grounds for criticizing and rejecting the precedents? In the event that precedents were at hand, where *else* did they look? Or, in the event that no judicial precedents were available or known, where did they find guidance in copyhold cases?

As we have seen in a number of instances, one strain of opinion held that in appropriate cases rules applied to freehold land ought to be applied to copyhold by analogy, assuming that manorial custom provided no rule governing the situation in question. I have argued that this opinion is defensible on grounds of utility. Although the common-law rules involved were themselves frequently of negligible practical use or positively inconvenient, there might nevertheless have been an advantage in having one set of rules for all landed property, insofar as local custom did not exercise its undoubted right to vary from the general. This argument from policy is not, however, the only defense of the opinion. Another argument may be made as follows: In copyhold cases, when there is no evidence before the court of a manorial custom governing the situation, the custom must be determined by inference. The best inference is that common-law rules, expressing as they do "the common custom of the realm," express, *mutatis mutandis,* the custom of particular manors which are not known to have divergent customs.

This argument seems persuasive at first sight. The best device for discovering rules to settle copyhold cases seems to be to assume, albeit fictitiously, that every manor has a sufficient body of law for all cases, and then to infer the content of that body of law, insofar as it is not given in evidence. The inference that the manor's law is probably the same as the realm's seems sensible enough. We have seen, however, that this procedure was not acceptable to all judges in all cases. Failure to follow it may reflect conscious or unconscious dissatisfaction with certain common-law rules on grounds of fairness and convenience. But such an explanation is neither safe nor necessary. Alternatively, the following argument may be made: Let it be granted that the correct procedure in copyhold cases is to construct the manorial law insofar as it is not known. Let it be further granted that in general manorial law probably corresponds with the custom of the realm. But this general presumption is open to question with respect to each particular rule. It must be asked in each instance whether the rule that expresses the common custom of the realm exists independently or as a dependency of another principle. If it exists independently, it may be presumed to be the custom of every manor not known to have a divergent rule. But if it is dependent, it must be determined whether the principle on which it depends probably expresses the custom of the manor with respect to its copyhold land.

At common law, for example, conveyance of land under certain circumstances will discontinue the estate and make it impossible for the entitled person to recover rightful possession by entry. If this rule expressed an independent custom, there would be no objection to presuming that manorial law regards copyhold estates as discontinued by conveyances made under similar circumstances. But the rule does not express an independent custom. It would not exist were it not for the fact that English law enables persons seised of freehold to convey, by livery, a greater quantity of interest than they have. It might of course be the case that the custom of a given manor would permit copyholders to convey a greater quantity of interest than they have. But ought it to be assumed, in the absence of direct evidence, that the custom of a manor does permit this? There is no conclusive basis for saying the presumption should not be made. For that reason, the whole attack on the procedure of applying common-law rules to copyhold by analogy is dubious. But once the question is put in the above form the problem deepens. Since the manor does not employ the machinery of livery, inasmuch as its custom has not provided different types of conveyances to serve different purposes, is it not the best guess that the custom does not seek to provide the same variety of potentialities to persons seised of copyhold as the common law accords to persons seised of freehold? Is it not the best inference that the manor adheres to the uniform practice of surrender and admittance in order to limit the range of things holders of copyhold land may do to obstruct the essential rights of others? Had it sought to do otherwise, would it not have found some way of discriminating conveyances capable of barring entries from conveyances not so capable, as the common law has done? It is tempting to answer these questions in the way that distinguishes freehold from copyhold, rather than in the way that assimilates them to one another. With appropriate modifications, similar questions may be raised with respect to other common-law rules, such as those affecting executory interests and contingent remainders.

The application of common-law rules to copyhold by analogy seems, though the pattern is not decisive, to have been more characteristic of the early Elizabethan courts than of the later ones. The explanation of this change may be simply that the arguments against applying the rules, which must be made separately for each rule, are more complex than the generalized argument in favor of applying them. It may simply have taken time for lawyers to develop and judges to digest complicated particular objections to a facile general policy. Insofar as this explanation is sufficient, the pattern of change need reflect nothing more than the newness and unfamiliarity of copyhold problems. One should ask, however, whether a larger movement of jurisprudence might not be reflected in the change. Were the arguments against applying particular rules conclusive, were the general line of inference obviously fallacious in some cases, it would certainly be sufficient to say that time and familiarity simply served to correct early mistakes. But since the shift does not seem to follow from conclusive reasoning, the possibility should be considered that it reflects an alteration of judicial habits which may have significance beyond copyhold law.

The arguments against applying certain common-law rules to copyholds require a degree of analytic understanding of those rules. It is necessary to think of the rules, not as discrete things, but as functions of ramifying legal ideas. The capacity and inclination to think of them in that way may be significant. There is perhaps some merit in the hypothesis, though its proof lies far beyond the limits of these studies, that the end of the sixteenth century and the beginning of the seventeenth was a period of rapidly growing sophistication and intellectuality among common lawyers. This tendency, one may suggest, manifested itself in part as greater interest in the theory of the law, in the interconnections among its specific contents and the general principles comprising them. Lawyers of the period did not have the historical knowledge or disposition to see the body of inherited doctrine as a socially meaningful whole. They were not ready to confront the law with philosophic criticism. Nor were they equipped with the abstract concepts and techniques for ordering ideas of later analytical jurisprudence. Nevertheless, according to this hypothesis, lawyers were in more and more ways transcending the limits of the craftsman. They were beginning to explore in greater depth and with greater self-consciousness than their predecessors the essences behind legal tradition; they were aspiring to a new elegance and subtlety of exposition and argument; they were displaying a new virtuosity in their sense of analogy and of the "reason" of the law. Although the results were often awkward, pedantic, and obscure, the way towards modern jurisprudence was being broken.

With this hypothesis in mind, it may be suggested that the tendency to criticize uniform application of common-law rules to copyhold is symptomatic of the new mood in jurisprudence. Such criticism calls for analysis of the nature of the rules and their relation to more fundamental principles; it replaces a simple sequence of ideas with greater complexity; it discriminates where the older approach conglomerates; it too easily confuses the appearance of logic with the reality and is too ready to sacrifice practical values. The criticism did not on the whole produce better law, but it may still represent, in a minor way, a phase in the growth of legal thinking.

The same point may be made, I believe more forcibly, with respect to another type of case presented by copyholds. The problem of coordinating customary with common-law interests and the problem raised by copyholds severed from the manor cannot be solved by reference to specific rules of the common law. If answers were discoverable, they could only be found in the most indefinite part of legal tradition—in lawyers' professionally conditioned ideas of justice and logicality in matters of property. The tendency in this area of copyhold law was for solutions sanctioned by familiar canons of fairness to give way before criticism claiming logical rigor.

This pattern is clear with respect to the coordination of interests. The early cases adopt a scheme of straightforward temporal priority: without regard to whether the interests are customary or common-law, the one which palpably existed first is to be preferred. This scheme not only has a utilitarian advantage but, in addition, implements the common notion that the fairest way to settle conflicting legal claims to the same property is to postpone the younger to the older, to make each acquirer bear the risk that there are prior encumbrances. The criticism that prevailed over this approach has been discussed above. In general, the critics won out by distinguishing copyholds from ordinary interests in land, largely because of the disproportion between the lord's estate and his power to grant copies. In part, the victory went to logical consistency: it was cogently represented as inconsistent to uphold the powers of the *dominus pro tempore* and at the same time to class copyholds, for some purposes, as posterior to common-law encumbrances. In part, it was the love of essences that prevailed: the visible fact that a copyholder comes to title and possession of his land at a specific time was subordinated to the intelligible truth that his interest, because it must spring from somewhere and cannot spring from the grantor's estate, issues from the timeless custom. Described in either way, it seems fair to relate the later and prevailing cases concerned with this problem to the incursion of a more rarefied, if more exacting, jurisprudence toward the end of Elizabeth's reign.

The cases on severance do not present a clear pattern of change. Their very confusion, however, may reflect a tension between justice and logic, and between an older and a newer approach to legal problems. Insofar as the courts were disposed to hold that severance will not affect existing copyholds, including their alienability, they may be thought of as implementing the basic principle that interests in being should be safe against the acts of strangers, that once a man definitely has rights the law will protect them throughout their natural life. Insofar as the courts doubted that this position is tenable, they were in part disturbed by the intellectual difficulty of conceiving how the custom of a manor could continue to sustain rights over land that no longer lay within that manor. In part, they were disturbed by the problem of how to do justice toward the copyholder, and at the same time, without loss of logical consistency, to prevent a proliferation of persons entitled to grant by copy. Both are the scruples of lawyers perhaps too intent on intellectual satisfaction.

In only one of the situations discussed above were the judges in a position to seek guidance from the statute book. If *De Donis* could be stretched to comprise copyholds, the awkward problem of how to construe conveyances of copyhold obviously intended to create entails would be solved. Again there is not a clear pattern of change in the prevailing opinion, but the confusion over whether or not the act was extendable to copyhold may again reflect a tension in judicial attitudes which is significant beyond the immediate issue.

The tendencies which I have tentatively suggested were present in late Elizabethan jurisprudence and detectable in the history of copyhold law are perhaps on the whole likely to seem unfortunate to modern eyes—necessary, perhaps, to legal progress, but in themselves inclined to take the law in an arid and overly technical direction. With respect to statutory construction, the direction of change is more likely to seem beneficent. What was probably taking place was an attenuation of the old doctrine of the "equity" of statutes. It is of course true that something of what was meant by the "equity" has survived in modern views of statutory construction. It continues to be held that judges applying statutes must look beyond the words in the narrowest sense and try to fulfill the purposes which Parliament intended to pursue by the act. This principle is partially equivalent to the old maxim that statutes are to be taken by the equity as well as by the words. But the modern dichotomy of words and intent, it seems to me, is a weakened version of the dichotomy of words and equity. The intent of the legislature is presumably what it actually had in mind, what there is solid reason to believe it consciously hoped to bring about by making the act, but has failed to express, or failed to express unambiguously, by the words used. The purpose of referring to intent is to avoid reading the words in the wrong way, as among alternative possible readings, or to avoid taking literally words whose literal sense may be reasonably thought the result of mistake or poor draftsmanship. In invoking the equity, the ancient courts were sometimes referring to intent in the sense I have given. But sometimes, it seems to me, they were doing somewhat more: namely, drawing implications from statutes without really believing the rule supposedly implied was consciously thought of and purposed by Parliament, without believing that failure to incorporate the implied rule in the express words amounted to an error. The line is admittedly thin between this practice and liberal forms of reference to intent. Possibly, on occasion, modern courts still go beyond reference to intent as I have described it. Pragmatically speaking, however, I think it is correct to say that modern courts are rarely prepared to stretch statutes to the degree that the old form of the doctrine of equity was employed to permit.

The question of the applicability of *De Donis* to copyhold involves the meaning of statutory equity. Whether or not the point was originally clear to all judges, it was cogently argued that copyholds are plainly not within the words of the act. It was probably agreed, at least after consideration, that if *De Donis* extended to copyhold at all it was by virtue of the equity. But some judges were unwilling to take the act by the equity in this case. The reason for their unwillingness is probably that they were disposed to restrict the meaning of statutory equity to intent in something like the modern sense. Because there is reason to doubt that Parliament was thinking about copyholders, or because there is no reason to suppose that the language that excludes them is careless language, there is, on this view, no warrant for extending the statute to them. Although it is possible that the judges on the other side only disputed the factual inference as to Parliament's intent, it is also possible that their position depends on a different and broader conception of the equity of statutes. They may have considered Parliament's laying down a principle in one type of case sufficient warrant for extending that principle to another type of case, even though Parliament did not have the latter in mind in any straightforward sense. *De Donis* prescribes a way of construing gifts in tail so as to preserve the real intentions of the donor, and it creates appropriate remedies to enforce such a construction. Perhaps the statute was made with the conscious purpose of favoring the intentions of freeholders only and therefore written as it was. At the time the statute was made, gifts of customary tenants, for whatever reason, may not have been thought to constitute a similar problem. Nevertheless, the policy of *De Donis,* sanctioned as it is by the highest authority, is to be taken for the policy of the law. It is consequently to be applied to copyholders when, in the course of litigation, the problem of how to construe their gifts and whether to enforce their intentions has to be faced. To allow the copyholder's intentions to go by the board, to allow the fee simple conditional to intrude into the law once more, is in effect to ignore the basic judgment Parliament made when *De Donis* was enacted.

The narrower conception of statutory equity is involved with the range of attitudes that define the relationship between Parliament and the judiciary as it has come to be in modern times. Judicial subordination to a sovereign legislature requires a doctrine of interpretation which incorporates the judge's duty to obey the clear verbal mandates of his superior, together with his duty to enforce a superior will and purpose which has not been clearly voiced. It must also incorporate the judge's duty to respect the silence of the legislature, a duty which, from another vantage point, is equivalent to his right to follow the common law and his own wisdom when the voice from above has not spoken decisively. The broader conception of statutory equity, on the other hand, seems to me involved with a range of attitudes stemming from the judicial character which Parliament originally bore. The courts were subordinate to Parliament, but somewhat as a lower court is subordinate to a higher. Unequivocal judgments from above were to be followed; the real purposes sanctioned by the High Court but not clearly expressed were to be sought out and enforced. But the duties and rights of the ordinary judge extended further, and in a somewhat different direction from that taken by the modern doctrine. The unvoiced implications of a "judgment of Parliament," its rationale as worked out by legal analysis of the sort commonly applied to judge-made law, were also to be taken into account. In this respect, the judge was less free than modern judges to go his own way when Parliament had not decisively intervened. But at the same time, because the lines of subordination between court and court can perhaps never be so clear as those dividing bodies with functions thought of as essentially distinct and bodies set apart by the theoretical distinction between sovereign and agent, the judge enjoyed greater freedom. He was freer to rely on what Parliament had done when he was seeking to effect purposes which no one could be sure Parliament had really considered or would really have approved. Conversely, he was freer to interpret Parliament's words away in a manner which, to say the least, can easily be confused with "judicial review." The controversy over the application of *De Donis* to copyholds may reflect uncertainty felt in the later sixteenth century over the kind and degree of liberality permissible in interpreting statutes, and hence uncertainty over the larger questions of the nature of Parliament, its relation to the judiciary, and the structure of authority in the state.

In discussing the possible implications of early copyhold law for the general history of Elizabethan jurisprudence, I have abstracted from the complexity of the material. There are many cross-currents, and the concrete cases rarely present issues of general judicial policy and technique in clear-cut form. In addition, I have used hypotheses, in part suggested by the history of copyhold itself and in part resting on other impressions, which stand in need of much more testing than I have furnished. Subject to all due caution, it remains my impression that copyhold law provides an insight into larger currents of legal development. As this new field of law developed over the first half-century of its life, its doctrines grew more subtle and complex, more deeply thought through, and more controverted. From one point of view, this development no doubt represents the natural accretion of time and litigation. Something of the sort might have happened in a different jurisprudential climate. But in the end the pattern of development seems too strong for such an explanation to suffice. It seems necessary to add the element of changing intellectual habits. The complication and confusion of early copyhold law must reflect the emergence of new standards of legal analysis, in themselves subtle, rigorous, and sometimes impractical, and the simultaneous persistence of older instincts and techniques.

BIBLIOGRAPHY

BIBLIOGRAPHY

Primary Materials (Manuscript)

The Public Record Office
  Early Chancery Proceedings
  Proceedings of the Court of Requests
  Star Chamber Proceedings
The British Museum
  Additional Manuscripts
  Hargrave Manuscripts
  Harleian Manuscripts
  Lansdowne Manuscripts

Primary Materials (Printed)

LAW REPORTS

All the following reports are most easily accessible in the Full Reprint of the English Reports (London and Edinburgh, 1907). They are also available in various old editions, of which those listed below have been primarily used in the preparation of this book.

Anderson, Edmund, *Les Reports* (London, 1664).

Bridgman, John, *Reports* (London, 1659).

Brooke, Robert, *Ascuns Nouell cases de les ans et temps le Roy H. 8, Ed. 6, et la Roygne Mary* (London, 1651).

Brownlow, Richard, *Reports (A Second Part) of Diverse Famous Cases in Law* (London, 1652).

——— and John Gouldesborough, *Reports of Diverse Choice Cases in Law* (London, 1651).

Bulstrode, Edward, *The Reports,* 3 pts. (London, 1688).

Cary, George, *Reports or Causes in Chancery* (London, 1650).

Coke, Edward, *The Reports,* 13 pts. (London, 1777).

Croke, George, *The Reports,* 3 pts. (London, 1661–1667).

Dalison, William, *Les Reports des divers special Cases Adjudge en le Court del Common Bank en les Reignes de les tres hault & Excellent Princes Hen. VIII. Edw. VI. Et les Reignes Mar. & Eliz.* (London, 1689).

Dyer, James, *Les Reports des Divers select Matters & Resolutions des Reverend Judges & Sages del Ley* (London, 1688).

Godbolt, John, *Reports of Certain Cases Arising in the Severall Courts of Record at Westminster In the Raignes of Q. Elizabeth, K. James, and the late King Charles* (London, 1652).

Hobart, Henry, *The Reports* (London, 1641).

Hutton, Richard, *The Reports* (London, 1656).

Jones, William, *Les Reports* (London, 1675).

Keilwey, Robert, *Relationes quorundum Casuum selectorum ex Libris Robert Keilwey* (London, 1602).

Leonard, William, *Reports and Cases of Law,* 2 vols. (London, 1658).

Littleton, Edward, *Les Reports* (London, 1683).

March, John, *Reports: or, New Cases* (London, 1648).

Moore, Francis, *Cases Collect & Report* (London, 1663).

Noy, William, *Reports and Cases Taken in the time of Queen Elizabeth, King James, and King Charles* (London, 1656).

Popham, John, *Reports and Cases* (London, 1656).

Plowden, Edmund, *The Commentaries or Reports,* 2 vols. (London, 1816).

Rolle, Henry, *Un Abridgement Des Plusieurs Cases et Resolutions del Common Ley; Alphabeticalment digest desouth severall Titles,* 3 *vols.* (London, 1688).

——— *Les Reports,* 2 vols. (London, 1675–1676).

Savile, John, *Les Reports* (London, 1675).

Tothill, William, *The Transactions of the High Court of Chancery* (London, 1649).

Yelverton, Henry, *Les Reports* (London, 1674).

MISCELLANEOUS

Bacon, Francis, *Works,* ed. J. Spedding, 15 vols. (Boston, 1864).

Bracton de Legibus et Consuetudinibus Angliae, ed. G. Woodbine, 4 vols. (New Haven, 1915–1942).

Britton, ed. F. M. Nichols (Oxford, 1865).

Brooke, Robert, *La Graunde Abridgement,* 2 vols. (London, 1573).

Calthrope, Charles, *The Relation Betweene the Lord of a Mannor and the Coppyholder his Tenant* (London, 1635; reprinted, London, 1917).

Coke, Edward, *The Compleat Copy-holder,* 2nd ed. (London, 1644).

——— *The First Part of the Institutes of the Laws of England; or, a Commentary upon Littleton,* ed. F. Hargrave and C. Butler, 1st

American ed., from 19th London ed., 2 vols. (Philadelphia, 1853).

A Commentary on the Tenures of Littleton Written Prior to the Publication of Coke upon Littleton, ed. H. Cary (London, 1829).

The Court Baron, ed. for the Selden Society by F. W. Maitland and W. P. Baildon (London, 1829).

Fitzherbert, Anthony, *La Graunde Abridgement* (London, 1565).

——— *La nouuelle natura Brevium* (London, 1553).

Fleta, seu Commentarius Juris Anglicani sic Nuncupatus (London, 1685).

Kitchin (or Kytchin), John, *Le Court Leete et Court Baron,* 2nd ed. (London, 1581).

Lambarde, William, Αρχαιονομια; *Sive de Priscis Anglorum Legibus Libri* (Cambridge, 1644).

Littleton, Thomas, *Les Tenures* (London, 1530).

Madox, Thomas, *The History and Antiquities of the Exchequer of the Kings of England,* 2 vols. (London, 1769). Volume II contains the "Dialogue of the Exchequer."

The Old Tenures of the Laws of England, reprinted with the 12th ed. of Coke on Littleton (London, 1738).

St. German, Christopher, *The Doctor and Student, or Dialogues between a Doctor of Divinity and a Student of the Laws of England* (reprinted, Cincinnati, 1874).

Select Cases in Chancery, ed. for the Selden Society by W. P. Baildon (London, 1896).

Select Cases in the Court of Requests, ed. for the Selden Society by I. S. Leadam (London, 1898).

Select Cases before the King's Council in the Star Chamber, ed. for the Selden Society by I. S. Leadam, 2 vols. (London, 1903–1910).

Select Pleas in Manorial and Other Seignorial Courts, ed. for the Selden Society by F. W. Maitland (London, 1889).

The Statutes of the Realm, 9 vols. (London, 1716–1722).

The Year Books. Numerous old editions, most convenient of which is London reprint, 1678–1680.

Year Books of Richard II. 13 Richard 2, ed. T. F. T. Plucknett (London, 1929).

Secondary Works

Ashley, W. J., "The Character of Villein Tenure," *Annals of the American Academy of Political and Social Science* 1:412–425 (1890–1891).

——— "The Character of Villein Tenure," *English Historical Review* 8:294–297 (1893).

The Cambridge Economic History, 2 vols., ed. J. H. Clapham and Eileen Power (Cambridge, England, 1941).

Fearne, Charles, *An Essay on the Learning of Contingent Remainders and Executory Devises,* 9th ed. (London, 1831).

Foss, Edward, *A Biographical Dictionary of the Judges of England from the Conquest to the Present Time, 1066–1870* (London, 1870).

Holdsworth, W. S., *A History of English Law,* 3rd ed., 13 vols. (London, 1926–1952).

Leadam, I. S., "The Inquisition of 1517. Inclosures and Evictions." *Transactions of the Royal Historical Society,* New Series 6:167–314 (1892).

——— "The Security of Copyholders in the Fifteenth and Sixteenth Centuries," *English Historical Review* 8:684–696 (1893).

Maitland, F. W., "A New Point on Villein Tenure," *Law Quarterly Review* 7:174–175 (1891).

Plucknett, T. F. T., *A Concise History of the Common Law,* 4th ed. (London, 1948).

Pocock, J. G. A., *The Ancient Constitution and the Feudal Law* (Cambridge, England, 1957).

Pollock, F., and F. W. Maitland, *The History of English Law before the Time of Edward I,* 2nd ed., 2 vols. (Cambridge, 1899).

Savine, A., "Copyhold Cases in the Early Chancery Proceedings," *English Historical Review* 17:296–303 (1902).

Scriven, John, *A Treatise on the Law of Copyholds,* 7th ed. (London, 1896).

Stephen, James, *A Treatise on the Principles of Pleading in Civil Actions,* 3rd ed. (reprinted, Cambridge, Massachusetts, 1896).

Tawney, R. H., *The Agrarian Problem in the Sixteenth Century* (London, 1912).

Victoria County History of the County of Hertford, ed. W. Page (London, 1914).

Vinogradoff, P., *Villainage in England* (Oxford, 1892).

Watkins, Charles, *A Treatise on Copyholds,* 2 vols. (London 1797–1799).

NOTES

TABLE OF CASES

INDEX

ABBREVIATIONS USED IN NOTES

C.	Early Chancery Proceedings in the Public Record Office. The first number following the letter C signifies bundle; the second number signifies the document.
R.	Proceedings of the Court of Requests in the Public Record Office. The first number following the letter R signifies bundle; the second number signifies the document.
St. Ch.	Star Chamber Proceedings in the Public Record Office. The first number following this entry signifies the classification Star Chamber 1 and Star Chamber 2; the second number signifies volume; the third signifies the document.
BM Add. MSS	Additional Manuscripts in the British Museum.
BM Harl. MSS	Harleian Manuscripts in the British Museum.
BM Lans. MSS	Lansdowne Manuscripts in the British Museum.
BM Harg. MSS	Hargrave Manuscripts in the British Museum.
EHR	*English Historical Review.*
TRHS	*Transactions of the Royal Historical Society.*

NOTES

Bills and pleadings from the Public Record Office are summarized. When this material, which is all in English, is quoted, the spelling is modernized. Comments on these summaries are in parentheses. Brackets are used when missing words in quotations are supplied.

To facilitate the reading of law reports transcribed from manuscripts, abbreviated standard words in Law French have been spelled out.

Full data on sources will be found in the Bibliography preceding the Notes.

Introduction

1. The background and history of copyhold are discussed in Holdsworth, *A History of English Law,* III, 198–213, and VII, 296–312; Vols. III and VII of Holdsworth *passim* for the general history and rules of real property. For unfree tenure in the Middle Ages, see also Pollock and Maitland, *History of English Law,* I, 356–383, and Vinogradoff, *Villainage in England,* especially pp. 78–83.

For medieval manorial courts, see the following Selden Society volumes and the introductions thereto: *Select Pleas in Manorial and Other Seignorial Courts* and *The Court Baron.*

For the general legal characteristics of copyhold, see Littleton, *Les Tenures,* secs. 73–84, and Coke's commentary thereon. See also Coke, *The Compleat Copy-holder.* The best modern books on copyhold law are Scriven, *A Treatise on the Law of Copyholds,* and Watkins, *A Treatise on Copyholds.*

For the manorial system from the point of view of economic history, see N. Nielson in *Cambridge Economic History,* vol. I, ch. vii, sec. 7.

2. The right of an ordinary tenant at will to maintain trespass against or re-enter upon one who had disseised his lessor was affirmed in 1459–1460 (Brooke's *Abridgement,* p. 256b). I have no evidence that such a right was recognized earlier, though it may have been. The tenant in villenage would presumably have the same rights in this respect as the ordinary tenant at will.

3. Vinogradoff, *Villainage,* pp. 79–81, including citations.

4. Holdsworth, III, 214. *Ejectio firmae,* or ejectment, lay against any

ejector, but originally could lead only to recovery of damages. Against the lessor, however, a lessee could recover the land itself in *quare ejecit infra terminum*.

5. Philipott v. Wade.

6. Littleton, sec. 82.

7. Savine, "Copyhold Cases in the Early Chancery Proceedings," *EHR* 17:296–303 (1902).

8. Leadam, "The Inquisition of 1517. Inclosures and Evictions," *TRHS* New Series 6:167–314 (1892); "The Security of Copyholders in the Fifteenth and Sixteenth Centuries," *EHR* 8:684–696 (1893). Ashley, "The Character of Villein Tenure," *Annals of the American Academy of Political and Social Science* 1:412–425 (1890–1891); "The Character of Villein Tenure," *EHR* 8:294–297 (1893).

CHAPTER I

The Protection of Copyholders in Equity

1. For example, by Coke and Bacon.

2. Savine, *EHR* 17:296–303 (1902); Holdsworth, III, 208; Tawney, *The Agrarian Problem in the Sixteenth Century*, pp. 288–294.

3. C.9/77; C.31/157; C.36/47; C.32/324.

4. C.19/237.

5. C.19/162.

6. C.16/376a–b.

7. *The Victoria History of the County of Hertford*, IV, 71.

8. C.9/139a–b.

9. C.31/342–345.

10. C.9/353.

11. *Year Book*, Michaelmas 7 Edward 4, pl. 16.

12. Fitzherbert's *Abridgement*, p. 116a.

13. E. Foss, *A Biographical Dictionary of the Judges of England*, pp. 388, 522.

14. Littleton, sec. 77. The fact that "poet" is used instead of "voet" in some editions is pointed out by an anonymous seventeenth-century commentator on Littleton. In all editions I have had an opportunity to examine, "voet" is used.

15. C.96/59; C.187/40; C.215/21; C.232/58–59; C.246/41; C.246/45; C.251/43; C.255/19.

16. C.96/59 could have been brought before 1493; C.255/19, after 1502.

17. C.232/59.

18. Most of the cases from Henry VIII's reign appear in the notes below. In the approximate figure of sixty, I include a number of fragmentary or doubtful cases, however, which are not separately noted.

19. See Holdsworth, vol. IV, for a summary of the scope of early equity.

20. Christopher St. German's *Doctor and Student* (first published in Latin in 1523) is contemporaneous with the material in this chapter. How much does it contribute toward answering these questions? It seems to me beset with many difficulties of interpretation. Until it is dissected more thoroughly than it has been, and its contents are coordinated with what can be found out about the actual work of the Chancery, one hesitates to say that it is authoritative for the theory and traditions of the court, or even to say exactly what detailed interpretations St. German gives to the principles of equity. (The larger and vaguer principles, such as the identification of equitable rights with conscience, reason, and nature, and their distinction from customary rights, are clear enough.) It should be noted that the *Doctor and Student* says nothing about the Chancellor's activity in protecting copyholders.

21. The common-law rule reflecting this "normal custom" is discussed in Chapter III, pt. 4, below.

22. (a) C.96/59 (1486–1493) is the earliest simple case illustrating these features. The complainant alleges that the lord has always been accustomed to grant the land by copy. It was let to the complainant for life and he paid his fine. The amount is not specified, however. Trusting to enjoy his term, the complainant spent great sums, of which the amount is again unspecified, on new buildings, repairs, and hedging, "whereby your said orator hath wasted his goods and right sore poverished himself." After he had thus increased the value of the tenement, and although he steadily paid the accustomed rent, the lord, defendant, put him out. He and his wife and children therefore have no house, and he has no remedy at common law "for reformation thereof."

(b) The following cases are only slightly later. Unlike the preceding case, they are specific about the amount of the fine, and the language of the bills suggests that pecuniary compensation is as much as the complainants hope for.

(1) C.232/58 (1493–1500). A prior, seised of a manor in the right of his house, "by his writing under seal" gave and granted a tenement to the complainant and another for life, to hold after the custom of the

manor. The fine of ten marks has come to the use and behoof of the monastery. "Within three weeks after the said grant made . . . and payment of the fine, and e'er your said orator had any part of the premises, the said prior for certain causes was deposed. . . ." A new prior was elected, and "incontinent after the said election the said . . . new prior commanded your said orators that they . . . not occupy the premises according to the said grant made by his said predecessor . . . and . . . will not suffer your said orators to occupy the premises." The complainant has often required the prior to suffer him to occupy the land or else to restore the fine of ten marks. There is no remedy at common law "to have recovery of any of the premises."

The answer says that the late prior at the time of his deposition was in possession to the use of the house. The land in question is "of such commodity to the same house that it should be a great loss and hindrance to the same house to put the possession and occupation thereof [out to a tenant]." The previous prior made no such grant unless he did so after his deposition. No such fine came to the use and behoof of the house. The complainants never took any profits from the land. The defendant has been prior for four years and had no knowledge of such a grant until lately, within the last half year.

The back of the bill carries an endorsement dated 14 Henry VII. It says that the complainant has not proved the matter contained in his petition, wherefore it is decreed that the prior is fully absolved and exonerated and dismissed out of court.

(2) C.187/40 (1493–1500). A copyhold was let to the complainant for life, for a fine of forty shillings and at an annual rent of six shillings, twopence. The complainant occupied the land for twenty years, during which time he erected a barn and other buildings to his cost of ten marks. The lord and grantor died. Then his wife, the defendant, "claiming the said mease and lands as part of her jointure and dower that unto her belongeth by reason of her said marriage had and after the said lease to [the complainant] for term of life made" expelled the complainant and will not let him take the profits. The complainant "can have no recompense for his said fine made of forty shillings, neither remedy by the course of the common law of this land for the great costs and charges that he hath done upon the same lands and tenements, and over that is without remedy to have any recovery by action of and for his said term."

(3) C.246/41 (1500–1501). It is alleged that a copyhold was

granted to the complainant and her husband for their joint lives, for which they gave a fine of ten pounds. The husband died. The defendant, lord and grantor of the joint estate, seeing that the complainant was a poor and friendless widow, put her out without cause. It is specifically alleged that this expulsion was "contrary to his own grant." (This feature, which occurs in some other bills, is perhaps more consistent with the first theory than with the second, since, under the usual custom that the *dominus pro tempore* can bind the entire fee by his copyhold grants, a claim based on customary title as such should be as good against any subsequent lord as against the grantor himself. Even under the second theory, however, such an allegation might serve the purpose of estopping the defendant from pleading that the land was not customarily demisable by copy.) The bill then goes on to say that the defendant has kept the petitioner out, "nothing recompensing her as executrix to the said John Gosse [the husband] of the said £10 nor of no part thereof." (Although the purpose of this allegation may be simply to show that no satisfaction in lieu of recovery of the land has been given, it may also be taken to indicate that the object of the bill is to obtain a money payment only.) Finally, after saying that there is no remedy at common law by action of trespass or otherwise, the Chancellor's intervention is requested in consideration of the lack of a common-law remedy "and of the great fine given for the same." (It is perhaps significant that the fine is specifically mentioned as a "consideration" why the case is appropriate for the Chancellor.)

(4) C.164/8 (1486–1493 or 1504–1515). The complainant alleges that he is a copyholder for life and that he paid one hundred shillings for his interest to the defendant, who himself granted the estate. The complainant has spent five marks and more on building and reparation. After the defendant expelled him, the complainant has often "desired the said Richard Trobrygge [defendant] to make him restitution of the said fine and also satisfaction for the said reparations and building," which the defendant has refused to do. (The last allegation suggests, more clearly than do the bills in the cases above, that the object of the suit is compensation rather than the land itself.)

(c) Specification of the fine or allegation of expenses, or both, occurs in the following later cases of simple expulsion.

(1) C.255/19 (1501–1504). Without elaborate pleading of the custom, the complainant says that he was a copyholder holding of the

Chapter of Hereford. He paid a four-pound fine for his interest. The defendant, Archdeacon of Hereford, entered upon him. There is no remedy at common law of and for the premises.

(2) C.615/9 (1529–1532). The defendant granted a copyhold to the complainant. The latter has paid all his duties and services and also incurred charges of unspecified amounts in building two houses on the land. The defendant seized the land and required a new fine of twenty-three shillings, fourpence, which the complainant paid in order to secure re-entry. Nevertheless, the defendant has expelled him again. There is no remedy at common law.

(3) C.840/42 (1532–1544). The defendant, lord, has expelled the complainant from a copyhold. The complainant pleads that he bestowed great cost, of unspecified amount, for repairs, and also that the expulsion was contrary to the defendant's own grant. He has constantly sued to the defendant to be restored. Because the lord is a man of great substance and much-friended and the complainant is very poor, he "is not able to sue for his due remedy therein at and by the due order of the common law of this realm."

(4) C.846/6–8 (1532–1544). The complaint is of expulsion by the lord and admittance of another, and the amount of the fine is specified. "Forasmuch as your orators can have no manner of justice at the said abbot's hands for that he is party to the said wrongs and also your orators be in great poverty having nothing to live withal but only the premises," application is made to the Chancellor.

The answer says the matter is determinable at common law, but as to the merits the tenement was forfeited.

(d) C.924/5 (1532–1544) varies from the simple cases of expulsion above but may be adduced for the same point. The complainant has a widow's estate in a copyhold. She pleads that her husband incurred expenses, of unspecified amount, in building on the tenement. The defendant is about to enter on her and is maintained by the lord so that she will not be able to defend her possession in the manorial court.

23. (a) The following cases are the simplest illustrations of this feature.

(1) C.551/20 (1515–1529). A copyhold was granted to the complainant for a fine of ten marks. He entered and enjoyed the land for a year, after which he went beyond the seas to the king's wars. While he was away, the lord granted the same tenement to the defendant for eight pounds. The defendant "at that time knew right well that the said Duke

and Lord had made a grant thereof before to your said orator." A remedy in the manorial court is unobtainable because the defendant is maintained by the lord.

(2) C.588/39–40 (1515–1529). A copyhold for life was granted to the complainant by the King, then lord of the manor, for a fine of eight pounds. Thereafter, the manor was granted to the Countess of Salisbury, and, for the better assurance of his estate, the complainant came into court and took a new grant from her. The first defendant, surveyor of the manor, thereafter let the land to the second defendant by deed. At that time, the second defendant knew full well of the complainant's interest in the land. There has been no actual expulsion, but the defendants have constantly vexed the petitioner, intending to defeat his estate, by driving out his cattle, taking distresses, and committing trespasses on the land. The complainant has made constant suit to the Countess for a remedy, but because of the surveyor's untrue representations to her it is unobtainable.

The answer on the part of the second defendant is preserved. After saying that the matter is determinable at common law, he goes on to respond to the merits, saying that the land is not demisable by copy. (This defense implies that the ultimate basis of the copyholder's right is custom as such. However, as pointed out in the text, allegation of notice might still be necessary when the defendant was a grantee by common-law conveyance, as he is here. In view of the fact that he took by deed, which probably means that he is a lessee for years, it seems questionable whether the lady of the manor would have jurisdiction to give the complainant a remedy even if she were inclined to. The bill nevertheless assumes that she has such jurisdiction. The preceding case is simpler, for there it appears, without being altogether certain, that the second grant was by copy.)

(b) An earlier case, C.117/16–17 (1486–1493 or 1504–1515) is essentially similar, except that no reason why a remedy within the manor is unobtainable is pleaded. It is alleged that the complainant's father and mother took a copyhold to themselves and their children jointly, for their lives and to the longest living of them. The father spent one hundred pounds and more for building on the tenement. Both parents, as well as all the children except the petitioner, are dead. "Because your said orator had no knowledge of the death of the last tenant, and also he lieth far from the said country and there [was] in manner forgotten," the lord granted the tenement to the defendant by copy. The defendant at that time not only knew that the complainant was alive, but actively misrepresented this fact to the lord—"alleging there that your said orator was deceased, and knowing that he was in life." Because of this "subtle and false pretensed craft and imagination," the complainant is kept from his own.

The answer says that the matter is not determinable in the Chancery, because the land is customary. (This amounts to a demurrer on the ground that the bill does not show why the case cannot be determined in the manorial court. The point is well taken, for in practically all cases where the defendant is another copyholder the bill alleges that a manorial remedy is unobtainable.) For the rest of his answer, the defendant says the land is his in the right of his wife, to whom it was granted by copy, but he does not properly rebut the complainant's title.

(c) In C.657/56–58 (1529–1532), the bill says that one R. L. was a copyholder in fee and surrendered to the complainant's use for life, with remainder over. The first of two defendants knew that R. L. had done extensive building on the land, to his charge of about one hundred pounds. He also knew that the land was copyhold, that it was surrendered to the complainant's use, and that the complainant had paid her fine, of unspecified amount. Having this knowledge, the first defendant came to the king's general surveyors (the manor in this case evidently being royal) and represented to them that the land was not copyhold, was not in anyone's possession, and might lawfully be let by indenture. The surveyors then let the land to him for years. The first defendant "letted and interrupted" the complainant's attempts to get admitted. He then made a sub-lease to the second defendant, who also knew of the surrender to the complainant's use and all the other things that the first defendant knew. The second defendant has put the complainant out and is now in possession.

Answers on the part of both defendants are preserved. The first denies having taken a lease or grant from the general surveyors. The answer of the second defendant is a demurrer like the one in the preceding case. As far as appears on the bill, the answer says, the matter is determinable in the manorial court only. (This exception seems to be well taken only if it is assumed that the manorial court has jurisdiction to give judgment for a copyholder against a common-law lessee of the same tenement. Cf. a–2 above.)

(d) C.215/21–23 (1493–1500) is a complex case which may have an over-all significance quite different from that of the cases above, but the form of the bill is such that it should probably be considered along with them. The land is alleged to be customarily grantable by copy and to have been granted to the complainant for life. He paid a fine of nine pounds and spent "great sums," of unspecified amount, for building. The defendant went to the lord of the manor in London, falsely told him that the land was let to him, and requested a renewal of the lease. The lord believed him and granted the new lease, whereupon the defendant put the petitioner out.

(Although this bill does not specifically charge the defendant with notice of the copyhold in being, it does charge him with active fraud. The effect is very much the same, for whether fraud or mere notice is attributed to the defendant, the claim may be interpreted as equitable in nature. It does not rest on the fact that the complainant had a customary title good against the lessor before the common-law lease to the defendant was made. It should be noted that the bill does not say why a manorial remedy is unobtainable. If this is not a defect in the bill, it must be because the manorial court would not have jurisdiction to give judgment against a common-law lessee.)

The answer begins with what is probably a token plea that the matter is determinable at common law and then goes on to plead to the merits. The essence of the defense is that the complainant's grantor was wrongfully seised of the manor. (The usual custom was that the copyhold grants of one wrongfully seised of the manor are not binding on the rightful owner, and the defendant here may be assuming such a custom. In that case, the defense should be construed as an attack on the complainant's customary title. However, even if the copyholder's rights arose purely from the equities of his situation the same rule should hold. If A disseised B and granted by copy, B's conscience would clearly not be affected, just as if A disseises B and covenants to stand seised to the use of C, B does not hold to the use of C after repossession.)

The answer proceeds to spell out the reason why the complainant's grantor was wrongfully seised. Sir William Barklegh was lord of the manor. He was married to Katherine. Sir William died, after which Katherine was entitled by "jointure or dowry." However, Sir Edward, heir to Sir William, entered into the manor. The defendant does not know whether or not any grant was made to the complainant by Sir Edward, as alleged in the bill, but if there was it was made "during the wrongful possession of the said Edward." Afterwards, Katherine and Lord Grey, her new husband, entered and put out Sir Edward and such persons as he had made leases to. "And also the Steward and officers of the said Lord Grey commanded every tenant that was tenant or had any interest by the said Sir Edward of any lands within the said manor to avoid their possession thereof, or else to agree with the said Lord Grey and Dame Katherine." The defendants subsequently took their interest from Lord Grey. In addition to making this plea (which by itself should be sufficient to defeat the claim) the answer denies that the complainant paid such a fine as he alleges to Sir Edward, that he did any building or hedging on the land, and indeed that he ever lived on the tenement.

The complainant's replication seeks to establish that Sir Edward's seisin was not wrongful. It says that Sir Edward entered as son and heir to Sir William and made the grant by copy. Afterwards, Katherine claimed a third of Sir William's land as her dower. After "strife and debate" between Sir Edward and Katherine, they submitted their difference to arbitration. The arbitrators awarded that Katherine should have the manor in which the tenement in question in this case lies in full satisfaction of her dower. Katherine having acceded to this arrangement, she and Lord Grey entered. The pleading then expresses the conclusion that Sir Edward was not wrongfully seised. It is denied that Katherine and Lord Grey commanded those who had their estates from Sir Edward to avoid their possession. The truth of the bill is reaffirmed in all particulars.

(Several questions are suggested by these pleadings. There is possibly a dispute of fact as to the nature of Katherine's interest. The answer suggests that it is a jointure or such an interest as dower *ex assensu patris,* in which case Sir Edward presumably had no right of entry after Sir William's death. On the other hand, if her interest is common-law dower assigned by agreement, as suggested by the replication, Sir Edward was hardly in wrongful possession before the assignment. The case is more interesting if the latter is true. Granted that Sir Edward's seisin was not, properly speaking, wrongful, ought the executed estate of dower after assignment not be dated back to the death of Sir William, and ought not Sir Edward's copyholds be as voidable as they would have been if he were a mere disseisor? This is of course a difficult question: the temporary possession of the heir under such circumstances is ambiguous. If we assume that the dowager after assignment ought, as far as the proper interpretation of customary rights is concerned, to be able to avoid copies granted during the heir's temporary possession, the question then arises whether circumstances of possible equitable significance—the payment of the fine and the expenses incurred—would alter the picture. It is at least worth noting that the defendant, in his catch-all answer, denies the truth of these circumstances, and does so even though he maintains that Sir Edward's possession was clearly wrongful.)

24. See Chapter III, pt. 5, below.

25. (a) C.392/21 (1515–1529) attempts to substitute an express promise to treat the complainants as if they were copyholders for a proper customary title. The bill alleges that the defendant granted the land "to have to them by copy of court roll for time of their lives after the custom of the said manor . . . the said John Butler [defendant] assuring the said [complainants] of his faith and truth that they should peaceably enjoy and have the same for time of their lives in as quiet and peaceable a manner as any other of his customary tenants holding of the same manor . . . and the said [complainants] having trust and confidence thereof, thinking the same to have had in as good case and assure [*sic*] unto the said [complainants] as though the same had been customary land used to have passed out of time of mind." The bill then states that the complainants have made considerable improvements on the land. Nevertheless the defendant has put them out.

(b) In C.773/34 (1529–1532), the complainant is not a grantee by copy, nor can she claim, like the petitioners in the preceding case, to have been promised the same treatment as copyholders of the manor enjoy. She is merely a tenant at will who, however, claims to be entitled in equity to treatment which might in effect make her comparable to a copyholder for life, and the equitable considerations are not unlike those pleaded in many proper copyholders' bills.

The bill says that the defendant, an abbot, was seised of "two parcels of land" in Chester. In consideration of services done for him by the complainant's late husband, and of forty shillings paid to him "in the name of a fine or income," the defendant let the land to the complainant and her husband to hold of him at will, paying an annual rent of six pounds. During the six years that have elapsed since the making of this lease, the husband built a barn on the land and made other repairs. After the husband's death, the defendant "in affirmance of the said lease took and received of your said oratrix one cow" by way of a heriot. Notwithstanding the fine, the charges incurred in building, the steady payment of rent, and the fact that the complainant's husband never had any other recompense for his service, and notwithstanding that "by the custom of that court . . . every tenant holding at will ought to have warning by the space of one whole year," the defendant has put the petitioner out. The complainant thereupon "exhibited a bill of complaint unto the right honorable the Earls of Sussex and Derby, then being the King's commissioners in those parts." The commissioners "directed their honorable letters willing and desiring him [defendant] . . . to restore your said oratrix [and] to make her sufficient amends for her wrongs and damages." The defendant has refused to obey these letters. The complainant is a poor woman and without remedy at common law.

(The alleged custom allowing tenants at will a year's notice perhaps does give the petitioner a customary right of a sort. What the court mentioned in the bill is is not clear, since it is not pleaded that the parcels of land lie in a manor. However, one gets the impression that the petitioner is seeking more than restoration to the tenancy at will until such time as notice is given and a year passes. Greater hopes than that would perhaps better explain the allegation of fine and expenses.)

(c) C.546/49 (1515–1529) seeks to establish a right to admittance on the lord's promise and other equitable circumstances, even though the complainant is not entitled to admittance by the custom and other persons are. The bill recites that Robert Smith was a copyholder in fee and died seised, leaving his heir Edmund. The homage presented that Edmund was entitled as heir. Edmund, who at that time was sick and weak, sought admittance to himself and his wife Eme, complainant in this suit, and their heirs. The lord was willing to admit Edmund, but unwilling to admit his wife jointly. Before anyone was actually admitted, Edmund died. By his will he bequeathed the tenement in question to Eme and her heirs. Eme then remarried, and she and her husband sought admittance without success. However, the lord, defendant, promised to admit Eme, in consideration of which promise she gave him her sorrel gelding. Later he made a second promise to admit Eme and her present husband, in consideration of which he received five pounds. The defendant has not honored these promises, but has instead admitted Edmund's sisters, taking a fine of five pounds from them. The petitioner has no remedy within the manor because the defendant "is lord and Chancellor within the same court and also party."

(The sisters who were admitted are apparently the heirs of Edmund, applying the doctrine of *possessio fratris,* or of Robert. From all that appears, and unless the custom was very unusual, the sisters were clearly entitled to admittance by the custom. The promises, Edmund's desires expressed while he was alive, and his last will must be considered as purely equitable circumstances in Eme's favor. As to the last will, copyholds were not normally devisable unless the testator was admitted and had made a surrender to the use of his last will. The complainant perhaps recognizes the equitable nature of her case when she points out that the defendant is lord *and Chancellor* within the manor. The suggestion is that if the lord himself were not party to the controversy—if, say, the dispute were between Eme and Edmund's sisters—the proper course would be to apply to him for equitable relief against the legally entitled persons. This is in keeping with the view, for which there is a good deal of authority, that the lords of manors have an equitable jurisdiction over and above the legal jurisdiction of the manorial court.)

(d) C.686/5–6 (1529–1532) differs from the cases above in that the complainants do appear to have a good customary title, but resembles them in that an express promise by the lord is relied on, making an equitable circumstance in addition to the legal title. The bill recites that a copyhold was granted to John and Joan for their lives. The grantor died, his heir entered and "compelled and caused" John and Joan to pay a new fine of thirty-three shillings, fourpence. Then the reversion of the copyhold was granted to Thomas, apparently for life. The second lord then died, his heir, the defendant to this suit, entered and compelled Joan and Thomas (John having died) to make a new fine. Thomas paid twenty-six shillings, eightpence. The defendant at that time "faithfully promised, granted, and agreed" that Joan and Thomas, complainants in this suit, should have the land without let and interruption during their lives. He also made new copies to them. The lord then wrongfully entered, "contrary to his said promise and agreement," and chased away complainants' cattle feeding upon the land. Later, the defendant caused his servants to expel the petitioners. They have requested him to permit them to enjoy the land "according to their said interest and title in and to the premises and also according to the promise, bargain and agreement of the said Sir Thomas [defendant]." The complainants have no remedy at common law, "forasmuch as your said orators have no sufficient writing nor especialty proving the said bargain, promise and agreement . . . and also for that the said Sir Thomas is a man of great power . . . and also lord and owner of the said manor."

The answer says that the matter is determinable by petition to the defendant, since the land is customary. As to the merits, the land was seized for forfeiture, which was committed by Joan when she was sole tenant after the death of John. The forfeiture was duly presented. The defendant denies having made the alleged agreement with Joan and Thomas and having granted them new copies.

(The bill in this case is in a sense an archetype for many other claims. On the one hand, it is more explicit than others in asserting customary title as one basis for the claim. On the other hand, in making the promise a second basis, it states an equitable consideration more explicitly than do those bills which merely allege a fine and expenses. What is the reason for this double-pronged attack? Possibly the promise is brought in to counteract the effect of the earlier forfeiture alleged in the answer, but the new copies, which are also pleaded, should serve that purpose equally well. If the basis of all copyholders' claims was an assurance implied in the grant, there might be some advantage in pleading the additional fact of an express promise given in conjunction with the grant, but then the customary right would as such be superfluous. The uncertainty of this claim is the more confusing since this suit was brought relatively late, long after an equitable remedy on one basis or another was established.)

26. In the following cases the defense that the land is not customary, or the estate not warranted by the custom, is used.

(a) C.585/35–38 (1515–1529). The bill alleges that the defendant's predecessor as abbot of a monastery granted the reversion of a copyhold to the complainant for a fine of forty shillings. The fine came to the use of the monastery. The particular estate ended and the complainant would have entered, but the defendant kept him from doing so.

The answer to this bill says that the land is parcel of the demesnes of the manor and not demisable by copy. The defendant claims to have explained this to the complainant and offered to refund the fine, which he is still ready to do. Although the bill only says that the complainant "would have entered," the answer says that he actually did and was put out. Finally, it is pleaded that even if the land were copyhold the complainant's entry was wrongful, because he entered without admittance or any claim made.

(b) C.672/5–8 (1529–1532). The bill alleges that the defendant, an abbot, granted the complainants a copyhold for life in reversion. A fine of four pounds, six shillings, and eightpence was paid, and the complainants admitted tenants of the reversion. The preceding life-tenant died, and the complainants would have entered, but the defendant kept them out and granted the premises to other persons. The defendant is said to be powerful and well-friended, in contrast to the complainants. Because the land is customary, there is no remedy at common law.

The answer says that the matter is determinable in the manorial court, but it then goes on to plead to the merits. The land has not customarily been granted by copy in reversion. The grant was made by the subchamberer of the monastery without the defendant's assent. Finally, the defendant adds an *absque hoc*—without that such a fine was paid or came to the defendant's use, or to the use of the monastery. The replication and rejoinder affirm the two preceding pleas and add no new facts.

(The answer has two implications which should be noted. It implies that the lord might be liable even when the complainant could not make out a good customary title, if he received a fine or if the grant was his own. For the defendant here takes care to say that the grant was in effect the unauthorized act of an agent, and that no fine was received to his use or the monastery's.)

(c) C.382/1–3 (1515–1529). The bill says that the defendant, again an abbot, granted the complainant a copyhold for life with common of pasture and other appurtenances. A fine of forty shillings was paid, and a larger rent than had ever before been customary. The defendant has recently enclosed, ditched, and converted to pasture land which from time out of mind has been common appurtenant to the complainant's tenement and others held of the defendant. The complainant does not fail to say that this is an unlawful enclosure, prohibited by statute. In addition, the complainant and other tenants are prevented from using a "market way" which they have been accustomed to use from time out of mind. Finally, the defendant's servants, at his command, took three mares belonging to the complainant on the enclosed common and conveyed them to an unknown place, so that they could not be repossessed by due order of the law. The defendant held onto the mares, intending to do so until the complainant would forsake title to the enclosed land. Certain of the petitioner's friends attempted to feed the mares, but the defendant put these friends in prison. Presently the mares foaled, "and for lack of sustenance and meat the said mares devoured and ate their own colts, and after for lack of sustenance the said mares died there in pound." The complainant is a poor man and unable to sue for the mares at common law.

In his answer, the defendant says that he took the mares as a distress and did nothing illegal in that matter. As to the land, it was indeed let to the complainant by copy. However, it had never before been let in this way, but had always been charter land. The enclosed land has always been the abbot's "several soil," and has been let and granted at his pleasure for such rent as he pleases. The tenants have not been stopped from using any customary highway. In contrast to the defendant in the preceding case, this one says nothing about the fine and does not deny that the copyhold grant was his own.

The replication says that the land has always been let by copy or by indenture, at the pleasure of the lessor, and that the common is appurtenant to the tenement. (This is an extraordinary plea, for by common-law standards it would have been a contradiction in terms to say that land was customarily demisable either by copy or by deed. If it was sometimes treated as if it were common-law land, it would have lost its special status and hence be incapable of sustaining customary estates. The replication therefore implies that something less than strictly continuous and immemorial distinctiveness is sufficient to make land customary in the Chancellor's eyes.)

(d) C.141/77–78 (1486–1493 or 1504–1515). The bill is brought by several tenants of Sir Richard Pole, as of his lordship of Long Wittenham, Berkshire. The complainants took lands by copy and peaceably occupied them for a long time, doing their services according to the custom. Before departing into Brittany, Sir Richard, "feeling the true dealing and minds of your said beseechers granted [by his receiver] to be their good master, and that they should so peaceably have and enjoy the said lands and tenements to them and their heirs without interruption and as largely as ever [they] had them of the said Duchess [of Suffolk, previously lady of the manor] or of any other person or persons holding of him and his heirs after the custom of the manor, doing their homage and service." The defendants, the bailly and farmer of the manor and his father, have put the petitioners out, "surmitting" that it is Sir Richard's commandment. The complainants know better, however, for they have recently been to Oxford, where they spoke with "Master Edward and Master John Hewes, which by the commandment of the said Richard now in his absence have the oversight and rule of the said lordship, and they, feeling the injuries of your said beseechers have advertised the said [defendant] to surcease of his malice and peaceably to suffer your said beseechers to have and occupy their said lands." The defendants have failed to do so.

(It should be noted that this bill is not directed against the lord, but rather seeks to compel the lord's agents to act in accord with his will. Though an unusual type of claim, it might have been good regardless of the liability of lords to copyholders.)

The answer says that the complainants held the lands mentioned in the bill at will simply, and that the lord had commanded that their tenancies be terminated. Thereafter, those lands were let to the defendants. The latter made no "sinister labor" to Sir Richard to have the petitioners put out. Finally, an *absque hoc* is added—without that Sir Richard of his receiver granted the complainants the land by copy, without that the complainants ever had any title or possession except at Sir Richard's will, and lastly, without "that the same tenements were customary lands, for he saith they were farm lands and not of custom tenure."

27.(a) C.246/45 (1500–1501). This is the only bill for admittance before 1515. The complainants say that one T. H. was seised of a copyhold, and that he came into court "and then and there showed and rehearsed to the said Steward after the order of the law and the custom of the said manor . . . [that] surrender should be sufficiently and surely made of the said lands" after the decease of T. H. to the use of the complainants and the heirs of their two bodies. The complainants were and still are ready to pay their fine, but they have not been admitted, and the land is "occupied to the lord's use against all right." *Subpoenas* are requested to the lord and to one R. W. (probably the steward, but this is unclear since part of the bill is torn off).

(It should be noted that the surrender in this case is to a future use. The common-law courts were later inclined to question the validity of such surrenders, on the analogy of the rule against interests to spring *in futuro*. There is no other evidence of the position of the Chancellor on this point. It may be argued that if the Chancellor purported to enforce legal manorial rights he should follow the common law in the absence of a special custom, but if the copyholder's rights were conceived as equitable the same latitude should be allowed as in the case of uses.)

(b) C.505/35 (1515–1529). The complainant requests that the lord be compelled to admit him as son and heir of a copyholder who died seised. The homage has lawfully presented that the ancestor died seised and that the complainant is her heir.

(c) C.575/20 (1515–1529). The right to a copyhold in fee has descended to the complainant. The lord, defendant, will not admit him but has instead admitted others. Unlike the two preceding cases, however, this one is complicated by other facts. First, the complainant claims to have compounded with the lord for a reasonable fine and to have actually paid it. Secondly, there is an element of fraudulence. According to the complainant, the other persons were admitted because one Eglysse, with the steward's connivance, forged a surrender by the said Eglysse, who in truth never had anything in the land. Those admitted claim under this surrender.

(d) C.657/49–52 (1529–1532). The right to a copyhold in fee has descended to the complainant. After the death of the complainant's father, his widow was admitted for life as of her freebench (a type of customary widow's estate), with a remainder to the complainant. The widow paid her fine. She has now died, the complainant has prayed admittance and is willing to pay a reasonable fine, but the lord, defendant, refuses admittance.

The answer alleges that the widow committed forfeiture by making an unlicensed lease and also that the complainant failed to present himself for admittance within the time required by the custom. The replication and rejoinder reaffirm the preceding pleas.

(e) C.793/25 (1529–1534). The complainant says that his parents were seised of a copyhold in fee and died. As son and heir he has often prayed admittance, but the lord, defendant, refuses it. One Bryde has entered into the tenement. "And forasmuch as the said Thomas Lyndley, now owner of the said manor, refuseth to admit your said orator as tenant unto the premises, he cannot maintain any action against the said Bryde for the said wrongful entry." There is no remedy at common law to compel admittance.

(f) C.811/8 (1532–1544). A copyhold has descended to the complainant, but the lord refuses to admit him. Instead he has admitted one J. B. The latter "hath your said orator . . . for the premises in suit in the common law in an action of Trespass, which are not of ability nor power to proceed in the same court nor yet determinable there." *Subpoenas* to both the lord and J. B. are requested.

(g) C.875/70–72 (1532–1544). The complainant is entitled to a copyhold by descent, and the lord refuses to admit him. One Stretor has entered by the lord's procurement and keeps the petitioner out. Application is being made to the Chancellor because there is no common-law remedy to compel admittance, and also "forasmuch as divers copies concerning and approving the title and interest of your said orator are comen into the hands and possession of the said Stretor, the number and certainty whereof unto your said orator are unknown." *Subpoenas* to both the lord and Stretor are requested.

The answer on the part of the lord says that the matter is determinable at common law, and as to the merits that Stretor is entitled. The replication affirms the bill.

(It should be noted that the formula by which Stretor is charged with detaining copies is the one used in all of the innumerable Chancery bills complaining of the detention of deeds.)

(h) C.920/39–40 (1544–1547). A copyhold has been surrendered to the complainant's use, and the lord, defendant, refuses to admit him until he has paid a fine in excess of the customary amount. The answer says that the surrenderor had committed forfeiture.

(i) C.501/35 (1515–1529). The complainant is the widow of a copyholder in a manor where the widows of customary tenants for life, in tail, or in fee, have a customary estate *durante viduatate*. The steward admitted the complainant, and she enjoyed the land for two years, but the lord refuses to admit her and has put her out. She is willing to pay the fine due.

(j) St. Ch. 2/10/8 (1515–1529). This Chancery Bill addressed to Wolsey is erroneously filed under the Star Chamber Proceeding. The bill states that the complainant's late husband and his ancestors long held a certain copyhold tenement. The lord, an abbot, put him out without cause. He sued the abbot (it is not clear where) and died before the matter was determined. The abbot then died and the defendant was appointed his successor. The complainant has petitioned the new abbot to be restored to her messuage. (She does not make it clear what her interest is, but presumably it is a customary widow's estate.) The defendant refuses to restore her unless he is compelled to by law. She is too poor to "pursue" the law against him.

(k) C.896/30 (1532–1544). The bill says that the complainant's ancestor was seised of a copyhold and died seised, after whose death the right descended to the complainant. The lord, defendant, has custody of the court rolls and also of "divers copies, muniments, and writings" concerning the land. He has made various unlawful entries into the land, occupying it and interrupting the complainant's possession. The complainant has requested him to give up the documents and let him enjoy the land. (It does not appear that he has been admitted, but he does not expressly complain of failure to admit.) For want of certain knowledge of the evidences, the complainant is without remedy to recover them at law.

(l) Like the preceding case, C.355/80 (1504–1515) is primarily a bill to recover evidences, but, as in that case, the attempt to do so is closely related to an entitled party's attempt to gain admittance. The bill alleges that the complainant is entitled to a copyhold as heir to her father, who died seised. "By covin had" between Aymer and Margaret, two of the defendants, the lady of the manor, and one J. C., who pretends to have a bargain made to him by Aymer and Margaret, these persons have counterfeited the rolls of the manor and entered matter which would give Margaret title. They have done so in order to disinherit the complainant. "So it is" that all the court rolls and other writings concerning the land have come to the possession of Aymer and Margaret, and they will not give them up. *Subpoenas* are requested to Aymer, Margaret, J. C., and the lady of the manor.

On the back of the bill is an endorsement dated 4 Henry VIII. The lady of the manor is acquitted of all the things alleged in the bill and dismissed out of the court. (*Quod nota.* She was apparently at least held liable to defend herself.)

28. (a) C.140/99 (1486–1493 or 1504–1515). The bill recites that the complainant's father was seised of a messuage and forty acres, held of the defendant by rent and suit of court after the custom of his manor, "which custom is that the heir of every tenant so seised of any lands and tenements within the said manor after the decease of his ancestor should enter, have and occupy the same lands and tenements to him and his assigns accordingly as his said ancestors it held and occupied, except that the heir so coming in to his lands and tenements should yield and pay to the lord of that fee for the time being as much money in the name of a fine as the rent of the said mease and land draweth to in a year." After his father's death the complainant tendered his fine and paid it, whereupon the defendant admitted him. But notwithstanding the admission and payment of the fine the lord will not suffer him to have and enjoy the land. Because it is held by the custom, there is no remedy by course of the common law.

(Because of the admittance, the complainant here is in essentially the same position as a copyholder who has actually gained possession and been expelled. Note that payment of a fine is pleaded even though the exact amount is not. More care than usual is taken to plead the custom.)

(b) C.393/14 (1515–1529). The defendant granted a copyhold to the complainant for life. He was admitted, paid the customary fine, of unspecified amount, and did fealty. The defendant expelled him "contrary to his grant (*quod nota*) and contrary to the custom of the said lordship."

(c) C.531/8 (1515–1529). Apparently upon a descent, the complainant was admitted to a customary widow's estate, for which she paid her heriot, of unspecified amount. The lord, defendant, has expelled her.

(d) C.676/13–14 (1529–1532). The complainant was duly admitted to a copyhold upon surrender and enjoyed the land for some time. The lord, defendant, then expelled him. Since the defendant is lord of the manor, there is no remedy by course of the common law. The petitioner's replication denies a forfeiture, which must have been pleaded in the answer.

(e) C.872/41–43 (1533–1538). A complaint of expulsion by the lord without special allegations. The answer and replication dispute whether there was a forfeiture.

(f) C.875/5 (1533–1538). A complaint of expulsion, without special allegations, by the lord, first defendant, who has granted the land to the second defendant. There is no remedy at common law "for the obtaining of their right title and possession." The complainant also alleges that the second defendant has contemptuously disobeyed an order of the Council of Wales, to whom the complainant first applied concerning the same matter. The defendants also detain deeds relating to the land.

(g) C.920/31–32 (1533–1538). The complainant's father died seised of a copyhold, the complainant, his heir, being within age. The custody of the tenement was given to the complainant's mother by the lord. The mother died and the lord then took custody for the non-age of the complainant. During this time, the lord did not account to the complainant for the profits, made no repairs, and suffered the tenement to decay. At full age the complainant was admitted. The lord then demanded that he make reparations and for his failure to do so seized the tenement as forfeit. There is no remedy at common law "to obtain again the possession of the premises nor to have recompense for the said profits."

The lord's answer alleges that the houses were not decayed by reason of the defendant's occupancy. He also apparently denies having been in occupation, saying that the custody was given to others.

(h) C.554/28–31 (1515–1529). The bill complains that the lord and steward devised a trick to "pluck away the possession" which the complainant had in a copyhold in fee. The steward asked in court to see the complainant's copies, promising to return them at once. They were handed over and then not returned. They were subsequently inherited by the lord's son, defendant to this suit. For lack of certain knowledge as to the number, description, and location of these evidences, the complainant has no means of recovering them at common law. The defendant has expelled him from the land, and without the copies he is helpless to maintain his title. He has requested the defendant to let him see the rolls upon which his title would appear, but the defendant has refused.

The answer makes separate pleas for different portions of the land. As to six acres, "sith the time of mind the lord of the said manor demised the same six acres to the ancestors of the said complainant to hold at the will of the said lord by copy of court roll. Without that the said complainant was seised of the said six acres in his demesne as of fee after the custom of the said manor in manner and form as by the said bill of complaint is alleged." (This would seem to be either a claim that the complainant has no *manorial* estate except at will or else an exception to the form in which the petitioner pleads his estate. He pleaded it by saying that he was seised in his demesne as of fee of the land "and that holden of one Thomas Pelham by copy of court roll as of his manor . . . after the custom of his said manor.") As to the rest of the land, the answer continues, the complainant has forfeited it by violating a custom which forbids copyholders to implead other copyholders of the manor for trespasses done on their copyholds in any court except that of the manor. The complainant impleaded such persons in the court of another lordship for trespasses done upon the tenement here in question.

The replication says that as to the first parcel of land the complainant should be restored, since the defendant has not sufficiently answered the bill. As to the rest, the complainant does not know about the custom, but he has never impleaded copyholders of this manor for trespasses done upon his copyhold in any other court. He did implead such copyholders in another court for freehold land held of a different lord.

The rejoinder says that as to the first parcel the answer is sufficient "for so much as by the said answer it doth appear that the grant by copy of court roll of the said six acres was but only a lease at will by reason whereof the said William Pelham might determine his will therein at his pleasure." The answer is otherwise true.

29. (a) C.410/8 (1515–1529). The defendant, claiming under an untrue title, has disseised the complainant of his copyhold. Because of the

favor and maintenance of the lord he can have no remedy in the manorial court. He is old and blind and has no remedy at common law.

(b) C.511/20 (1515–1529). The defendant has disseised the complainants of their copyhold. They have sued to recover the land in the manorial court and also to recover rolls wrongfully detained by the defendant. By reason of the lord's maintenance, they cannot have justice.

(c) C.922/77 (1532–1544). Unlike the preceding cases, the bill in this one names the lord defendant rather than the party with whom the complainant has a dispute governed by manorial law. Against this stranger the complainant has a claim in the nature of mort d'ancestor, but the lord will not hear the complaint or do justice. The bill requests a *Subpoena* to the lord in the alternative: he is to be directed either to hold a court and do justice or to appear in the Chancery, the matter to be determined there.

30. (a) C.251/43 (1501–1502). A tenement customarily demisable by copy was granted to the complainant for life, whereupon he paid a fine of twenty-six shillings, sevenpence. The manor subsequently changed hands and the new lord, defendant, expelled the complainant.

(b) C.325/52 (1493–1500 or 1515–1529). The lady of the manor granted the complainants a copyhold in fee in full court according to the usage there. The complainants paid "a great sum of money," the amount unspecified. The lady then married the defendant, who is now lord in the right of his wife. He has expelled the complainants. The complainants' crops are growing upon part of the land, and part of it is ready to be sown with corn.

(c) C.681/7–8 (1529–1534). The complainant was a copyholder in fee. The lord of the manor died, and his widow, defendant, "had" the land (whether as dower or jointure is not clear). For ten years she received the complainant's services. Of late she put him out for the reason that he gave evidence concerning the manor upon a writ of *Subpoena*. The complainant is aged, impoverished, and has no remedy at common law.

The answer says that from time out of mind the land has been pleadable in the manorial court only. As to the merits, the complainant committed forfeiture by giving false and malicious testimony tending to defeat the defendant's interest and that of the infant heir to the manor.

(d) C.354/114 (1504–1515). The complainant pleads that the land in question has customarily been let by copy in fee, in tail, and for life. The complainant was a copyholder in fee, having taken his interest from the Earl of Shrewsbury, then lord. The Earl subsequently sold the manor to the defendant, who recovered it against the Earl in a writ of entry in the post upon a feigned title. The defendant has expelled the complainant. There is no remedy at common law "because of the said feigned recovery." The expulsion was "contrary to all good conscience and contrary to the custom of the said lordship."

(It would seem that the complainant in this bill has no strict legal or customary right to the land. The usual rule was that the grants of one lord were binding on subsequent lords, provided that such subsequent lord did not enter or recover in virtue of a better title to the manor than the grantor's. Here, despite the collusive nature of the recovery, it would be matter of record that the Earl was wrongfully seised vis-à-vis the defendant. Therefore the complainant would seem to be claiming that this legal result is unconscionable, even though he says that the expulsion is a violation of custom. Note also that the feigned recovery is the only reason given why a remedy at common law is unobtainable. This suggests either that the expression "common law" is used loosely to include manorial proceedings, or that a remedy in the royal courts of common law was available at the time of this case. The latter possibility is at variance with most of the evidence.)

31. The following are bills to compel persons holding copyholds to the use of others to carry out the trusts: C.184/48; C.229/33; C.327/43; C.389/6; C.389/45; C.663/18.

32. (a) C.472/36–37 (1515–1529) recites that a copyhold has been entailed and that the complainant is heir under the entail. After the death of the complainant's ancestor, the defendant, who is a steward of the manor, entered and remains in possession. Inasmuch as the defendant is steward, the complainant cannot obtain copies of the court rolls by means of which she would be able to make her title for the land in the manorial court.

The defendant's answer says that the matter is determinable in the manorial court. As to the merits, the land is rightfully the defendant's, by virtue of a surrender by one of the complainant's predecessors in title.

(b) C.783/25 (1529–1532). The bill says that the complainant was admitted to a copyhold upon inheritance, but "forasmuch as the steward of the said court by negligence left out of the copy eight acres, parcel of the premises" the lord has entered upon the said eight acres. The complainant is poor and will be driven to beg if she does not have the Chancellor's aid. (It is not clear, however, whether this petitioner intends that the lord should be subpoenaed, or only the steward to repair the evidences.)

33. (a) C.302/57 (1504–1515). The complainant says that her late husband was a copyholder for life, and that the custom gives the widows of such tenants estates *durante viduatate*. After her husband's death, the complainant came to court, paid her heriot, and was admitted to her widow's estate. After being in possession for many years, she let the land to the defendant from year to year for the space of four or five years. The defendant "labored unto" the petitioner to have the land, which she refused. He then "labored unto" the steward, who, for "reward and pleasure given" granted him the land by copy for life. The defendant then expelled the complainant, since which he has been in possession for sixteen years. The complainant had her right and title found by the homage, but because the steward maintains the defendant she cannot obtain a remedy in the manorial court. She is too poor to sue for the land in any other court.

(b) C.568/76 (1515–1529), the complainant is heir to a copyhold in fee. The defendant has entered into this tenement. Justice is unobtainable in the manorial court because the defendant is maintained by certain "chief head tenants" of the manor and is himself one of the chief men of the lordship. Without these men, there are not enough other tenants to make an homage. The maintainers are of such importance "that in manner there is nothing done in that court but after their wills."

This bill is endorsed with a decree enjoining the steward to admit the complainant and the complainant to pay his fine. (It should be noted that the case terminated in this decree despite the fact that the bill does not name the steward as a defendant.)

(c) C.581/59–63 (1515–1529). The bill alleges that the complainant's great-grandfather was a copyholder in fee and surrendered to the use of John the elder and Margaret for life, "wherefore the lord had a heriot price of six shillings," remainder to William and the heirs male of his body, remainder to John the younger and the heirs male of his body. After the deaths of John the elder and Margaret, Kyng's father entered and was seised of wrong. William is dead without heirs male of his body, and the complainant is heir male of the body of John the younger. The complainant accordingly brought a plaint in the nature of formedon in the remainder against Kyng. While this plaint was pending, Kyng, "for only maintenance," surrendered to the use of Wharley. The complainant continued to pursue his plaint against Kyng, and the parties were at issue. The steward awarded a *Venire facias* directed to the bailiff to return a sufficient inquest at the next court. Twelve men were returned, all of whom appeared except one Pydok, who, by the labor of Wharley, absented himself. Since then, the complainant has not been able to have an inquest to try the issue. Subpoenas to Kyng and Wharley are requested.

An answer on the part of Wharley says simply that the matter is determinable in the manorial court. This pleading is stricken and marked "Vacat." In his final answer Wharley says that the matter is determinable in the manorial court but then proceeds to plead to the merits. He alleges that if any such gift in tail was made it was "avoided and annulled" by the donor's wife, "according to the law and custom of the manor aforesaid." Wharley's title may be traced from the wife of the said donor, and he and those through whom he claims have been in possession since 19 Henry 6.

The complainant's replication affirms the truth of the bill generally and specifies why the case is not determinable in the manorial court. He "hath no remedy by the course of the common law nor in the court of the lord of whom the said land is holden by reason of the forcing and brassing, bolstering and bearing of the said Raffe Wharley, which Raffe hath a fee of the abbot of Halysown [lord of the manor in question], and also the said Raffe Wharley is bailiff of the said lordship of Horborne under the said abbot." The rejoinder adds nothing new to the defense.

(d) C.401/11 (1515–1529). The complainants were admitted tenants of customary land by copy of court roll for life and to the longest living of them. Later, the land was granted to the defendant by deed, the grantor surmising that the land lies in grant by deed and not by copy. The complainants can get no remedy in the manorial court "by reason of divers and sundry untrue informations made so well to the said countess [lady of the manor] as to other her officers."

34. (a) C.465/31–33 (1515–1529). The bill says that Thomas, the complainant's ancestor, was seised of a copyhold and disseised by Robert, who was succeeded in title by Elizabeth. The complainant sued a plaint in the manorial court "in the nature of a writ of entry in le quibus in le per and cui," and had judgment to recover. In spite of the complainant's willingness to pay a reasonable fine the defendant, steward of the manor, will not admit him.

The defendant's answer is mutilated. The replication says that it is not the custom that recoverers in the complainant's position may not enter without a grant from the lord, which presumably indicates the nature of the defense. The complainant says that the answer was feigned to put him to the expense of copying it and to "fatigate" those hearing or reading it.

(b) Unlike the preceding case, C.885/26 (1533–1538) does not directly charge the defendant with unconscientious performance of his office, but it does seek to defeat the effects of conscienceless behavior on the part of homagers by compelling the manorial officers to override a false presentment. The bill alleges that the complainant is rightful heir to a copyhold, but the homage presented that one Roger was heir. There are no tenants or suitors within the manor other than those who found the false verdict, and they will not reverse themselves in any other action brought by the complainant in the manorial court. An injunction requiring the officers of the manorial court to annul the false presentment is requested.

This bill is endorsed with an injunction as requested by the petitioner. The injunction is crossed out, however.

(c) C.462/25 (1515–1529) is distinctive in that removal of a manorial suit to the Chancery by *Certiorari* is requested instead of injunctive relief. According to the bill the complainant has been impleaded in the manorial court by plaint in the nature of formedon in the remainder. He cannot have justice because the suit is brought by procurement of the bailiff, who will be judge in the cause. The bailiff has bought a "feigned title" to the land from the demandant in the plaint in the manorial court.

(Two cases which may involve copyhold land but do not clearly do so may be cited as evidence that *certiorari* would lie from the Chancery to manorial courts. According to the bill in C.207/38, the complainant brought a suit in the Chancery for recovery of evidences. The defendant to that suit then brought a plaint of trespass in a manorial court for the land to which the evidences related. The Chancery suit was still pending at that time. In his pleading in the manorial court, the complainant's adversary made allegations at variance with those he made in the Chancery suit. On the basis of these facts, the complainant requests that the manorial suit be removed into the Chancery by *Certiorari*. In C.347/11, *certiorari* is requested because the complainant has been sued by plaint of trespass in a manorial court and the officers are prejudiced in favor of the adverse party.)

35. E.g., BM Add. MSS 25,196, pp. 372b–373a, a report of Browne v.

Foster in the Queen's Bench, Michaelmas 37/38 Elizabeth, where the justices say ". . . le Seignor est Chancellor inter ceux copiholders. . . ."

36. (a) In the following cases the bills contain allegations which seem to attempt to establish that equitable resources on the manorial level have been exhausted:

(1) C.314/8 (1504–1515). The bill says that one Childwell was seised of a copyhold in fee. He bargained and sold the land to one Dolnes. Dolnes conveyed it to the complainant, who was admitted tenant. The complainant spent more than five hundred pounds in building, whereas the yearly value of the land was before about ten shillings. After the surrender to the complainant, Childwell lived fully twelve years "without any manner of claim making." Childwell "verily sold the said cottage and garden unto the said Robert Dolnes and was well and truly by the said Robert paid." "Yet forasmuch as certain rolls, by the space of three years, wherein the same surrender [to the complainant] was entered cannot be found or seen," Childwell's son and heir, defendant, intends to recover the land from the complainant in a manorial proceeding, supposing that Dolnes disseised his father. If the defendant were to recover, he would get land of vastly increased value, but the complainant has no remedy, "by the order and custom of the said court, for lack of the said rolls." This being the case, the complainant "exhibited a bill containing all the said matters" to the lord of the manor, "as Chancellor in conscience of his said lordship." The lord refused to take any action, "saying that he would not let the said John Childwell and the other parties to sue for their remedy after the order and course of his customary court . . . and over that saying that if the said parties or any of them should recover the said lands by and after the custom and order of his said court . . . then he would have the said lands himself by the reason of a custom within the said lordship as he affirmed is, that is to say, if the heir of any customary tenant decease, and his heir cometh not into the court and claim his right as heir unto his ancestor within a certain time, that then he shall be excluded of his title and right thereof and the lord to seize and have the land forever. . . ." The defendant and his sisters did not make claim within the prescribed time, so that if they should recover the lord would have the land himself. A *Subpoena* to Childwell is requested.

(2) C.406/52–55 (1515–1529). A copyhold was surrendered to the complainant's use, and she appeared in court to claim admittance. By labor of the defendants, she was adjourned to the next holding of the

court. The defendants then corrupted the steward and got the court held secretly, the complainant being in London and having no knowledge of it. The complainant was openly called in court and made default of law, after which the defendants were admitted tenants. "Whereupon, for the reformation thereof, your said oratrix . . . often and many times made suit and labor by petition and otherwise unto my lord of Winchester, lord of the lordship, to have the said matter heard and the wrong thereof reformed according to right and conscience, for that your said oratrix was without remedy by the course of the said court. And the said lord of Winchester committed this matter unto his steward and officers of the same court, telling them to examine the said matter by the tenants and homage of the said lordship, which to do his said steward and officers, forasmuch as they were privy and party to the great untruth and open wrong before rehearsed, have always refused and delayed. Wherefore your said oratrix is not only without remedy by the course of the common law, but also without remedy in that court after the custom of the said lordship there used, except your gracious favor and charitable help be showed unto your poor oratrix in this behalf. In consideration whereof, and forasmuch as your said oratrix hath been always delayed to her utter undoing and can have no remedy by petition in conscience nor otherwise within the same court," a *Subpoena* is requested.

The answer says that the matter is determinable in the manorial court, and, as to the merits, that the true title is in the defendants, who were duly admitted, the complainant's pretended title having been proved false. The replication and rejoinder add nothing material.

(3) C.406/3–4 (1515–1529). The complainant says that his father was seised of a copyhold, after whose death the land should have descended to him. But one Knolles entered without right and persuaded the lord to make a new grant to him by copy, supposing that no heir had presented himself after the death of the complainant's father and that the land had reverted to the lord. Knolles sold the land to the defendant, who is now in possession. ". . . Your said orator can have in the said prior's court no indifferent justice. Yet that notwithstanding, your said orator hath sued from time to time by petition to the said prior for remedy therein, the which prior gave in commandment that the homage of the court of his said manor should inquire of the title of your said orator of and in the premises. The which homage presented that your said orator was son and heir to the said Robert and also that he had title to the premises in manner and form as is before rehearsed,

and that the said John Knolles had no right nor title to make sale of the said mease and other the premises but by abatement and wrong. . . And that notwithstanding, the said Thomas Wilson [defendant] by great might and power as yet keepeth your said orator out of possession thereof, of the which your said orator hath no remedy by the course of the common law nor yet in the court of the said manor, forasmuch as the said Thomas is supported, borne, and maintained by the officers of the said manor in such manner and form that your said orator can in no wise have the law and justice indifferently ministered unto him."

The answer prays remittance to the manorial court, saying "all matters concerning the same lands have been used out of time of mind to be determinable in the said court according to the custom of the manor before the steward there, and not elsewhere." (This demurrer is surprising. If other bills similar to the one in this case are good, the maintenance of the officers would seem sufficient to make out a cause of complaint.)

(4) C.382/41–42 (1515–1529). The bill alleges that Thomas Perse was tenant by copy and in consideration of a bargain and sale surrendered the land to the use of Sir John Dall, "by force of which bargain the use of the same lands and tenements was in the said Sir John Dall in fee after the custom of the said manor." Thomas Perse died "afore that the said surrender was testified in the court of the said lady." Dall then bargained and sold the land to the complainant, who was admitted tenant. The defendant, Thomas' son, "forasmuch as the said Thomas Perse, his father, died seised of the said lands and tenements by course of the law, because the said Sir John Dall was not admitted tenant in the life of the said Thomas Perse, sued a plaint in the nature of Assise of Mort d'ancestor in the said lady's court and by the common law recovered the same . . . and thereof is now seised." The complainant has requested the defendant to surrender to him. He has also "made great and humble suit to the said lady to compel the said Robert Perse to make surrender. . ." The lady of the manor refuses to do so because of the great favor she bears to the defendant.

In his answer the defendant says the matter is determinable in the manorial court, and, saving this advantage, denies that the bargain and sale to Dall was ever made. The complainant entered of wrong after Thomas' death and the land was duly recovered from him in the manorial court.

(b) C.515/88–90 (1515–1529) is not evidence that equitable remedies on the manorial level had to be exhausted before applying to the Chancellor, but the case illustrates the operation of manorial equity. The complainant says that she is heiress to a copyhold and that after her father's death she paid her heriot and entered. She cannot be admitted because one of the defendants pretends title and makes labor to the officers of the manor. The second defendant abets him in this. The complainant also says that she is ready to pay the fine, that she is young and of small substance, and that the first defendant detains deeds relating to the land.

The first defendant claims in his answer to be the rightful owner of the copyhold and says that the complainant's father obtained it by virtue of an untrue presentment of a surrender. At the time the complainant's father obtained his interest, the defendant was an apprentice in London and "could not resort into the country to have knowledge of his said true and just title." When he found out about the untrue presentment, he "sued by way of petition to the said reverend father [Bishop of Winchester and lord of the manor] . . . having power as well to minister and execute justice [to them] that would sue according to the custom of the said manor by plaint as to examine the conscience of every matter concerning the copyhold land holden of the said manor. . . The which complaint the said reverend father, upon long suit to him made, remitted and sent to the homage and tenants of the said manor." The homage found that the earlier presentment was untrue and that the defendant was entitled. The officers of the court were therefore instructed to defer admitting the complainant. Also, the lord commanded the defendant to "sue to divers of the learned counsel of the said Bishop, whom the said Bishop had sufficiently advertised to examine the right and also the conscience of the said whole matter and to set such direction therein as might stand with equity, justice, and good conscience." The defendant had accordingly sued to the learned counsel. He has made no labor to the officers and has not withheld the deeds.

In his answer, the second defendant says that he has made no "sinister labor," but "in discharge of his conscience against God hath divers times testified before the officers and homage of the said manor" concerning the matter in dispute. His testimony was to the same effect as the other defendant's allegations.

(c) A special form of manorial equity is illustrated by two cases where the manors are royal. The regular procedure (and, in the second case, what may perhaps be taken as equitable resort to the General Surveyors) has failed to produce a remedy, and consequently the King's Chancellor is applied to as the lord would be in the ordinary manor.

(1) C.327/53 (1504–1515). The manor was royal at the time of the transactions mentioned and presumably still is, since nothing is said of an alienation. The complainant is a copyholder there. One Alice Hyggyn pretends title and at a recent court "labored and caused" by crafty means twelve persons to be impaneled to inquire whether she had the better right. She has given money to the twelve men to induce them to return a verdict in her favor, "which is contrary to the custom of the said manor and against right and good conscience." The bill requests that "the King's writ of special *Certiorari*" be directed to the steward of the manor to certify into the Chancery "all the copies, processes, actions . . . and judgments touching or concerning the premises or depending in the said court between the said parties."

(2) C.469/2 (1515–1529). The complainants are a copyholder of a royal manor and his farmer, the latter holding under a lease from year to year. The defendant, pretending title, surmised to the King's General Surveyors that the lands in question were demesne lands and demisable by indenture rather than by copy. By such labor, the defendant obtained a grant of the land for twenty-one years by letters patent. The defendant has entered upon the complainants, distrained and driven away their beasts, "subverteth and turneth" the ground, and "so useth himself that your said orators can take no profit thereof." The petitioners have complained in the manorial court and also before the General Surveyors, but they can have no remedy.

37. *Select Cases in the Court of Requests; Select Cases before the King's Council in the Star Chamber*. See the introductions to these volumes. See also Leadam, *EHR* 8:684–696 (1893).

38. (a) R. 6/234. The initial bill in this case is comparable to several Chancery bills discussed above. It alleges that the complainant and her late husband were jointly admitted to a copyhold for their lives. They paid a fine of forty-six shillings, eightpence. "Upon hope and trust" that they would be permitted to enjoy the land for their lives, they spent forty marks for repairs. The defendant, lord and grantor, has nevertheless put the complainant out. It is requested that he be made to appear before the Council at Whitehall to answer for these things.

A second bill alleges that when the complainant's son tried to serve the defendant with the King's Privy Seal writ, awarded on account of the first bill, the defendant's son assaulted him, in contempt of the court. It is further said that the defendant is a powerful man and the complainant of small power.

The next document for this case, the defendant's answer, contains several points of interest. The defendant begins by admitting that he expelled the complainant's late husband, but he denies that he did so "of his extort power." According to the answer, the husband fled to a sanctuary town in order to defraud his creditors, and the complainant meanwhile enjoyed the land. She then made a lease without the lord's license and went to sanctuary herself. In their absence, the defendant let the land to others. The defendant then goes on to plead that the fine given by the complainant and her husband amounted to only forty shillings. He also denies that money was spent on building and fencing, "for the whole homage and other honest men hath viewed the same and cannot find neither in fencing or otherwise that ever he bestowed the value of 4 £ sterling in and upon the presaid tenement." Then, the answer continues, the complainant and her husband returned from sanctuary and demanded the land, which the defendant did not at that time have in his hands. The husband accordingly sued a *Subpoena* in the Chancery (*quod nota*—he elected the Chancery first), which the defendant "did humbly receive." At this point the document becomes partially illegible. It is clear, however, that the defendant was urged by someone—possibly persons commissioned by the Chancellor to determine the case—to refund part of the fine to the husband. The defendant then agreed with the husband "of and for the interest of the same tenement. And thereupon, of his own gentleness and good will, and in discharging of his conscience, gave unto the said Thomas [the husband] 4 marks sterling . . . which the said [defendant] need not so to have done, inasmuch as the said Thomas had forfeited his copy." At the next court Thomas made a surrender to the defendant. He was to have delivered up his copy at the same time, but the complainant said she had lost it. The contempt alleged in the second bill is denied.

The record also includes a replication, a rejoinder, and a letter from the defendant to the Council. These add nothing to the pleadings above. In addition several depositions are preserved, to the effect that the land was forfeited according to the custom.

(b) R. 2/59 (1540) contains no pleadings, but only the return of commissioners of an inquisition taken by authority of letters under the Privy Seal. The commissioners report that they were commanded to examine the right and title of one Margaret Kirby in a certain copyhold held of the Bishop of Chichester and to try to bring the matter to a final determination. They have examined Margaret and others who might know about the matter and reached the following results: "We find not that ever the said Margaret Kirby had any good or just title to the said copyhold, but further we find that about xiii years past the said Margaret Kirby, by complaint made against Robert Sherber, late Bishop of Chichester, in the King's High Court of Chancery for and concerning her pretended right in and to the premises, obtained a commission from the said court directed toward [several gentlemen] giving unto them full power and authority by virtue thereof not only to examine the right of the said Margaret of and in the premises, but if by ways and means they might to end and determine the same. Whereupon they calling before them as well the said Bishop and the said Margaret as also all other persons by whom they might be informed of the truth, after long examination of the matter found that the said Margaret had no right unto the premises . . . [a few words are illegible] but for that the said Margaret was a widow . . . the said commissioners required the said Bishop "to give her iiii nobles, which he did, and the said Lord Laware [one of the commissioners] also in compassion of her poverty gave unto her a noble, all which money the said Margaret at that time accepted and so bargained and sold unto the said Bishop all her pretended right of and in the said copyhold and was therewith contented and acquieted, unto now of late and sithens the death of the said Bishop." The members of the earlier commission are ready to testify to these matters. Margaret, "notwithstanding this our examination nor any persuasion that we can give her will not thus be acquieted," wherefore this return is made.

(It should be noted that Margaret in this case, like the complainant in the preceding one, resorted to the Requests after bad luck in the Chancery but went first to what was probably the usual court for such cases. The inclination of the Chancery commissioners in both cases to recommend some compensation of the complainants despite the failure of their titles perhaps suggests that in copyhold matters the Chancellor was frequently unwilling to settle cases merely on the basis of customary title. In the preceding case the bill raises, and the answer meets, equitable considerations in connection with the fine and expenses; the return in this case suggests that whatever equities may have been involved the commissioners were primarily concerned with legal title.)

(c) R. 6/246 (1545) is a claim adverse to the lord which relies on customary right free of special equitable considerations. The bill alleges that the reversion of a copyhold was granted to the complainant and his daughter for their successive lives. The particular estate ended, so that the complainant should have had the land. The first defendant occupies it, however. He is the lessee of and maintained by the lord, who is also named a defendant.

An answer says that the custom is that reversions of copyholds may not be granted without the assent of the particular tenant, which was not obtained in this case. Consequently the grant to the complainant was void.

In his replication, the complainant denies that there is any such custom. He also pleads that such a custom ought not to be allowed if it did exist: "Without that any such custom ought to be used and allowed if any such pretensed custom were within the said manor." (This second plea is the only instance of a challenge to the reasonableness of a custom that I have found among the Chancery and Conciliar records. There are many such challenges in common-law cases from Elizabeth's reign and after. The alleged custom in this case requires a procedure in the nature of attornment, which does not seem highly unreasonable. The record includes depositions on both sides as to the existence of this custom, but there is no evidence of whether it was allowed.)

(d) The following claims are not adverse to the lord and are indistinguishable from comparable Chancery cases:

(1) R. 2/26. The defendant has entered into a copyhold in an ancient demesne manor which of right should be the complainant's. He maintains his wrongful possession by forged copies and also wrongfully detains documents of title so that the complainant has no remedy to recover the land. The formula for alleging detention of deeds is identical with that used in countless Chancery cases concerning evidences for land of all sorts.

(2) R. 6/170. The defendant detains a copy which he obtained by trickery. He is a powerful man and the complainants powerless. The usual formula for detention of deeds is used. The answer says the matter is determinable in the manorial court but proceeds to dispute the substance of the claim.

(3) R. 3/22. The bill complains of forcible ejection from a copyhold held by the petitioner in tail. The defendants are favored and maintained by the bailiff and steward of the manor, and with their help

have "taken up" the land in the court of the manor. One of the defendants answers that another of the defendants was rightfully seised by copy, he himself having only taken the profits as the latter's farmer. The complainant had no interest except in virtue of a surrender to him upon condition, for breach of which the defendant, who is rightful owner, entered. The replication denies the essential points in the answer.

(4) R. 8/326. Among other things, the bill charges the defendant with procuring an unjust and partial verdict in a manorial court, contrary to the evidence.

(e) The following claims involving copyholds are properly within the class of "poor men's causes." There is no indication that a remedy could not be obtained in the manorial court, but complaint is nevertheless made to the Council on the ground of poverty or, as in case 4 (R. 2/95), for another special reason.

(1) R. 6/172. The complainant says that the right to a copyhold descended to him, but that the defendant claims to have "taken" the land at a certain court. The homage says he did not "take" it, and they are ready to so testify, according to the bill. The complainant is a "poor man, a daily laborer, and not able to shewe [*sic*] by course of your laws."

A second document indicates how the Council handled the case. This is a letter from the steward of the manor where the land lies to the Council. The steward recites that "at the King's last being in Sussex, ye did direct unto me a certain complaint made to his highness . . . against [defendant], tenant unto the late Abbot of Brenston of the manor of Roughton, where I am Steward, and the same complaint by me to be examined." He has examined divers tenants and finds that, whereas the complainant claimed an estate of inheritance, there is no custom warranting more than estates for life. Enclosed with the steward's letter are excerpts from the copies of tenants of the manor showing that they all have estates for life only.

(2) R. 1/82. The petitioner complains of expulsion from a copyhold demised to him by the copyholder for seven years. The defendant is not lord of the manor, but a stranger, from all that appears. The petitioner says he is too poor to sue at common law.

(This is the only case of its type I have found among the Chancery and Conciliar records. It is doubtful whether a copyholder's lessee could maintain a termor's common-law remedies in the early sixteenth century. Presumably manorial courts had jurisdiction to defend such interests even though the lessee had not been admitted by the lord, but I have no evidence on this point.)

(3) R. 5/130. (Although catalogued with cases mainly from Henry VIII's reign, this case is clearly from Edward VI's for reference is made in the bill to an admittance in 8 Henry 7, "your most noble grandfather." It is consequently probable that copyholders had a common-law remedy at the time of this case.) The complaint is of expulsion from a copyhold. The defendant is widow of a late lord of the manor and has apparently acceded to the manor by way of jointure. The complainants say they are "aged and weak and not able to follow the common law."

The defendant's answer prays remittance to the common law but answers to the merits. A replication and rejoinder disputing the facts are also preserved.

(4) R. 2/95. Without specifying the nature of the tenure, the complainant says that land which ought to have descended to his wife is wrongfully occupied by the defendant. The complainant's reason for application is that he is the king's messenger and because of his attendance on the king is unable to sue at common law.

The second document in the record is a commission to inquire into the matter, do justice if possible, and otherwise to certify to the Council what can be found out. A third document is the commissioners' return. This reports first how the defendant replied to the bill: The defendant first said the matter was determinable in a manorial court. But for the declaration of the truth he said that the complainant and his wife had previously brought an action against him in the manorial court. To this action the defendant answered that the land was forfeited after the death of the ancestor whose heir the complainant's wife claims to be. The reason for the forfeiture was failure of an heir to present himself within the customary time. The tenancy thus being vacant, the land was granted to the defendant. In the manorial proceeding, the complainant then replied that his wife was only five years old at the time of her ancestor's death, and because of her infancy no forfeiture for non-claimer occurred. Upon trial of the manorial suit, the homage found that the complainant's wife was not next heir. The next heir was rather one Alice, who was alive and of full age when the ancestor died, and for the failure of Alice to present herself in time the land was forfeited. The defendant accordingly had judgment in the manorial action.

The commissioners' return also includes depositions taken before them on the question of when Alice died. (This is presumably relevant for determining whether Alice was alive when the ancestor died. It is noteworthy that the commissioners seem not to have felt bound by the determination of the manorial court that she was alive at that time. This is the only case I have found which suggests the question of whether the Chancery and Conciliar courts would be concluded by findings, and particularly by judgments, of manorial courts.)

39. (a) The following cases may be assigned to Henry VII's reign:

(1) St. Ch. 1/2/99. The complainant says that he came to the court of the Abbot of Malmesbury and took a tenement by copy, "like as his father . . . held before in his life." The grant was to the complainant and his wife for their lives, and they gave a fine of four pounds, six shillings, eightpence. The complainant spent great sums in building and increased the value of the land by careful husbandry, and, perceiving this, the defendant, Kitchener of the abbey, riotously put him out. The complainant adds that he is not "of power" to sue for his remedy at common law.

In his answer, the defendant denies the riot and says that the complainant forfeited the land for non-payment of a customary fee for pasturing his swine in a certain waste of the manor. The forfeiture was duly presented, and the defendant only acted as the abbot's representative.

(2) St. Ch. 1/2/110. A copyholder's claim to security in his manorial estate is no part of the complaint in this case, for the suit is brought by the lord of the manor. He complains that he was peaceably seised of certain lands when the defendants riotously, with force and arms, entered upon him.

The answer says that the matter is determinable at common law. It then proceeds to say that at a court of the complainant and Alice his mother the land was granted to one of the defendants for life, in exchange for a fine of forty shillings. This defendant occupied the land until he was expelled by the complainant. The complainant has not been expelled or menaced in any way.

For replication, the complainant says that the land belonged jointly to Alice and Thomas her husband. Thomas died, Alice was seised by survivorship, and at a court held by her the defendant took the land "to hold of the same according to the custom of the said manor by copy of court roll and at the will of the said Alice." After Alice's death, the land descended to the complainant under an entail to the heirs of the bodies of Thomas and Alice. "Withouten that the said Alexander [complainant] made any lease of the said mease . . . as is surmised." (Is this replication good, in view of the usual rule that the grants of the lord for the time being bind the fee?) Depositions in the case survive and are in part concerned with whether the defendant took a copy from the complainant, as opposed to Alice. One deponent says that he did not and another says that he himself was admitted tenant at the complainant's first court but never had a copy from him.

(b) The following cases are from Henry VIII's reign:

(1) St. Ch. 2/10/109–110 combines a copyholder's claim with an allegation of riot. The complainant says that his father devised a copyhold to him, in virtue of which he entered. The defendant, a manorial officer, riotously expelled him and has also refused to admit him. He has in addition cut and carried away trees and crops growing on the land.

The answer first excepts to the sufficiency of the bill on the ground that a devise is alleged in the bill, but no surrender to the use of the father's will. Nor has the complainant made out a sufficient title as next heir. The defendant then pleads further that after the death of the complainant's father contention arose because the complainant refused to take up one third of the copyhold land held by his father. The lord of the manor complained to the Chancellor ("the late Lord Audeley"). The Chancellor ordered the complainant in this suit to take up all the land held by his father and decreed that if he failed to do so his copyhold lands should be forfeited and the lord might enter. (Note this unusual Chancery proceeding.) The complainant still refuses to take up the disputed third, although the lord made copies to him and made livery by the rod. The complainant also refuses to pay his fine and rent in accord with a further provision of the Chancery decree. He has also committed forfeiture on other grounds. The defendant entered at the lord's command.

(2) St. Ch. 2/6/366–367. The bill complains simply of riotous expulsion from a copyhold. The defendants deny the riot and allege that the complainant forfeited the land, that the forfeiture was duly presented, and that the tenement was subsequently granted to the defendants by the lord. (Note that allegation of riot in the bill removes the necessity of showing why a remedy in the manorial court is unobtainable.)

(3) St. Ch. 2/11/32–34 consists of two answers and a replication. From these it appears that the complaint was of riotous and wrongful entry into the petitioner's copyhold. The defendant justified his entry by saying that the copyhold was only granted to the complainant's wife for life, that she died, and that the holding was subsequently regranted to him.

(4) St. Ch. 2/7/141–142. The bill complains of riotous ouster from a copyhold. The answer denies the riot and justifies the entry as servants of the true owner, who has a better title than to the freehold than the complainant's lord.

(5) In St. Ch. 2/6/181, both riot and illegal enclosure serve as grounds for the complaint. The complainants are several copyhold tenants of the defendant's manor. They say that the defendant "hath wrongfully vexed, unquieted, and disturbed your said poor subjects, being copyhold tenants of the said manor as is aforesaid, contrary to all equity and the custom of the said manor." He has taken the complainants' pastures and enclosed them. "By compulsion [he] hath caused some of your said poor subjects to take other lands being none of his own further off at his pleasure, being worse lands and not like in values nor number of acres nor the title thereof clear, and to some of your said poor subjects he hath appointed no lands at all nor other recompense." He has violently attacked those who would not agree to these exchanges, and "after most riotous and forcible manner beset their houses about and threatened them to imprison, whereupon your said poor subjects, perceiving his mischievous intent, for the salveguard of their lives shut up their doors against him and durst not for fear and peril of death come forth." Some of the complainants said to the defendant "Jesu . . . in the name of God what mean you thus to handle us poor people?" To which the defendant replied, "Do ye not know that the King's Grace hath put down all the houses of monks, friars, and nuns, therefore now is the time come that we gentlemen will pull down the houses of such poor knaves as ye be." The defendant has served notice on certain of the complainants to vacate their tenements, so that the manor is likely to be depopulated.

(6) In St. Ch. 2/11/83, the defendant is not charged with riot, but is accused of illegal enclosure. The complainants are inhabitants of two towns and tenants of three different persons, including the defendant. The bill says that the defendant has enclosed a moor in which the complainants have common by reason of their tenures, that he has enclosed another common in which the inhabitants of one town have used to have pasture, and that he has stopped a way which the complainants have used by reason of their tenure. He also took the tenements and pulled down the houses of one of the complainants and two widows for the purpose of enclosing their land in a park and nevertheless compelled them to pay rent. He demanded the evidences of his tenants in court and

erased parts of them before handing them back, by color of which altered deeds he threatens to put them out of their tenements. He has failed to make estate by a sufficient deed to one of the complainants in spite of a promise to do so and a substantial fine paid. He has ejected some of the complainants from their tenements. He has compelled them to do labor services without paying them and used their horses, nearly working them to death before returning them. He has let his deer lie on the complainants' crops and killed their dogs if they try to chase the deer away. Finally, he has allowed the church to fall into decay by preventing the parson from enjoying a common which he should have. The complainants are not of power to sue for their remedy elsewhere, and if they cannot have a remedy they will be forced to leave their holdings.

Copies of two pleadings by the defendant are preserved. The first is a counter-bill, in which he says that certain of the complainants in the bill above assembled riotously, in the manner of rebellion, broke his palings, and committed an assault upon his person. The second document is the answer to the first bill. In this, the defendant says that those of the complainants who are not his tenants have brought the bill of pure malice. Those who are his tenants include life tenants by deed, copyholders, and ordinary tenants at will. As to those who are his tenants, "they ought not ne may by the common law prescribe to have common against the said Sir John [defendant] owner of the said manor and if they might, as they may not, yet the said Sir John saith that it is lawful for him that is their lord and owner of the said manor . . . to improve himself in his own ground, leaving his said tenants sufficient common there." The moor mentioned in the bill is more common that the tenants can occupy. As to the common way, there are two ways, equally convenient, to the same place, and the defendant has shut off one because it came so close to his house as to constitute a nuisance. The house allegedly pulled down had fallen into decay and was demolished with the tenant's agreement, and that tenant continues to enjoy the land. The other land which the defendant is alleged to have taken is copyhold and was forfeited. The erasure of deeds is denied. As to the breach of promise, he has always been ready to seal the deed if requested. He has already made amends for any damage his deer may accidentally have done. Common has not been withheld from the parson.

(7) St. Ch. 2/10/128 is different from the cases above in that there is no allegation of riot or enclosure. The complaint is indistinguishable from those brought in the Chancery and the Requests. The petitioner

says that she is a copyholder in fee in a manor where the custom is that copyholders shall have all timber on their tenements without impeachment of waste. The defendant, a new lord of the manor, sold the wood on the petitioner's land to two purchasers, who have cut down the trees. To prevent the complainant from interfering with this woodcutting, the defendant and his vendees caused surety of the peace to be taken against the complainant. Moreover, because the complainant objected to the woodcutting, the defendant, sitting as steward in his manorial court ("which appeareth to be against all conscience that any man should be judge in his own court") discharged the complainant from her tenement and will not suffer her to occupy it in peace. The petitioner has no remedy at common law because the defendant is lord of the manor and a man of great substance and many friends.

(8) St. Ch. 2/2/110 is like case a–2 above in that the complaint is brought by the lord of the manor. The bill alleges that much of the land in the complainant's manor is copyhold, and that John Barbor, one of the defendants, is a copyholder of the manor. Barbor, being confederate with the other defendants, claims that his tenement is ancient demesne and that he has an estate of fee simple therein. At a manorial court, the defendants other than Barbor were sworn to "inquire of such things as they should be charged withal." However, they "would make no presentment but after their own pleasure and would not find that the said John Barbor held the said tenement . . . by copy of court roll . . . notwithstanding good and sufficient matter then showed unto them for the proof of the same as well by court roll as other, saying that the stewards of the manor and the lord may at their pleasure make what precedents they will." The complainant commanded the defendants to show their copies by which it would appear by what tenure they held, but they refused to do so. The defendants "occupy their tenements and lands against the will and mind of your said orator and contrary to his mind keep the possession thereof, and in such wise that your said orator cannot come to the possession thereof . . . unless he should raise great hurt, danger, and inconvenience. And thus, most dread sovereign lord, the said John Barbor and the other persons before rehearsed not only wrongfully keep the possession of such tenements . . . as they severally have and occupy within the said lordship, by means whereof your said orator in time coming is like to sustain much hurt . . . and be disinherited."

An answer on the part of the defendants other than Barbor is preserved. They say first that the complainant has already brought a suit concerning the same matter in the Chancery and ask recovery of their expenses incurred in defending the Chancery suit. As to the merits, the manor is ancient demesne, some of the tenements being held by base tenure and some by free tenure. Those held by base tenure have been used to pay one half-year's rent at every alienation, "in the name of a release" and the tenant's best beast at his death and no other payments. The heir or alienee of such land, "being sworn to be true tenant or offering himself to be true tenant" in court may enter "without taking of any copy, payment of any fine, or any other act." Before the complainant sued his *Subpoena,* in the Chancery, John Barbor died. His heir, Thomas Barbor, came to court to be sworn. The steward refused to swear him, whereupon he entered anyway. Because the steward would not accept the defendants' true presentment that the land was not copyhold, they went away.

(c) It should be noted that there is a great deal of unindexed Star Chamber material in the Record Office which it was not feasible for me to use. The conclusions suggested here may, therefore, be based on only a small part of the surviving copyhold cases before the court.

In Leadam's *Select Cases before the Star Chamber,* II, 4–67 a long series of proceedings involving copyhold among other things is published under the name of Inhabitants of Thingden v. Mulsho. Among the documents are two copyholders' complaints, 15–27. One of these is interesting as an example of a complaint brought in the Star Chamber without any special allegation of riot or other similar offense. Like b–7 above, it counts against the view that an element of public liability was essential to a properly drawn Star Chamber bill.

40. Ford v. Hoskins. Croke's Reports, I, 368–369; Moore's Reports, p. 842.

41. For the concurrent role of the Chancery in Elizabeth's reign, see Tothill's Chancery Reports, pp. 44–46, and Cary's Chancery Reports, pp. 3–7. These reports are too scanty to be of much value. However, it does appear from several brief entries in Tothill that customs of relatively short duration would support temporary protection by the Chancellor. Scriven, *Copyholds,* pp. 462–473, summarizes the modern law on the role of equity in copyhold matters.

CHAPTER II

The Acquisition of Common-Law Remedies

1. Littleton, *Tenures,* sec. 77.
2. *Year Book,* Michaelmas 7 Edward 4, pl. 16.
3. *Year Book,* Hilary 21 Edward 4.

4. Pointed out by Ashley in *Annals A.A.P.S.S.* 1:412–425 (1890–1891).

5. *Ibid.*, pp. 421–422; Maitland, "A New Point on Villein Tenure," *Law Quarterly Review* 7:174–175 (1891); Holdsworth, III, 208–209.

6. See above, Chapter I, pt. 1.

7. For the doctrine of color, see Stephen, *A Treatise on the Principles of Pleading in Civil Actions,* pp. 233–246.

8. Foss, *Biographical Dictionary,* p. 158.

9. C.246/41.

10. Coke, *Compleat Copy-holder,* sec. 9.

11. Keilwey's Reports, pp. 76a–77a (Michaelmas 21 Henry 7 and Michaelmas 22 Henry 7).

12. See the material in Chapter I generally.

13. See Chapter III below.

14. Calthrope, *The Relation Betweene the Lord of a Mannor and the Coppy-holder his Tenant.* A MS version of the Readings exists in BM Lans. MSS 738, pp. 280a–294b. The MS differs from the printed version in some details, is more intelligible at some points, and is quoted here.

In addition to the general character of the Readings, note the opening passage: "The great inuryes which ar offered and small remedyes that are used in cases of Copyholdes wch as it seemethe dothe growe by the obscure knowleidge, what lawe & custome iudgethe in theise matters movethe me to shewe you somme pte of my pooer travell in theise poyntes. . ." See also the passage quoted from the MS version below. There Calthrope says that the justices of the present day *seem* to be of an opinion favorable to copyholders. In the printed version he is more positive, saying they *are* of that opinion.

15. As can be seen from the material in Chapter I above, it was good form, whether or not legally essential, for Chancery bills to say that there is no remedy at common law. As a rule, the bills plead this somewhat vaguely, so that it is not clear whether they mean that any sort of remedy is lacking, or only a fully adequate one. Probably if they meant only to say that the common-law remedy is inadequate they would show in what way it is inadequate more often than they do. The best course is to suppose that the frequent occurrence of Chancery complaints drawn in the conventional language implies that no relief was obtainable at common law. There are, however, a few bills which do specify a reason why no common-law remedy is available but give some reason other than the mere fact that the petitioner is a copyholder. In C.774/9,

for example, the complainant justifies applying to the Chancellor only because he is a poor man, while the defendant is rich and friended. In C.840/42, an expelled copyholder who has incurred charges on the land says that he "is not able to sue for his due remedy therein at and by the due order of the common law of this realm" only because his lord is of great substance and acquaintance. In C.856/46, the complainant is seeking admittance to which he claims to be entitled by descent. He says that he is poor and the defendant rich and that "your poor orator dwelleth lxvi miles of where as the said land doth lie, and also far from the law holden at Westminster" so that he is unable "to sue for his right." The language of these bills implies that in the absence of the special circumstances alleged a common-law remedy might be obtained. It should be considered, on the other hand, that if a complainant had one sufficient reason for proceeding in equity, such as poverty, he might well rely on that without citing another, such as the absence of a common-law remedy for copyholders generally. Also, since there was disagreement among common-law authorities in the early sixteenth century, a petitioner who asserted outright that there was no common-law remedy for copyholders might run the risk of being challenged.

16. Dalison's Reports, p. 8. It should be noted that Saunders speaks from the bar, Montague and Browne from the bench.

17. This case is unprinted. It appears in two MSS in the British Museum, Add. MSS 24,845, pp. 40–41, and Harl. MSS 5154, p. 3a. The case is dated Trinity 7 Edward 6 in the former, Michaelmas 6 Edward 6 in the latter. The transcription in the text follows the Harleian MS. Variations in the Additional MS. are insignificant except that that version says simply that it was agreed that the lord may not oust his copyholder, instead of giving this as the opinion of Hales and Portman only.

18. 32 Henry 8, ca. 2, principally set the period of limitation on writs of right at sixty years. According to Hales, this act implies that continuous demisability by copy for sixty years makes land good copyhold and entitles the tenant to security. Although this may seem a strained interpretation, it is based on good authority. Littleton (sec. 170) interprets the act of limitation in the Statute of Westminster I, ca. 39, in the same way. That statute disqualified, for purposes of writs of right, evidence of an ancestor's seisin before 1189. Littleton reports as a current opinion, with which he appears to agree himself, the view that any evidence of conditions before that year is by implication disqualified from being

used to defeat a prescription. The rationale of this interpretation is probably that in making statutes of limitation for the highest of real actions Parliament essentially gives a general judgment on the reliability of ancient evidence. If Parliament says that evidence before a certain date is too remote to count for or against a man's claim to ownership, it must think that equally ancient evidence is unreliable for any other purpose.

That Hales's opinion on this point was not followed appears from several pieces of evidence, but that evidence does not point to a single doctrine on the period of prescription for copyholders. The earliest Elizabethan case on this matter with which I am acquainted is Lord Dacres's Case, Michaelmas 8 & 9 Elizabeth. (Printed in the published version of Calthrope, pp. 63–64. A slightly fuller report, quoted here, is in BM Add. MSS 35,940, pp. 326a–b.) The main point in this case was whether a lease of 12 Henry 6, which proved the lands to be demisable by deed and not by copy at that time, was outside the time of legal memory. The court held that it was: ". . . le rentall que prove destre lease terre fuit devant temps de memorie car fuit 12 H6 que fuit plus que 120 ans mes sil mostre ascun Indenture fait deins 50 ans ou deins 80 ans issint que home poet remember ceo car home poet remember 80 ans et 90 ans car ascun homes sont del age de 100 ans et tiel evidence serra bon de prove les terres demease terres et semble que le statute de limitations ne extend al ceo car les Justices disont que tiel Evidence que prove le Copihould de comencer deins le temps de memory est bon et defeater le Interest del tenant."

Lord Dacres's Case thus rejects Hales's device. It proposes that the period of prescription be the time any living man anywhere might possibly remember. Perhaps this is an attempt to take literally the phrase used in pleading prescriptive titles, "time whereof memory runs not to the contrary," but the standard is obviously imprecise as well as contrary to the authorities that hold that written evidence from a time more remote than any living man could remember may defeat prescriptions. (See Coke on Littleton, sec. 170.)

Howard v. Basse (Michaelmas 15 & 16 Elizabeth. BM Add. MSS 24,845, p. 278) probably rejects both Lord Dacres's Case and Hales's opinion in favor of the view that the immemorial continuance of customs may be disproved by written evidence as ancient as would ever be likely to occur in practice. This interpretation of the case depends on taking the last sentence, giving the court's opinion, to mean that a record from Edward I's reign may defeat later usage. It might, of course, mean that it is outrageous to allow such ancient documents to defeat such an accumulation of usage. The report of Howard v. Basse is as follows: "Replevin per Howard vers Basse issue pris si custome del manor soit que copiholder poit fair leas pur 3 ans ou meins ou tenents del Manor fuer suffer pur donor evidence et per eux et auters estrangers fuit mostre que tenants ad use per le space de 80 ans de fair leas pur 3 ans sans licens et dauter parte fuit mostre divers presentments en temps El et E2 E3 et R2 que terre fuit seisie pur ceo que les tenants ad devyse ceo pur ans sans mostre quel ans Auxi divers court roles fuerunt mostre que tenants ad prie licens de seignor de fair leas pur 3 ans et ad pay VI d. ou meins ou pluis et en cest case fuit dit per court que si record en temps El disprove un custome tout usage ou prescription de puis ceo est que void. . ."

Calthrope (printed ed., pp. 15–16) rejects the relevance of the new Statute of Limitations for determining the period of prescription. He says that long usage will establish a presumption that land is copyhold, but that such a presumption can always be rebutted by testimony from the memory of a living man, however remote the events testified to. He does not make the role of written evidence clear. In 32 & 33 Elizabeth, Justices Anderson and Periam repeated the point that long usage raises a rebuttable presumption and clearly implied that there is no practical limit on the antiquity of written evidence for purposes of rebuttal. (BM Harl. MSS 1588, 5a–b. ". . . il sufficit a doner in evydence que ceo ad este demise pur 50 ans ou 60 ans per Copy et issint repute in le pais & ne besoigne de prover expressment que il fuit Copyhold ut fuit tenus per Anderson et Peryam et per eux si ne poet estre prove per testimoignes ou per escript que il nest copyhold et custome de antiquity serra intend per le vehement presumption del usage. . .")

The best conclusion is that the courts rejected both Hales's opinion and the somewhat vague approach of Lord Dacres's Case and accepted written evidence as far back as Littleton's 1189 to defeat copyhold prescriptions. This is exactly the position the courts took with respect to prescription for incorporeal hereditaments, where the issue is the same (see Holdsworth, VII, 343–345).

19. Dalison's Reports, p. 62. The issue in this case—whether demises by copy are within the Statutes of Monasteries—is the same as in the better-known Heydon's Case in the Exchequer (Coke's Reports, III, 7a–9a). The opinion of Walshe (Welch) and Dyer here accords with the decision in Heydon's Case.

20. BM Harl. MSS 5143, p. 72a.

21. BM Add. MSS 35,940, pp. 650b–651a. The case is probably from the Common Pleas. "Auter question fuit move si un coppiholder que fait lease pur ans per custome si le lesse averra Eiectione firme per le comen ley et le dout fuit intant que le lesse est un customarie tenant come le Coppihould mesme et il suer in le Court le Seignor et nemy per Comon ley mes semble que lesse pur ans per liscence le Seignor per Indenture suer al comen ley per eiectione firme. . ."

22. BM Harl. MSS 5143, p. 175a: ". . . fuit teigne en banke le Roy que sil soit eiecte il poet meintener Eiectione firme al Comon ley mes le melior opinion de Justices de comen banke fuit contrarie pur ceo que il ne poet estre mys en possession de Copyhould per Habere facias seisinam quere. . ."

23. Moore's Reports, p. 128.

24. Melwich v. Luther, note 78, Chapter III below; Combe's Case, Coke's Reports, IX, 75a–77a.

25. Downing's Case, BM Add. MSS 25,196, p. 353b, Trinity, 36 Elizabeth: ". . . auter matter fuit move all barre que fuit si copyholder fait lease pur ans que nest garrant per le custome si ceo lease soit bon ita quod le lessee poet mainteine un eiectione firme et tenus clerement que cy car parenter lessor et lessee et touts auters forsque le seigner del mannor le lease est bon et issint ad este sovent foits adiudge in cest court."

Sprake v. Sprake, BM Add. MSS 25,203, pp. 75b–76a, Trinity, 41 Elizabeth: "HEALE seriant move comment un speciall verdit fuit done en eiectione firme a tyel effect coppyholder fait lease pur un an except un iour que est garrant per le custome et lessee est ouste per estranger et port eiectione firme et tout le court tyent clerement que laccion gist et POPHAM dit que sil ne fuit ascun custome uncore serra bone lease vers touts forsque cesty que ad le franktenement et issint est si tenant a volunt al comon ley fait lease pur ans a que GAWDYE assent car en tyel case le tenant a volunt serra disseisor mes vers luy le lease est bone come est 12 E4 12b Et FENNER dit que per loppinion en auncient temps eiectione firme fuit forsque en nature de trespass et nul terme fuit recover pur que nest reson mes que tiel accion soet bien maynteyne per lessee dun coppyholder Mes POPHAM dit que tenant pur ans que prist son estate per coppy navera laccion."

In one case, however, the Common Pleas denied that a copyholder can make a lease without warrant which will be valid and support ejectment: BM Harl. MSS 1588, pp. 153b–154a, Trinity, 36 Elizabeth. "Sur evidence concernant un copyhould deins le mannor del Paris gardein fuit tenus que si Copyholder fait lease pur ans al intent de porter eiectione firme que cest est void lease car copyholder nad que a volunt hors de quel il ne poet deryver un terme et coment que le lease fuit fait sur le terre ceo ne enable le matter car il ne poet estre disseisor eo que son entry fuit loyall in regard del son precedent interrest al volunt mes le lessee per son entry cause le disseisin accordant al 12 E4 Mes fuit obiect per les Sergeants del cest partt que le lease fuit bone et coment que soit un forfeiture et issint le lease parenter le seignor et le lessee void uncore parenter lessee et lessor & quant al touts estrangers ceo est bon lease Sed le Corte tient ut supra. . ."

The best later position was that unwarranted leases are good except against the lord. (Scriven, *Copyholds,* p. 223.)

26. How much, it is of course impossible to say without extensive local research. Legal sources give only vague indications—e.g., "great part" (Heydon's Case, Coke's Reports, III, 8b.) Coke indicates that many men who could not be called peasants were interested in copyholds (*Compleat Copy-holder,* sec. 8).

27. Ford v. Hoskins. Croke's Reports, I, 368–369; Moore's Reports, p. 842. The reasoning in this case seems to be that admittance is not a conveyance from lord to surrenderee but only a formal act necessary for passing an interest from surrenderor to surrenderee. An action on the case was not allowed in various similar situations where the wrong consisted in failure to do a formal act.

28. See J. G. A. Pocock, *The Ancient Constitution and the Feudal Law,* for an illuminating discussion of relations between legal thinking and historical sense.

29. *Year Book,* Michaelmas 7 Edward 4, pl. 16.

30. See Holdsworth, III, 166–171, for the relevant rules on prescription for incorporeal hereditaments.

31. For the distinction between personal and local prescription, see Coke on Littleton, sec. 170.

32. Keilwey's Reports, pp. 76a–77a. "Kingsmill. Jeo agrea que un particuler tenant a volunt ne poit prescriber en son sole tenancie, mes quant le prescription & le custome curt per mye tout le manor, Moy semble que per cest voie il poit bien giser en custome, car le Seignor poit eux suer pur lour fines & rents surdants sur le tenure, donques il est auxy graund reason que ils purront prescriber vers luy, car lour estate ad son respect a le seygniorie pur ceo que il curt per tout le manor."

33. *Year Book,* Hilary 21 Edward 4. Catesby seems reluctant to say that the copyholder prescribes against his lord, presumably because he is using the word "prescription" for a personal claim. However, he considers the case of a special custom under which land is devisable relevant, and that is a clear example of the local type of prescriptive claim.

34. Littleton, sec. 82. See Coke on Littleton, sec. 82, for the importance attached to the passage.

35. BM Harg. MSS 3, pp. 13a–b. The case must fall between 1522 and 1529, the years when both Richard Brooke and Anthony Fitzherbert sat in the Common Pleas. (Foss, *Biographical Dictionary,* pp. 129, 258). "Nota per Brooke & Fitzherbert Justicez si home ad copie dascun terre a luy & ses heirz & sil devi son fitz ne poet enter en le terre come ceo sera forfetur mes il convient destre restore come tenant soloncque le custome del manor & si le Seignor devant que le fitz est restore come tenant graunt ceo ouster a un auter donques le fitz poet aver pleint de mortdancestor quod nota."

36. Quoted from MS version. See above, note 14. The printed version of this passage is not different in any essential way, but the MS, at a few points, is clearer and fuller.

37. Coke on Littleton, sec. 73. The passage is taken from William Lambarde's Αρχαιονομιχ; *Sive de Priscis Anglorum Legibus Libri.* (The definitions of folkland and bookland occur in the *Glossarium,* at p. 222 of the Cambridge ed. of 1644. In this edition, the only one I have been able to obtain, the following sentence is added: "Illam nos vulgo *frehold* & *per chartam,* hanc ad voluntatem Domini appelamus." The additional sentence, if included in the editions known to Calthrope and Coke, would seem to be the basis for their identification.)

38. Coke on Littleton, sec. 73.

39. For the history of tenure in ancient demesne, see Pollock and Maitland, I, 366–389; Holdsworth, III, 263–269; Vinogradoff, *Villainage,* pp. 89–126.

40. Lib. I, cap. 9, fol. 7.

41. E.g., at fol. 26a, cited by Coke, Bracton makes it clear that the familiar "copyhold" conveyancing procedure applied to ordinary tenants in villenage as well as to villein socmen.

42. *Year Books of Richard II. 13 Richard 2,* pp. 122–128.

43. Fitzherbert's interpretation of *The Old Tenures of the Laws of England* is in his *Natura Brevium,* tit. "De recto clauso." The relevant titles in the *Old Tenures* are "Fee base" and "Villenage." See also tit.

"Socage," where "Socage of base tenure" is not associated with the little writ, but is connected with the *Monstraverunt,* a second ancient demesne writ.

44. Littleton, sec. 72.

45. Kitchin, *Le Court Leete et Court Baron.* The relevant passages are at pp. 86b and 94a–95a.

46. Coke on Littleton, secs. 73, 74, and 77.

47. The citation is to *Britton,* ed. F. M. Nichols, fol. 165a.

48. The citation is to *Fleta,* lib. 1, cap. 8, fol. 4.

49. Madox, *History and Antiquities of the Exchequer of the Kings of England,* II, 391–392. The *Dialogue* is cited by Coke as "Ockham (who wrote in the reign of Henry II)." The identification of "Ockham" with the *Dialogue* was made by Dugdale and is pointed out in the Hargrave-Butler edition of Coke on Littleton.

50. Coke, *Compleat Copy-holder,* secs. 3–10, 18, 32.

51. *A Commentary on the Tenures of Littleton Written Prior to the Publication of Coke upon Littleton,* ed. H. Cary, pp. 163–164, 187.

52. *The Works of Francis Bacon,* XIV, 302–303. Cf. *ibid.,* p. 404, where, in the treatise called "The Use of the Law," once erroneously attributed to Bacon, the view is again stated that copyhold evolved gradually out of villenage.

53. BM Add. MSS 25,196, pp. 17–18. ". . . et Bracton dit que un copiholder doit restore les terres al Seignor quant il eux convey ouster car le Seignor doit estre privie al departure ou alienacion. . ."

BM Add. MSS 25,199, p. 18b. ". . . et Bracton dit que le tenant doit restituere domino. . ."

54. E.g., see Chief Justice Popham's opinion in Gravenor's Case, note 44, Chapter III, below.

CHAPTER III

The Elizabethan Courts and the Common Law of Copyhold

1. See next note, (c) and (d), and Gravenor's Case, note 44 below.

2. (a) BM Add. MSS 35,940, pp. 549b–550a, Michaelmas 13 & 14 Elizabeth, Common Pleas: "Copihoulder en fee in droit sa feme fait surrender le feme nest examyn per le Seneschall ne per ascun de les tenants le custome ceo permittant le barron devi si cest surrender soit discontinue quel mitter le feme a son plaint en natura de un cui in vita ou si poet enter nient obstant fuit move per MANWOOD Serieant et semble a lui que son entre congeable sicome in Litt case Si tenant in taile enfeoffe

cesty in le revercion ceo nest discontinuance nient plus icy poet le surrender fait al Seignor que est en revercion que ad le franktenement faire un discontinuance del feme et DYER WESTON et HARPER, absent WELSH, tenus que ceo fuit un discontinuance et nient resemblable al case a quel fuit resemble Et DYER dit que nient obstant le surrender fuit fait al Seignor et le tenant admitt per le Seignior uncore la ley dira que il est eins per le barron et quel dout si le feme ust este examyne serroit barre a touts iours."

(b) BM Add. MSS 35,940, p. 602, Michaelmas 14 & 15 Elizabeth: "Jeo vey in la raport Mr Ffleming de 13 Eliz T. Mich: que DYER & [touts?] Justices del comon bank dit il fuit sur argument in le Chancery determyne si coppihould dinheritance discend al deux sours quel entront et devant le Court et admission un de eux devy le uncle a luy avera le moitie et nemy soer et auter parcener eeant de demy sanke et auxi si coppihoulder in taile surrender al auter use que est admitt tenant est discontinuance et issint le barron de Coppihould le feme et auxi il dit remitter serra de coppihould come serra de franktenement et inheritance al comen ley."

(c) BM Harl. MSS 5143, pp. 179a–b, Michaelmas 15 & 16 Elizabeth, Common Pleas: "[Knight surrendered his copyhold to the use of his wife for life, remainder to his own heirs in fee. Later, Knight surrendered to the use of Baxter in fee, who was admitted accordingly. Knight died and his wife entered. One of the questions moved by MEADE was whether the entry was legal] Et DIER dit que primes il semble que le entre le feme nest loyall car le surrender al use de Baxter fait discontinuance et Copiehoulders ne sont deins lestatute de 32 H8 per que le feme ne poet enter mes est mys de recontynue ceo en Court del Manor per suite in nature de Cui in vita. . ."

(d) BM Add. MSS 24,845, p. 221, Michaelmas 15 & 16 Elizabeth, Queen's Bench: "Si le Baron seisi dun copyhold en droit sa feme surrender ceo al use destranger le feme ne puit enter apres le mort del Baron car Copyhold est hors del estatute de 32 H8 car ceo est entend de Freehold, mes el duist faire son pleint en nature de cui in vita fuit agree."

(e) BM Add. MSS 24,845, p. 287, date uncertain, but after 1582, the year of Anderson's appointment to the Common Pleas: "Tenant en tail dun copihold surrender al use un pur vie etc. et devie devant ascun court Jour et devant ladmittance et pur opinionem curiae absent ANDERSON ceo est discontinuance et yssue est mis al formdone nient obstant le mort tenant en taile devant admittance."

3. Executory interests and warranty, discussed below, exemplify situations in which there was some question about the lord's role in surrender and admittance.

4. Dyer's Reports, p. 264a. In this case, a woman who was a copyholder for life took a husband. The lord granted the reversion of the copyhold to three persons for their lives successively. The husband surrendered to the use of the first reversioner, who was admitted and died. The second reversioner predeceased the first. The third reversioner prayed admittance, and the question was whether he should have it. All Dyer reports is that some Serjeants and Justices thought the third reversioner should not be admitted, because there was the chance that the wife would outlive the husband and be entitled to regain the land by *Cui in vita* or entry. Later advocates fastened onto the words "or entry," which the report indeed contains, and used this to prove that a husband's surrender will not discontinue his wife's estate. This seems to be making a lot of very little.

5. Croke's Reports, I, 148–149.

6. Moore's Reports, p. 596. A much fuller report is given in BM Add. MSS 25,196, pp. 334a–b: "Fuit trove per speciall verdict que Alice Butteler fuit seisi de un copihold in sa demesne come de fee que fuit demisable et ad este touts temps demise per copie de court rolle . . . et el prist baron George Bullocke que surrender ceo copihold al Seignor del dit mannor al oeps et use dun Mathew Willer in fee et il fuit admitt tenant et il surrender al oeps Tho. Dilbye le defendant in fee que fuit admitt tenant et puis le feme George Bullocke devi aiant issue Robt Bullocke et Edward Bullocke Robt Bullocke enter sur Dilbie sans ascun admittans et fait leas al Edward B. son frere et Dilbie lui ouste et il port Eieccione firme Les points sur le verdict sont forsque 2 le primer si cest surrender fait per le baron eant seisi in droit sa feme soit un discontinuance ou nemy le auter si lease fait per Robt B. devant admittans soit bone ou nemy Et fuit argue per un Brocke utter barrester del inner Temple que nest discontinuance et auxi que le lease est bone et issint leieccione firme maintenable Primes il dit que discontinuance de copihold ne poet estre fait put 4 reasons le primer pur le imbecilitie et feblenesse de son estate le 2 pur ceo que un garranty ne poet estre annex al estate le 3 pur ceo que nad son estate per livery de partie que surrender le 4 reason est pur ceo que nad son estate de lui mes del seignor del mannor Primerment a consider lestates del tenant per copy il dit que le comen ley ne eux regard mes come tenant in villenage et

tenants in bondage et nont estate forsque al volunt le seignor come appiert per FF [Fitzherbert] in son Na Br fol 12 et in 6 R2 avowrie 86 avowrie fuit fait per un Seignor sur son tenant per copie de Court rolle pur rent et iudgement fuit demande si fuit bone pur ceo que il nad riens de freehold mes come a volunt per base tenure et in bondage et Belknap agard le avowrie bone car auterment le Seignor perdera les services de eux et est dit in 3 E3 corone 300 que tenants in auncient demesne forfeitra annum diem et wastum mes Brook in abridginge de ceo case dit que si sont Copiholders que ils ne forfeitra annum diem et wastum 13 R2 faux iudgement 7 14 H4 35 tenant ad voluntatem domini ne poet porter briefe de faux iudgement car sil serra restore il serra restore al franktenement et ceo il ne poet car le franktenement est in le Seignor et sur ceo il inferr que son estate est cy feeble que le ley ne ceo regard mes come tenant a volunt al comon ley et pur ceo ne poet faire discontinuans Car si tenant a volunt al comon ley fait feffment et le feffee enter ceo est un disseisin come 12 E4 est Et quant al 2 reson il dit que est plaine que garranty ne poet estre annex a lestate pur ceo que va per voy de surrender et nemi per feffment Et auter reason est que ne poet estre discontinuans est pur ceo que null livery fuit fayt de ceo et issint ne poient estre discontinuans come si home seisi in droit sa feme pur vie del feme surrender al cestui in revercion et devi le feme poet enter car nest discontinuans pur ceo que livery la nest fait Le 4 et darrein reason pur que ne poet estre discontinue est pur ceo que il nad son estate del discontinuer mes dun auter et donques per un rule in 21 H6 ne poet estre un discontinuans mes lou lestate est prise del discontinuer mesme et ceo il nest icy car copiholder prist estate del Seignor del mannor et sic est lentrie in le Steward liver quod cepit de domino mesuagium a tener a volunt &c et 9 Eliz Dier 264 que non obstant tiel surrender come ceo est le feme poet enter ou aver cui in vita per plaint in court le Seignor Et il cyte le case de Foxlie et Colson adiudge in Comon Banke in 32 et 33 Eliz rot 937 que fuit cest verie case et adiudge null discontinuance et in ceo case fuit teng auxi que tenant in taile dun copihold ne poet discontinue per Surrender Quant al 2 point si copiholder poet faire lease devant que soit admitt ou nemy il semble que cy car poet prender les profitts et le freehold serra in lui devant admittans issint que serra un possessio fratris et tenancy per le courtesie come appiert per 12 Eliz Dier in Alderman Dixies case Et copiholder per discent poet surrender al use dun auter devant admittans et auxi ceo lease nest in question inter le Seignor et lui mes inter estranger et luy et vers touts estrangers il est sicome tenant de freehold devant admittance et poet maintein accion de trespas GAWDIE semble que ceo est discontinuance et il vouche Litt que le means pur un copiholder pur alien son terre est pur faire surrender et ceo est un livery accordant al custome car quant copiholder voyt surrender il convient faire surrender in les mains le Seignor et ceo convient estre per bayler dun petit verge al seneschall et le seneschall ou baylie delivera ceo al cestui a que use le Surrender fuit fait in nosme de seisin et ceo baylement del verge est cy notorious come livery et seisin al comon ley per livery dun clodd ou ascun auter chose et intant que ad este obiect que ne poet estre discontinuans pur ceo que ne vient eins in le terre per cesty que fist le discontinuans mes per le Seignor ceo nest issint car il vient eins per cestui que fist le Surrender car le Seignor nest forsque instrument pur conveier le terre come attorney pur faire livery et Litt dit que poet aver plaint in nature dassise de novel disseisin ou assise de mord al comon ley et GAWDIE dit que ceux poient estre in le per cui et post que prove que vient eins per cestui que surrender et issint teignont les auter 3 Justices FENNER dit que nest discontinuans car nest discontinuans car tenant in taile dun copihold ne poet discontinuer per null means forsque per recovery in court le Seignor car per surrender null discontinuans car nest forsque grant de son estate CLENCHE que nest discontinuans et ne poet estre compare al livery al comon ley car per livery al comon ley home poet faire tort mes per surrender il done nient pluis mes ceo que il poet loyalment faire et cestui a que surrender fuit fait convient estre admitt per le Seignor POPHAM in 9 Eliz 246 le feme poit enter ou aver cui in vita et si ne soit difference inter ceo case et le case de Foxlie et Colson il ne voit estre de contrarie opinion et il dit que est differens parenter copiholder pur vie et copiholder denheritans car si copiholder pur vie surrender in maines le Seignor al use dun auter cestui a que use le surrender fuit prendra del Seignor car ceo drowne in le Seignor mes le copiholder denheritans sil surrender cestui a que use le surrender fuit fait prendra riens del Seignor Et fuit teng in le Seignor Arundells case in que il argue si copiholder pur vie surrender al use dun auter pur ans ceo estate drowne in le Seignor car si copiholder pur vie surrender al Seignor al use dun auter que ne voit prender tenant pur vie ne ceo avera arere mes contra de copihold denheritans et si copiholder in droit son feme surrender il done nient pluis mes ceo que il loyalment poet faire et le Seignor nest forsque instrument dadmitter quod FENNER affirm et POPHAM dit que si le case ne fuit adiudge ceo fuit un dubious case a lui et il fuit dit per TANFIELDE que ad este adiudge que si infant surrender al use dun auter al plein age ceo non obstant il poet enter arere quod Curia concessit Et puis ultimo die termini GAWDIE mutata opinione tient que nest discontinuance car in touts les cases de Littleton le convient estre un livery et auxi convient estre per son owne act mes in le case icy il ne poet done mes per lact del Seignor et per surrender home ne done riens mes ceo estate que il poet loyalement come 35 H6 home seisi in droit sa feme pur vie la feme et le baron voile surrender et devie le feme poet enter car est loyal act et lou home fait act quel per le ley il poet faire ceo nest discontinuans come le case 35 H8 Di 57 cestui que use pur vie fait lease pur vie le lessie ceo nest discontinuance al cestui in remainder in tail car serra intend que poit loyallment faire per lestatute de 2 R3 POPHAM in le case de cestui a que use il ne fait ascun wronge car il fait act que lestatute de R3 lui autorise de faire mes quant al case de surrender est avoier si ceo drowne in le Seignor ou nemi car si copiholder surrender al use dun auter et il ne voit prender ceo retornera a lui arere mes sil surrender absolutement donques ceo drowne mes in lauter case le Seignor nest forsque un instrument et issint difference FENNER est nul discontinuans car surrender est loyall act et quant est per loiall act ne poet estre discontinuance car il ne comitt null wronge come si tenant in taile graunt son estate ceo est null discontinuans et il dit que il fuit a councell ove le case in le comon banke que tenant in taile fait lease pur 3 vies garrant per lestatute de 32 H8 et fait livery et ceo fuit adiudged null discontinuance pur ceo que il fait riens mes ceo il poet loyalment fair per lestatute et lou nest wronge null discontinuance CLENCHE ove lui et iudgement fuit done que ne fuit discontinuans mes que lheire le feme poet bien enter et nest driven a son accion et POPHAM ne ceo contradixit.

7. Moore's Reports, p. 753.

8. BM Add. MSS 25,203, pp. 463a–b, Easter 44 Elizabeth: "Nota que sur un evydens enter Elbridge et Norris fuit tenus que si le Coppyholder en tayle fait un surrender et morrust lissue en tayle ne poet enter car le surrender est un discontinuance car POPHAM dit que un tenant in taile dun coppyhold ne poet faire discontinuance per ascun auter voye Mes Litt prove quil poet faire discontinuans car il tient que lissue in tayle avra pleint in nature dun formdon en le discender al comon ley et ceo ne poet il aver vers ascun mes vers cesty que est eins per surrender car pleint in nature de formedon ne gist vers luy que enter de son tort demesne puis le mort del coppyholder eo que il devest le francktenement hors del seignor per disseisin pur que le surrender doet estre discontinuance et GAWDYE dit que coppyhold convient imitate le cours del

francktenements al comon ley sinon que soet ascun custome al contrary et pur ceo sicome tenant in tayle poet discontinue al comon ley per feasans dun livery issint auxy poet le coppyholder per surrender mes uncore ils advise le Jurye pur trover un speciall verdit que fuit fait accordant Et in mesme cest terme sur un auter evydens enter Gurrey plaintiff en eiectione firme vs. Sanderson et alii deffendants fuit tenus accordant per lauters 3 Justices POPHAM eeant absent in Camera Stellata mes en ceo case auxy le Jurye per le direction del courte trove cest matter specialment. . ."

9. BM Add. MSS 25,204, p. 3b: "HUBBERD move que tenant in tayle de coppiehold que surrender in fee que nest un discontinuance et vouche Case Bullocke et Dilby que baron per surrender ne discontinue terre del feme et ANDERSON accord Sed WAMESLEY KINGSMILL WARBURTON et DANIEL contra Et ils deny le case de Bullock supra et vouche iudgments al contrary et auxy iudgements in le point Car ils diont que le livery del verge in coppyhold est auxy fort come livery del terre de freehold. . ." [The rest of the report is illegible.]

10. Coke, *Compleat Copy-holder,* sec. 50.

11. Oldcot v. Levell, Moore's Reports, p. 753; Galawaie's Case, Trinity 24 Elizabeth, Common Pleas, BM Add. MSS 24,845, p. 256: ". . . per curiam il est nul forfeiture dun copihold que tenant pur vie surrender al use un et ses heires."

12. Note 44 below.

13. BM Add. MSS 25,200, p. 201a: "In trespass per Joiner vers Lumberd le case fuit que le seignor de un mannor grante le terre que un ad come copiholder in fee al un auter per copy que morust seisy et son heire auxi admitt le heire del copiholder que avoit droit enter et devant ascun admittance surrender al un J. S. et tenus que le discent dun copihold ne tollera entre & que le surrender devant admittance fuit bone auxi mes sil ust surrender devant entre auxi ust este clerement void per POPHAM."

14. BM Add. MSS 25,208, p. 52b: "Nota per WILLIAMS Justice que discent dun Coppihold toll lentry dauter que ad coppihold droit coment nemy dauters que ad droyt al franktenement al comon ley YELVERTON Justice contra et FLEMINGE Chief Justice doubta ideo quere." It should be noted that Coke (*Compleat Copy-holder,* sec. 50) thought that descent of a copyhold will not toll the entry.

15. Stanton v. Barnes, 1594, Queen's Bench. Croke's Reports, I, 373. A fuller report appears just below. Stanton v. Barnes is a strong case because the custom, as found by the jury, could be interpreted as expressly

forbidding conveyances by way of remainder. It is not absolutely clear that the court accepted this interpretation. It is probable, however, that they did, in which case the holding means in effect that the custom cannot prevent the creation of remainders once it has sanctioned demises in fee. I know of no denials of Stanton v. Barnes or of other cases in which the copyholder's power to create remainders without an express custom was challenged.

The MS report, BM Add. MSS 25,196, pp. 369b–370a, is as follows: "Stanton port eieccione firme vs Barnes sur speciall verdict trove al Oxon le case fuit tiel Hughe Higden copiholder in fee (lou le custome del mannor est que le Seignor del mannor poet solumodo demise son copihold terre in fee) surrender al seignor del mannor al intent quil regrantera ceo a lui et a sa feme pur lour vies remainder al Alice son file et heire et a les heires de son corps ingendres le remainder al droit heires del H. H. quel estate fuit fait accordant et le iury trove ouster quod numquam antea facta fuit talis copie &c le question fuit si ceo estate fuit garrant per le custome BURDEN argue que cy que ceo paroll solumodo doit aver un favorable construcion et nemi a lier le Seignor tantum a demise in fee et nemi auterment et pur ceo lestatute de 1 Eliz dit que touts leases fait per evesques other then for 21 yeres or three lives shalbe void uncore fuit agree in Fox et Colliers case 23 Eliz et issint est le comon experiens a cest iour quils poient faire leases pur 20 ans ou meinder ans ou pur un vie ou deux vies uncore lestatute dit precisement al leases other &c et pur 20 ans ou un an est other uncore est deins le meaninge del statute car quant lestatute ou custome garrant home a faire greinder estate a faire meinder estate est inclusively garrant per mesme lestatute et custome car in omni maiori includitur minor et in mesme le case et pur mesme le reason fuit lopinion de mon Seignor Chief Justice al St Albons terme M 35 et 36 Eliz in Rake et Groweners case Auxi Pas 36 in ceo Court parenter Hopkins et Downes fuit ceo case le custome del mannor fuit que Seignor poet demise son copihold terre pur vie ou vies et le Seignor demise ceo al un durante viduetate et adiudge que ceo est garrant per le custome et issint icy in nostre case Et quant a ceo que est trove ouster quod nunquam antea facta fuit talis copia ceo nest materiall mes lestate est bone nient meins car si touts lour copies ont use destre fait in Frenche ou Lattine et le Seignor ore fait copie in Englisshe ne voit estre denie mes que ceo est bone et uncore il est voier quod nunquam antea facta fuit talis copia &c per que COWFIELDE al contra un custome ne poit garrant ascun estate destre fait per copie sinon tiel que ont estre use destre fait de temps dont memorie &c et pur ceo si custome dun mannor soit que le Seignor poyt demise pur 3 vies et il demise pur 4 vies ceo est void FENNER moy semble que ceo est bone demise garrant per le custome car 17 E3 est custome que home poyt devise son terre pur vie et il devise ceo in fee quel nest garrant per le custome uncore ceo est bone devise pur vie car lestate pur vie que est garrant per le custome est done inclusive in le devise in fee issint icy per le custome il poet demise in fee ergo il poet demise in tayle ou pur vie que est include deins le custome GAWDIE estate taile del copihold ne poet estre sans expresse custome a garrant ceo et in le case in St. Albons terme le court fuit divide Mon Seignor Chief Justice et mon frere Fenner incounter mon frere Clenche et moy mesme et issint verament ieo teigne le ley que ceo estate nest pas garrant per le custome FENNER ieo mise cest case si le Seignor demise al 2 homes et al hieres de lun lou est tiel custome come devant nest ceo garrant per le custome CLENCHE ceo est un bone case TANFIELD ieo poy bien denie vostre case nest question mes que est bone per le custome car customes ne sont expownde cy strictment mes que semblable estates in substance ou meinder estates que le common usage est bone per le custome et pur ceo 11 H4 est custome que infant del age de 15 ans poet faire feffment uncore sil fait lease pur ans et releas ceo est bone GAWDIE nostre livers sont contrarie Adiornatur Ad alium diem GLANVILLE seriant si ceo estate ne soit bone et garrant per le custome uncore est estate in fee determinable come fuit al comon ley Auxi le surrender eant a ceux uses coment que tiels estates ne poient estre faits accordant al uses donques ceo remains al Surrenderor et donques nous sumus droit heire a lui et issint nous avomus bone droit daver le terre et donques nest pluis mes Copiholder surrender al use del roigne ore est al use del copiholder et riens remaine in le Seignor TANFIELD est trove per lespeciall verdict que le custome est solumodo ea capienti extra manus domini ergo nest garrant per le custome mes ieo agree que per cest custome un demise pur vie ou in taile al primer priser est bone mes remainder al estranger ne poet estre garrant car est directment incounter le custome car est ea solumodo capienti &c Auxi le surrender icy nest al use car donques le ley serra come ad este prise mes est surrender absolute ea intentione que fait greind diversitie car in le primer case le Seignor ne voit faire estate accordant le surrenderor poet enter mes in le darrein case il nad remedie forsque in Chauncerie mes icy le surrenderor mesme reprist estate ergo de necessitie le revercion remaine in le Seignor del mannor. POPHAM le case al St Albons que fuit adiudge est ceo verie case et la vous touts agree que estate pur vie est garrant per le custome que fuit a demiser in fee mes lou seroit estate taile ou fee conditionall fuit ascun contrariety de opinions CLENCH lestate pur vie et le remainder est un estate in ley ergo cibien come poet demise in fee al un il poet auxi demise al un pur vie le remainder in fee al auter et ceo serra garrant per mesme le custome FENNER est bien dit car per nostre livers si tenant pur ans fait lease pur vie le remainder in fee et tenant pur vie morust et cestui in remainder enter ore il est disseisor et assise gist vers lui et issint per iudgement del ley il est in mesme le condicion come le primer priser serra Issint iudgement fuit done pur le plaintiff que est bone demise garrant per le custome GAWDIE fuit absent al ceo iour vide postea Hill 37 Eliz p. 14 [Under Hillary 37 Eliz., pp. 374b–375a, the judgement is repeated as above.] However, on this occasion, ". . . CLENCH et FENNER disont que si le custome dun mannor soit que le copiholder poet surrender pur 3 vies et il surrender al use de 4 ceo est void pur tout car nul tiel custome poet garrant ceo mes sil surrender al use dun pur vie le remainder al 2nd pur vie le remainder al 3rd pur vie le remainder al 4 pur vie ceo est bone pur les 3ois et est voyd pur le quart et il resemble ceo al case lou lesse pur ans fait lease put vie le remainder pur vie la si lesse pur vie morust et cestui in remainder enter il est novel disseisor. . ."

16. (a) For the printed authority, see Coke, *Compleat Copy-holder,* sec. 56, and the cases cited in Scriven, *Copyholds,* pp. 131–132. Though the printed reports are not all decisive in the sense that they recount majority holdings, as opposed to the views of individual judges, they nevertheless entirely support the position that admittance of the particular tenant vests remainders.

(b) Alverie v. Kippinge, however, holds that ordinary admittance of the particular tenant, without special words to indicate inclusion of the remainders, will not serve them.

BM Add. MSS 25,196, pp. 125–126, Trinity 30 Elizabeth: "Eieccione firme per Alverie vs. Kippinge et auters le case fuit que Jo. Kippinge fuit seisi de copiholde et ceo devise a son feme pur sa vie remainder a W. Kippinge son fits et al heires de son corps et puis J. Kippinge surrender in maines le Seignor al use de son volunt et puis devi et le tenant pur vie fuit admit et puis cestui in remainder devant admittans surrender in maines le Seignor al use del defendant in cest eieccione firme et lissue in ta: que fuit lissue. W. fait leas al un que port eieccione firme et le question est si cestui in remainder poet surrender devant que soit admitt per le Seignor et per GODFRYE ne poet et donques le plaintiff avera iudgement de recover et il mist diversitie inter discent et purchase car lou copihold discend cestui a que ceo discend poet surrender devant admittans pur ceo que le possession in ley est iect sur lui et de ceo serra possessio fratris mes poet estre obiect que admittans del tenant pur vie est admittans pur cestui in remainder mes ceo ne poet estre nisi soit per speciall admittans scilicet a aver a lui pur vie le remainder ouster et per cest speciall admittans fait al tenant pur vie serra admittans a cestui in remainder auterment nemi et ne semble al case que est al comon ley lou home fait lease al un pur vie remainder al auter in fee si livery soit fait al tenant pur vie ceo serra pur lui in remainder mes poet estre resemble al cest case lou home devant lestatute de 27 H8 que transfer uses al possession fait feffment al un in fee al use destranger pur vie remainder al auter in fee si cestui a que use pur vie grant son interest a cestui a que use in fee ceo nest execucion del remainder car convient estre execute per le Seignor ou auterment ne poet estre unques execute donques si ceo ne fuit execution de remainder le surrender devant admittans fuit voide et donques quant lheire W. Fait lease de port eiecttione firm leieccione firme voit bien giser Auxi pur auter reson laccion voit bien giser car si ceo soit bone admittans serra preiudicial al Seignor car il perdera un fine et il dit pur faire cest case clere mesme le case in reson fuit devant le Seignor Wray al St Edmonds Burie et semble a lui donques que tiel admittans ne servera pur lui in remainder si admittans ne soit special come devant et que devant admittans cestui in remainder ne poet surrender COKE econtra et semble que le plaintiff serra barre et ceo pur 2 resons un quia ladmittance de tenant pur vie est admittance de cestui in remainder et uncore cestui in remainder paiera un fine apres le mort le tenant pur vie et si cest remainder ne soit execute per ladmittans le remainder serra void et ne unques serroit in lui et pur prover que admittans del tenant pur vie est admittans de cestui in remainder il cite 7 H2 [*sic*] scire facias ou scire facias fuit sue pur execute un remainder sur estate pur vie que fuit grant per fine et pur ceo que appiert que lestate pur vie fuit execute le scire facias ne voit giser car ceo execute le remainder et Fitz N.B. 206 si devise soit al un pur vie remainder ouster si le devise soit execute in le tenant a terme de vie donques ceo est execution del remainder car donques cestui in remainder avera accion per course del comon ley et ne ex gravi querela et in [—?] E2 attornement 22 home grant seignory pur vie remainder in fee le tenant attorn al tenant a terme de vie per que cestui in remainder fait avowrie per cest attornement Auxi 14 E4 7 attornement al tenant pur vie est attornement al cestui in remainder si ne soit issint que le tenant est daver acquittall cestui in remainder come sur grant de mesualtie al un pur vie remainder in fee la coment lattornement soit bone uncore cestui in remainder ne distreinera tanque ad grant son acquitall al tenant car auterment il serra 2 foits charge ove le Seignory et ove le mesne et navera unques son acquital Auxi tempore Eliz un devise un terme a sa feme et que si el devi deins le terme que remain al auter si executors assent que feme avera durant sa vie si el morust ceo cest assent al remainder donques pur auter reson le plaintiff serra barr car sur le surrender fait per cestui que fait le devise si le remainder ne serra in lui donques est in le Seignor vers que il navera remedy Et puis al auter iour per loppinion de touts les iudges le generall admittans ne servera a lui in remainder mes uncore pur auter cause COKE move que iudgement ne doit estre done car ne unques appiert in pleadinge que cestui que fait le lease sur que leieccione firme fuit port fuit unques admitt et quant a ceo touts les judges agree que ne poet aver eieccione firme devant admittans et per le Seignor WRAIE est diversitie lou Copihold discend a un et lou vient merement come purchasor car in le primer case in respect del interest suspend serra possessio fratris et auxy il avera accion mes in case de purchase come cest case est doit estre admittans ou auterment ne unques avera action."

(c) In Coke's Reports, IV, 23a, Gravenor's Case is reported as authority that admittance of the particular tenant serves remainders, but it appears from the MS. report in note 44 below that that was only the opinion of Gawdy and Fenner, and that counsel challenged their view, though indecisively.

(d) Dell v. Higden, note 46 below, is a 3–1 holding that admittance serves remainders, one Lake's Case being cited as authority.

(e) The reports of Tiping (or Keepinge or Gyppyn) v. Bunning (or Bunney) vary slightly. Moore's Reports, p. 465, says that the case held that the first admittance is good for the entire estate, including remainders. Croke's Reports, I, 504, gives this as Popham's opinion only. A MS. report accords with Croke in this but includes a dissenting opinion by Fenner: BM Add. MSS 25,198, pp. 239b–240a, Easter 39 Elizabeth: "En accion de trns [Trespass] le case fuit que copiholder in fee devise son Copiholde terre al feme pur vye remainder ouster et devye le devise est present et pur ceo le particuler devisee pur vye admitte que apres morust et si cest admittance servera pur cestui en remainder fuit le question et semble al POPHAM que ladmittance va a tout lestate pur ceo que a diverse intents le particular estate et le remainder sont tout une come daver une an pur mortmaine et daver forsque une attornement et ils payeront forsque une fine lou le heire payera novell fine apres le mort son piere et pur ceo ladmittance dun eeant forsque consent avaylera lauter FENNER quant le particuler lessee est admitte lentre est cui dominus concessit et riens est mencion de Remainder et cest entre per tiels parols est quasi une graunt del Seignor et graunt fait al particuler tenant est riens in availe al Remainder per que apres son morte duist novell entre fait quod dominus auxi concessit al cestuy en le Remainder POPHAM le ley est clere que dissesor ne poet graunt copies ne faire ascun chose per voye de graunt de lyer le dissesye apres son entre mes uncore sauns question il poet faire admittance al Copiholds et est indefeasible le quel prove que admittance al Copiholds nest ascun graunt nient obstant lentre soit come adevant mes solement une consent et lou assent est requisite de perfect lestate et le partye assent al parcell de ceo il servera pur tout adiornatur Et vide 18 E4 7 Com 545 ou le case paramore et Yardley revercion graunt pur vye remainder en fee attornal lessee pur vye enurera al Remainder et si segnor et tenant sont et le tenant fait lease pur vye remainder in fee si le lessee done notice il servera pur le Remainder apres son morte de faire le seignor avowe sur luy Enfant lessa pur ans Remainder ouster rendant rent et al plaine age il accept le Rent del lessee ceo est affirmance dambideux estates et accordant si tearme soit devise Remainder ouster assent per lexecutor al primer devise est assent al tout lestate subsequent issint icye si admittance soit forsque assent admittance del particuler estate est admittance de cestui en Remainder."

(f) In Calchin v. Calchin, the Queen's Bench upheld a surrender by an unadmitted remainderman. Three separate grounds for so holding were discussed, and it is not clear which was decisive. Only Popham and Fenner explicitly agreed to the general proposition that the life-tenant's admittance serves remainders. Croke's Reports, I, 662; BM Add. MSS 25,203, p. 58a, Easter 41 Elizabeth: "Enter Calchin et Calchin le case fuit tyel baron et feme sont coppyholders a eux et lheires le baron, baron devye fits vivant sa mere et devant admittance surrender son reversion in maines de 2x tenants hors del Courte queux per custome poient prender un surrender si cest surrender fuit bone ou nemy fuit le queestion Et loppinion del courte fuit clere sans argument que le surrender est bone et POPHAM mitt un case que si home enseale et deliver un fait conteynant un estate pur vye et devant livery fait le lessee surrender que livery ne serra fait apres et issint il dit si Coppyholder surrender al use dun estranger et le cesty que use devant ascun graunt fait a luy per le seignor surrender al seignor cest assetts bone et que cesty que fist le surrender et auxy cesty a que use sont forclose de claym le coppyhold. Et COOKE Attorney generall mit un case que si coppyholder surrender al use dun vye le Remainder al auter en fee et le tenant pur vie soit admytt que cest bone admittance pur le Remainder quod POPHAM et FENNER concesserunt Et il mitt un auter case que si coppyholder surrender al use dun en fee et devant admittance le cesty que use surrender cest bone surrender et un implicatum admittance quod POPHAM concessit mes FENNER negavit et POPHAM dit que cest differens fuit tenus en le Seignior Arundells case que si disseisor soet dun Manor et un coppyholder en fee surrender al use dun estranger que est admitt accordant per le disseisor le disseisee navoidra unques cest surrender graunt et admittance mes si un coppyholder pur vie surrender auter est car ceo aler en advauntage del disseisee quant il enter Mes COOKE Attorney generall tyent le ley clere en cest darrein case que si le surrender soet al use dun auter pur vie de cesty que surrender cest assetts bone et le disseisee navoidra ceo mes POPHAM teigne touts foits son former oppinion."

(g) In Fish v. Hokely, Common Pleas, two judges held that admittance of the particular tenant serves remainders and one dissented. BM Add. MSS 25,196, pp. 17–18, Michaelmas 37 Elizabeth: ". . . ANDERSON Chief Justice fuit necessarie dalledge ladmittance del Richard Fish accordant al surrender come il ad fait et ceo admittance del particular servera touts ceux in remainder BEAUMOND accordant sicome livery fait al particular tenant servera touts ceux in remainder . . . OWEN Justice cestui quel est admitt pay argent et lauter in remainder non per que nest reason que ladmittance dun particular tenant serroit un admittans de ceux in remainder. . ."

17. Coke, *Compleat Copy-holder,* sec. 54, for the Statute of Uses. BM Harl. MSS 5143, pp. 118a–b, lists the Statute of Wills as one of those which do not extend to copyhold.

18. Fearne, *An Essay on the Learning of Contingent Remainders and Executory Devises,* pp. 276–278; Scriven, *Copyholds,* pp. 107–108.

19. Croke's Reports, I, 29–30.

20. Bulstrode's Reports, II, 272–276; Rolle's Reports, I, 309–310.

21. BM Add. MSS 25,208, p. 46b: "Eieccione firme per Palmer vers Walter Peacocke et count de lease de Edmonds et son feme et sur generall issue appiert que le Auncestor del defendant et son feme fueront

Jointenants pur vie del terre in question eeant coppihold terre le remainder al dit Auncestor del defendant in fee et le dit Auncestor vend le remainder al Edmonds lessor del plaintiff et surrender ceo remainder al use del vendee et plaintiff alleadge tiel surrender nient obstant le iointenancy del franktenement fuit bon del remainder per le custome del mannor et in proofe de ceo il mostre que le vendee enter in le terre puis mort del vendor et son feme et le heire del vendor port briefe de droyt in le Court del seignor del mannor devant Brograve Senescall del Seignor vers le vendee que fuit trove la per le homage que le vendee (sur tout cest matter mostre) avoyt pluis droyt que le heire del vender et que surrender de tiel remainder est bon per custome le Senescall advise et deferr le iudgment et puis al auter court Judgment fuit la entered vers le heire del vendor (et nota que cest matter fuit issint trye per Order et direccion hors del Chauncerye de Sir Nicholas Bacon Seignor Keeper del graund Seale &c) WILLIAMS Justice le point est si tiel coppiholder poet surrender son remainder al auter et reteyner a luy mesme le particular estate in le franktenement ove son feme semble que nest bone car coment tiel coppiholder poet surrender le franktenement et le Inheritance sur ceo en fee uncore ne poet in tiel manner ove reservacion de particular estate in luy mesme &c fuit 12E4 cyted Cook 2 Rept in Wiscott's case mes si estate ad este fayt al baron et feme pur vy et puis le revercion ad este grant al baron la le baron poet bien granter ceo mes si soyt tiel custome come est alleadge supra et que le terre sur tiel surrender ad este enioy per les purchasors per tiel custome ceo voet alter le matter car le custome serra observe et accordant a ceo fuit lopinion de Wray et Manwood quant cest case fuit in question devant eux &c MOORE Apprentice vous mesme Mr. Justice Williams le darrein iour que surrender de coppiholder serra prise accordant al entent come volunt serra et icy le intent fuit a passer le remainder WILLIAMS Justice vous oyes mon opinion ore in cest case et pour ceo mostre a nous ascun president que le terre sur tiel surrender ad este enioy per le surrenderee car custome doit estre prove per le usage de ceo auterment est vaine dalleadger ceo Et puis il mostre lou in tiel case come le principall case supra le baron surrender son remainder al use de son eigne fits que enioy ceo accordant WILLIAMS Justice ceo fuit per discent come heire al comon ley puis mort del pere et pur ceo mostres president de tiel surrender al use de estranger auterment vous proves riens mes uncore le councell ne mostrent ascun tiel surrender al estranger pur Evidence mes mostrent le case escrye alarge et le opinion de Anderson Popham et Bromley 20 Eliz. ove lour nosmes subscribe a ceo per eux mesmes que tiel surrender bon les parolls fueront tiels: Wee take yt this surrender of Roger Peacocke que fuit le Jointenant pur vye ove son feme le remainder al droit heires del dit Roger come supra doth carry away le fee simple of the coppihold dependinge upon the ioint estate of Roger et Johan son feme put lour vies &c et WILLIAMS Justice dit quant les dits 3 deliver ceo opinion adonque ils fueront forsque councellors et ils escryent pur lour client mes le councell al barre dit que cest matter fuit referre al eux hors del Chancery pur le point in ley et ils certifie lour opinion al Chancery come supra mes dauter parte fuit dit que lopinion de Wray et Manwood Justices in 21 Eliz fuit auterment viz que surrender del revercion in ceo case le coppihold in remainder ne passe sinon que soit speciall custome que garrant ceo Nota las testimognes mostre que fuit tiel custome de surrender &c mes quia nul president fuit mostre lou le terre fuit enioy per vertue de tiel surrender ideo les Justices teigne que le custome nest sufficiament prove pur le reasons de WILLIAMS Justice supra &c mes uncore le councell dit que speciall verdict poet estre trove del matter et evidence &c mes uncore (come remember) ne fuit mes verdict (come ieo oye) fuit per le plaintiff que claime desouth le purchasor &c fuit dit per ascuns que le feme que avoyt iointe estate ove son baron pur lour vies fuit in vie al temps de le recoverye in le briefe de droyt supra et avoyt le terre per le survivor pur que quecunque [? two words illegible] le heire del vender navoyt droyt al possession &c quere de ceo ulterius durant le vye del feme il ne poet per ascun meanes coment que il enter in le terre avera droyt et tytle daver briefe droyt come de coppihold estate in fee quant son entry fait tort al feme car si revercioner de coppihold in fee sur estate pur vye ouste le coppiholder pur vye semble que est disseisor al seignor et nient semble al 9 H7 25a in case de franktenement al comon ley &c Auxi fuit dit per que cy longe come ceo iudgment in briefe de droyt fuit in force le possession doit vaer accordant &c."

22. BM Add. MSS 25,208, p. 48b: "En Ejectione firme per Midleton vers Holmes et son feme pur coppihold terre deins un Manor ou fuit pretend per le Court que le custome del Mannor ne allowe ascun estate ta. mes que chescun estate ta. deins cest manor est fee simple condicionall al comon ley pur ceo que ils ad custome que chescun tenant in ta. per surrender al auter use poet barre son issue sans ascun fine ou recoverye &c et ils ne poient bien prove que sur ascun tiel estate ta. le remainder ad este lymitt ouster al estranger et enioy accordant et pur ceo chescun estate ta. eeant prise per le Court destre fee simple condicional deins cest

mannor un coppiholder surrender al use son eigne fits in ta. soe as hee pay 10£ al puisne fits ses heires ou assignes a tiel iour et sil ne pay ceo al iour que donque serra al use le puisne fits leigne fits fuit admitt largent ne fuit pay al iour si ore le puisne fits poet aver le terre per le lymittacion supra sur cest cesser destate G. CROOK et TOWSE que nemy car leigne fits ayant fee le pier que fist le surrender nad ascun remainder de lymitt ouster ergo &c WILLIAMS Justice Will, use, et surrender sera prise accordant al intent des parties et lintent des parties fuit icy que le puisne fits averoit vel largent vel le terre et entant que leigne fits ne voile pay a luy largent est reson que il averoit le terre come si home devise terre a son eigne fits in fee payant 10£ a son file et sil ne pay a luy largent que el avera le terre si largent ne soit pay a luy al iour assigne el avera le terre car lintent le testator fuit que el averoyt lun ou lauter issint in nostre case YELVERTON Justice contra et il denye le case de devise mise per WILLIAMS Et puis les parties compound al barre."

23. Paulter v. Cornhill. Croke's Reports, I, 361.

24. Allen v. Palmer, Leonard's Reports, I, 101; note 26 below.

25. For the effect of a common-law feoffment with a remainder to the right heirs of the feoffor, see Coke on Littleton, sec. 19. For conveyances under the Statute of Uses, see Holdsworth, VII, 125–126.

26. BM Add. MSS 24,845, pp. 208–209: "Copyholder en fee simple surrender en mains del Seignor al use de sa feme et puis al use de ses droit heires demesne le Seignor graunt ceo per copie al feme pur sa vie Remainder as droits heires del baron accordant al Surrender et ore si ceo soit revercion en le baron ou que son heire prendra ceo come remainder per purchase fuit move per GAWDYE et HARPUR et MANWOOD, le heyre aura ceo come per purchase Et il est un Remainder car per le Surrender lentier estate del fee simple passe a le Seignor et si le Surrender ust este al use del feme pur vie sans dire plus, donques le Seignor avera le Revercion en fee simple, et nemi le baron que surrender Et donques quant le Signor ad lentiertye per le Surrender et demise ceo per copy al feme pur sa vie Remainder as droit heires le baron per ceo le baron prist riens forsque en droit sa feme et le heire del Baron prist le Remainder come purchase mes si le baron aura prise estate en son droit demesne pur sa vie Remainder a ses heires donques il aura estate en fee simple en possession pur vie conioyne et couple ove le fee, mes auterment est quant il prist riens forsque en droit sa feme pur terme de sa vie MONNSON econtra Jeo ne poy agreer le case que si le Surrender ust este al use del feme pur sa vie, sans plus, que per ceo le Seignor mesme aura le

Revercion car en ceo case ieo entend que le revercion en le Seignor est solement come instruement de transferre lestate a le feme accordant al entent del surrender et nemi auterment et si issint soit donques en nostre case le fee simple est en le baron et ses heires, et ne fuit unques hors de luy come si home fist lease pur vie ou done en taile a estraunger Remainder as droit heires del lessor ore ceo est revercion en le lessor mesme et son heire aura ceo per discent, et nemi come remainder per purchase et issint en le comen case si home fist feoffment en fee a J. A. al use destranger pur vie ou en taile et apres al use des droit heires del feoffor ore en ceo case ceo est un Revercion en le feoffor mesme et son heire serra adiuge daver ceo per discent et nemi come remainder per purchase et pur leire serra en gard, car le feoffor mesme est partie al fait et est le person hors de que lestate et use fuit deryve et pur ceo est conserve destre un revercion en luy MANWOOD en vostre case le ley est prise come vous dits, en le court de wards sur lestatute de willes mes si fuit al comen ley et destre adiuge sur reason et authorytie voet estre dure de prover la ley destre issint car per le feoffment lentier fee simple passa hors del feoffor al feoffee et ses heires et donques ieo ne voy coment le lymytacion del use al heirs del feoffor puit reduce le fee simple a luy mesme et si home seisi de terrs de parte sa mere fist feoffment al use de luy mesme et ses heires le use discende as heires de parte le pier car il est un novell purchase en luy. Et MANWOOD dit que si lease soit fait a J. pur vie Remainder a estranger entaile, Remainder as droit heires de J. la remainder del fee est en J. pur cause del possibility a ceo temps del estate fait que le remainder puit conioyne a le particular estate mes lease a un pur vie Remainder a auter en taile, Remainder as droit heires J. la si J. purchase lestate pur vie, uncore le remainder nest passe en luy."

27. Cf. discussion of the theory of surrender in connection with discontinuance and warranty.

28. It was held that in the event an admittance failed to follow the uses designated in the surrender, the surrenderee nevertheless had the land in such estate as if he had been admitted properly. See Scriven, *Copyholds,* pp. 101–102, and the cases cited there.

29. I know of no sixteenth-century cases directly in point. However, the rule follows from the practice of observing an analogy between what could be done under the Statute of Uses and under the Statute of Wills. See Holdsworth, VII, 119–135.

30. BM Harl. MSS 5143, pp. 179a–b. Knight surrendered to the use of his wife for life, remainder to his own right heirs. Knight then sur-

rendered to Baxter in fee and died. The wife entered. Aside from the question of whether there was a discontinuance, Dyer spoke as follows to the point of whether the wife's entry could reduce the fee to Knight's right heirs: "Mes si son entre fuit loyall donques si le fee simple ne fuit en le baron mes demurre en expectancy de prender effect en son droit heir come Remainder donques percase lentre le feme reducer le frank-tenement a luy mesme pur vie & Auxi le Remainder al heire le baron mes si le fee simple fuit en le baron donques si revercion poet estre surrender per Custome le surrender de ceo est bon al use de Baxter et ne serra reduce per lentre le feme mes le quel ceo soit revercion en le baron ou Remainder expectant de vester en son heire voit faire question."

31. BM Add. MSS 24,845, pp. 275–276: "Trespas enter Sere et Baker et casus fuit que un George Seare esteant copiholder en fee symple surrender ceo al use sa feme Remainder a ses droit heires et fueront admitt accordant et puis George surrender ceo al use Baker et ses heires que fuit admitt et puis George morust et feme enter et puis feme devie et fitz George ore plaintiff enter et question fuit si cest remainder al droit heires George soit bone ou que soit voide et revertion remain en George et ses heires et fuit argue per SNAGGE que ou estate est limitte al heir quel le ley iect sur luy ceo voide come home devise a son eighne fitz en fee 3H6 vide 32 H8 Garranty 93. 4 H6 19 Champnon case et il dit home ne poit done al luy mesme, et que seignor est que instrument et nul droit ou interest passa de luy et FLOWERDEWE argue del auter part et puis fuit move per court si leir George poit enter devant lestate et copie fait al Baker soit avoide et adnul per accion en le court et ils ad iour ouster a parler al ceo, mes pur lauter matter le court dit que ils fueront resolve et videtur que remainder est bone car coment home fait lease pur vie remainder al droit heyres lessor soit voyde remainder, uncore ceo esteant de copiholde il passa come de seignor home fait feoffment a faire lease pur vie al A. Remainder al droit heyres Feoffor quere pluis."

The case is completed at p. 277:

"Residue Sere et Baker devant fol 275 fuit agree per court que si home fait done en tail, Remainder al droit heires donor que ceo est revertion en lui mesme accordant al Champnon case mes a cest temps fuit dit per ANDERSON et PERIAM que le principall case differ de ceo car lestate est surrender al seignor et issint lestate devest come del seignor mes MEADE dit que seignor fuit que instrument de conveyer ceo car si home surrender al use un en tail et seignor admitt luy en fee uncore ceo void et si home surrender al use dauter sur condition ceo bone et il recovera son terme mes PERIAM et ANDERSON diont que ceo est condicionall surrender al seignor come si ieo enfeoffe A. de enfeoffer B. sur condition si B. ne paia X £ que il poit enter ceo bone condition uncore B. et eins per A. et nemy primer feoffer et donques mitt [MEADE] prist cest diversity que si home surrender al entent que seignor regraunt al un pur vie remainder al ses droit heires que la leir prist per purchase contra ou home surrender al use etc. quant al auter point, si heir poit enter sans suit en le customarie court fuit admitt que [—?] poit enter et ideo videtur que leir poit auxi enter et sic pendet et ils ad Jour al mesme Terme."

32. Leonard's Reports, I, 101.

33. Fearne, *Contingent Remainders,* pp. 60–70.

34. Gravenor's Case, note 44 below; Stanton v. Barnes, note 15 above.

35. BM Add. MSS 35,940, pp. 549b–550a.

36. For the general principle, see Coke on Littleton, sec. 170. Cf. Coke's argument in Hill v. Morse, Moore's Reports, pp. 188–189.

37. The passage from Littleton cited is sec. 76. See also sec. 73, where Littleton lists the fee tail as one of the possible copyhold estates. The citation to Plowden is Plowden's Reports, II, Appendix, pp. 1–15. The third citation is to Brooke's *Abridgement,* p. 257a.

38. BM Harl. MSS 1543, p. 185a: "[A copyholder in fee surrendered to the use of A. and the heirs of his body, remainder to B. in fee, and admittance was had accordingly. A. then surrendered to the use of J. S. in fee. A. then died without issue and B. brought a plaint in the nature of Formedon in the Remainder against J. S. The question was whether the action lies. BENDLOES moved the question, and HARPUR and MONSON agreed that the action lies] car de puis que le custome extende al estates en tayle home avera tiels accions sur ceo come apperteyne per le ley al nature de lestate come Litleton dit . . . et uncore Copieholds ne sont deins lestatute de W. 2 . . . [MANWOOD thought the action will lie although copyhold is not within the Statute] car en ascun cases formedon en Remainder fuit a le comen ley puis mort tenant pur vie et coment que lestate tayle soit fait per lestatute uncor tiel manner de dones condicionall fueront devant cybien de copiehold come freeholde et accordant al nature des dones nous poyomus presume que tiels suits fuer de copieholds devant lestatute si ont use issint et issint ieo intende Litleton est destre pris que tiel estate et tiel accion avera este use de tout temps &c car si ne poet estre mainteyne issint que tiel accion ad este la per prescripcion voit estre dure de mainteyner ceo entant que est hors de lestatute

MEADE donques tiels accions voet estre mainteyne en poyes manors en Angleterre et sic tiels Copieholde estates serra de petit force car surrender tant solement lyer ceo donques a touts iours BENDLOES ceo est use ore al Stepney et de suffer comon recovery en briefes de droit de lour copieholde."

39. BM Harl. MSS 5143, pp. 215a–216a.

40. *Ibid.*, p. 216a: "Termino Trin. a 21 Roigne Eliz. en un case en le duche Chamber enter Haselrigge & Grey lopinion de Wray chiefe Justice Sir Tho. Gawdy Justice Sir Gilbert Gerrard lattorney generall & George Bromley lattorney del Duche fuit accordant a le dit opinion del Judges pur lentayle del copiehold." The later citation of Haselrigge v. Grey is in Hill. v Morse, Moore's Reports, pp. 188–189.

41. Coke's Reports, III, 8.

42. Moore's Reports, pp. 188–189. Hill v. Morse is cited in Warne v. Sawyer, Rolle's Reports, I, 48–49. The account of the case in Rolle gives a somewhat different picture of Coke's role and says that it was held that the second custom was good, on the assumption that the estate tail was supported solely by the custom.

43. Croke's Reports, I, 148–149; Leonard's Reports, I, 174–175.

44. Coke's Reports, IV, 23a; Croke's Reports, I, 307; Popham's Reports, p. 33. A fuller report is in BM Add. MSS 25,196, pp. 328a–329a: "En Gravenors case fuit trove per special verdict que un Hall fuit seisi de copihold terre in fee et ad issue 2 files et devised in ta: le remainder in ta: ove remainder ouster in fee Et ils trove ouster expressement que cest terre ad este demised et demisable per copie de Court Roll pur vie ou in fee et nemi in tail et ore le question move fuit si copihold terre est deins lestatute de Westminster 2 ou nemy. COKE sollicitor le Roigne semble que est un estate ta: deins lestatute de Westminster 2 car null remainder fuit sur estate condicionall al comon ley nec revercion mes ore poet estre un remainder ou un revercion dun copihold apres estate ta: ergo ceo est created per lestatute et le reson pur que un quid iuris clamat ne gist sur grant de tenant in ta. per fine est pur ceo que la fuit nul revercion al comon ley et cest briefe fuit al comon ley et est plaine que nul custome poet comence puis lestatute car appiert 8 Eliz 247 lou un Tofte fuit indebt al un Foxcrofte in C£ et Wilkingson fuit indebt al Tofte per obligation et Tofte morust intestate et lordinarie comitt administracion al un Marshall apres que Foxcrofte port dett in London vers et sur le [dett?] del Ordinarie ad forrein attachement per le custome del det in mains de Wilkinson et recover et apres Marshall port dett in

le Common Banke come administrator de Tofte et le custome de forreine attachement pled in barr et le plaintiff demurre et pur ceo que al comon ley nul det gist vers lordinarie devant lestatute de Westminster 2 ca 19 que fuit puis le temps de memorie que ne poet faire costume le plaintiff avoit iudgement et auxi il cited 47 E3 de unitie de possession et Lit. 16 dit que tenant per copie de Court rolle poet aver plaint in nature dun foremedone in discender et cest accion ne fuit al comon ley ergo est done per lestatute Et Mr Plowden in Manxells case in les Comentaries dit que chescun chose que concern [?] le terre et est inheritans poet estre entailed come use rent et honor mes auter est dannuitie ou office de garder ses Haukes et similibus et 14 H8 B 3 dit que estate tail de copihold poet et poet per le custome et poet per lestatute. Et lestatute de 31 H8 yf annie estate or interest be in beinge it shalbe void et fuit adiudge in lexchequer que copihold estate est deins ceo statute car le Seignor cheif baron dit que ceux sont tiels estates quex doient estre regarded in ley Et un copiholder serra resceive per lestatute de Glocester ca 11 et issint moy semble que cest est estate ta: deins lestatute de Westminster le 2 TANFIELD econtra car touts copiholds sont grounded sur custome et nul statute trenchast al Copihold si non que soit nosme deins ceo et pur ceo si feme indowed de copihold pur vie et el levi fine ceo nest deins lestatute de 11 H7 ca 20 nec si le baron alien le Copihold le feme ceo nest deins lestatute de 32 H8 Et ore serra intend que le custome fuit ab initio que poet estre estate ta: de copihold et que ceo nest created per lestatute de Westminster le 2 et issint est 14 H8 B3 et 26 H8 et issint fuit decreed in le Dutchie come est la reported et a nostre case est expressement trove que nul demise poet estre in ta. et issint nul custome est icy pur garrant estate ta. et il semble in cest case que le limitinge del remainder ouster fait le primer estate determinable per un condicionall limitacion car quant un condicionall limitacion est fait la ceo est parcell del estate et doit estre mostre in conveians al estate come si ieo face leas pur ans si J. S. tam diu vixerit le lessee in pledinge doit avere le vie de J. S. JUSTICE GAWDY semble que Copihold terre nest deins lestatute de Westminster 2 car devant le temps de E4 le Seignor puissoit ouste son copiholder car il fuit esteeme forsque pur un tenant a volunt et pur ceo quant cest statute fuit fait les iudges semble lour estate nul estate in ley et les parols del statute sont de tenementis datis sub condicione et issint cest estate a volunt ne poet estre construe deins lestatute mes custome taile poet estre dun copihold mes ceo serra per prescripcion de temps dont memorie &c Et donques quant surrender fuit fait al use dun et ses heires de son corps ceo poet estre fee simple condicionall &

issint nest incounter le custome et pur ceo prover il cite Amy Townesends case in les commentaries CLENCHE a mesme lentent car les parols del statute sont quod voluntas donatoris secundum intentione in charta expressa observetur issint appiert que lestatute intend tiels estates queux poient aver lour essens per fait et ceo ne poet estre intend dun Copihold Auter reson est le briefe de formdone que est sett downe in lestatute et touts foits quant le briefe est sett downe in un statute le forme de ceo est destre observe mes de Copihold terre nul formedon gist mes un plaint in nature de formedone et pur ceo cest plaint nest warranted Auxi lestatute dit et si finis super huiusmodi tenementis imposterum levetur ipso iure sit nullus issint lestatute intend de tiels chose dont fine poet estre levied et ceo ne poet estre de Copihold et issint moi semble que nest deins lestatute FENNER econtra car copiholds sont guided per reson del comon ley et un copihold est incorporate ove le reson del comon ley et avera son accion in nature dun accion al comon ley et devant lestatute heire doit aver assise de mordancestor mes ore il avera formdon mes voile estre dit que in London vous ne averes formdon veray ceo car vous averes briefe de droit car le custome nest altered per le statute en assise de mordancestor Copiholder doit faire prescripcion deins les 30 ans come al comon ley et issint moy semble que estate taile est created de Copihold per equitatem statute POPHAM a mesme lentent car devant lestatute de Westminster 2 estate ta. ne fuit oonques et issint ceo ne poet estre warranted per custome mes per equitie del Statute dit quod voluntas donatoris in carta expressa &c uncore si done in ta. soit fait sans fait ceo est bone et un estate ta. poet estre dun use deins lestatute et uncore ceo est pluis strange case que cest est car pur un use est nul remedy per formdone nec auterment per le comon ley mes in le Chauncerie et in temps E2 [1?] uses fueront cy petit regarded come copihold mes apres quant eux comence destre pluis comon ceux fueront provided for et uncore nul formdon gist dun use mes ceo est construe deins lestatute Et copiholders estates sont pluis regarded ore que in temps praeter car ad este adiudge quils ont interest certein incounter lour Seignors et le remedy de Copihold est in nature dun formdon al comon ley et devant cest statute fuit nul formdon ergo il ad son remedy per lestatute Et per lestatute de Westminster 2 cui in vita est done al feme sur alienacion le baron et si baron de copihold alien le feme poet aver plaint in nature de cui in vita mes ieo voile agree que ceo nest deins lestatute de 11 H 7 car feme navera dower de Copihold terre et issint les auters statutes poient estre [intend?] mes si soit trove que custome garranteth fee coment que ne unques fuit estate pur vie fait de cest copihold uncore tiel estate poet assetts bien estre fait pur ceo est meins que lestate garranted et issint est destate ta. et si custome garrant estate pur un vie ceo ne poet estre lesse pur 2 vies nec si custome garrant estate ta. ceo ne poet estre lesse in fee mes pur un auter point le quel ieo ne poy bien intend touts les judges agre que iudgement serra done CROKE move que cestui in remainder que est ore lessor fist cest lease devant admission et pur ceo le leas est void GAWDIE et FENNER semble que ladmittans del particular tenant est admittans de cestui in remainder TANFIELD CROKE SNAGGE et ALTAM certes ceo fuit adiudge in un Greindells [?] case que cestui in remainder doit estre novelment admit car per ALTHAM le case la fuit que surrender dun copihold fuit fait al use dun per vie remainder ouster in fee et cestui in remainder voilet aver surrender durant le particular estate et adiudge quil ne poet SNAGGE fait un differens quant ladmittance fuit in le singular nomber et lou in le plurall car si in le plurall ceo voile serve pur ambideux TANFIELD ieo ne remember ascun tiel differens prise in le case mes le reason del iudgement fuit pur ceo que si un admission serveroit ambideux donques le Seignor perdera le fine due a lui per cestui in remainder Et le recorde fuit view et ceo fait le case plaine car ceo fuit le particular tenant fuit admitt le remainder ouster et admissi sunt inde tenentes et perinde fecerunt finem issint que les parols del admission va al ambideux CROKE move que fuit un discent de toller lentrie de cestui in remainder et discent de copihold tollera lentrie cibien come de fee simple et issint fuit adiudge 9 Eliz in le case de Syon GAWDIE si puissoit appier que fuit un discent in le case ieo voile estre in oppinion que ceo voile toller lentrie cibien come discent al comon ley come si le baron soit seisi de copihold in droit son feme surrender ceo al use dun auter in fee le feme apres mort son baron ne poet enter mes est mise al sa plaint in nature de cui in vita FENNER econtra mes al auter iour POPHAM agree ove GAWDIE car auterment plaint in nature de briefe dentrie le per fuit invent in vaine."

45. Note 15 above.

46. Moore's Reports, pp. 358–359. For a fuller report, BM Add. MSS 25,198, pp. 48b–51a: "En eiectione firme sur non culp pled fuit trove per speciall verdict que per le Custome dell Mannor de A. lou terre ou etc eant parcell fuit devant temps dount etc demisable per Coppie de Court Roll en fee simple ou fee taile ou pur vie et que fuit present per le homage en temps H8 que B eeant seisie dell dit mannor avoit done cest terre en question per copie all un pur vie remainder al auter en taile

remainder al 3d en taile et que lessee pur vie fuit admitt et devie et apres le primer tenant en taile en remainder enter et surrender al use J. S. et ses heires en fee vers que estranger comence un plaint en nature de briefe de entrye sur disseisin en le courte dell dit mannor en que J. S. vouch tenant en taile que vouche ouster et issint recovery fuit ewe et execucion accordant et le recoveror admitt et que tenant en taile devye sans issue et que cestui en le darreine remainder en taile enter et fait lease all plaintiff et que le defendant enclamant desouth le title dell recoveror luy eiecte et fuit trove ouster que devant cest temps ne unques fuit ascun tiell recoverye en le dit Courte adevant et sur tout ceo les iurors prie ladvice dell Courte FOSTER arguast que cest recovery est voide pur ceo que coppieholds sont transferre accordant a le custome per conveyance scilicet per surrender en manus domini et icy cest recovery est founded [?] sur garranty que est all comon ley et nient garrant per le custome eeant presisement trove per le verdit que null tiell recovery fuit ewe la adevant et il cite 23 H. 8 Br pl 39 Recoverie in valu 27 que pleint de terre tenus per Coppiehold et recovery ewe per garrantye nest bone pur ceo que ne poet garrant contra est de terre in auncient demesne et il cite auxi le case de Glun [?] et Pease que fuit en Comon banke a mesme le purpose et si le recovery soit bone ensuera inconvenience car donques le seignor avera un tenant sans son privity et auxi le tenant poet creater estate sans paiant ascun fine per que le title de celuy que claime desouth cest recoverye nest bone TANFIELDE dit que si coppiholde soit done pur vie le remainder en taile le remainder ouster que le admittance dell tenant pur vie est admittance dell touts les remainders et pur ceo icy eeant trove que le tenant pur vie fuit admitt et devie et cestui en le remainder devie sans issue lentre de celuy en le auter remainder et son lease est bon et il compare ceo all reason dell case en 18 Ed 4 lou revercion est grant pur vie remainder en taile remainder al J. S. en fee attornment all grauntee pur vie est attornment touts les remainders et il ne doubta mes que estate taile poet estre de Coppieholde assetts bien pur ceo que Littleton dit que briefe en nature de formedone poet estre sue en le Courte dell mannor pur Coppiehold terre et auxi est expressment trove icy que le custome avoit garrant cest estate et il vouch un Lakes case destre adiudge pur le point dadmittances que admittance del particular tenant est admittance de touts les remainders et quant al recovery si lessee pur vie ou ans avoit surrender all use all Comon ley que cest surrender ne fuit unques bone mes percase lestatute ore save ceo uncor un garranty ne poet estre annexte a tiell use a fortiori en cest case le garranty ne serra bone pur ceo que celuy que ceo fesoit est forsque tenant a volunte et pur ceo le recovery est voide auxi eeant ewe per reason de ceo et ne poet estre ascun discontinuance pur ceo le tenant en taile ne fuit tenant all temps issint lentrye del tenant en taile en remainder bone et donques son lease est bone et le recoverye vers luy de null effect GRAYE contra et il dit que estate taile de Coppieholde ne poet estre create per ascun custome car cest estate est founden solement sur lestatute de donis condicionalibus et est clere que copieholde terrs ne fueront deins cest statute nient pluis que ils sont deins les statutes de uses and prier [?] volunts etc et 21 [?] H4 90 est que tenant a volunt fuit ouster dell aide pur ceo que il navoit ascun certenne interest et tenant per coppie en le reputacion dell ley nest pluis que un mere tenant a volunt et donques si le terre ne fuit deins lestatute le custome ne poet creater estate en cest customary terre per garrant dell statute pur ceo que il est tenant en fee simple sur condicion come devant all comon ley et issint post prolem suscitatam il avoit potestatem alienandi come absolute tenante en fee simple et donques ayant surrender all use lissue ne poet enter mes soit ceo admitt que il fuit tenante en taile soit ceo per le custome ou per le statute uncor per le surrender en fee ceo est discontinuance de lestate taile come est mise en le Seignor Barkley's case Comentaries 233 pur ceo que il navoit ascun auter mesnes per livery ou auterment de ceo discontinuer quod CLENCH concessit mes touts les auters iustices quant a ceo fueront de contraria oppinionem et TANFEILDE dit que il ad este darreinement adiudge destre null discontinuance donques all recovery ove voucher ceo est bone ou all meines forsque avoidable et il cite une iudgement 36 et 37 Eliz destre en comon banke lou pleint en nature de briefe dentrye fuit porte vers tenante en taile de Copiholde et recovery et execucion ewe ceo fuit discontinuance issint est Litt 154 et donques celuy en remainder fuit toll de son entrye mes il duist aver porte son accion et avoyder le recoverye ou fauxifier ceo ou auterment per son entrye il est torte feasor et son lessee navoit ascun titell de claimer encounter le recovery et lestate derive hors de ceo durant le temps que le recovery remaine en force touts les Justices agree ni un que admittance dell particuler lessee pur vie lou sont divers remainders ouster est admittance de touts les remainders auxi car per POPHAM quant le tenant pur vie vient destre admitte il mostre le Coppie en Courte all Stewarde en que auxi touts les remainders sont comprise et le Senescall fait entrye en son roll ou liver que super hoc admittitur mes ils en remainder paiera lour fines ou auterment est forfeiture dell Coppiehold sur lour refusall et nest pluis preiudice a le Seignor de aver son fine de cesty en remainder sans admittance de luy que dell heire dell tenante en fee apres le morte son pier per que il est tenant devant admittance CLENCHE le custome ne poet create estate taile en Copiholde terre sinon le custome auxi prove que per formedone en discender ou remainder il avoite este recover apres discontinuance fait et donques ceo est estate taile per reason dell custome de recoverye nemi per le done car le done solement sans le custome de recover fait estate in fee simple condicionalment all comon ley et icy nest trove per le verdictt que le custome fuit de recover apres discontinuance per que null estate taile GAWDYE estate taile poet estre de Copieholde per 14 H8 Br t. per coppi 24 pl3 et formedone in discender gist de ceo per Custome all comon ley et serra intende que ceo ad este un custome la de tout temps dount &c nient obstante que le briefe de formedon en discender est done per lestatute de Westminster et pur ceo cest custome que le terre tenus per Copie fuit demisable per Coppie en taile eeant trove ceo est bon taile accordante all Custome et quant Copieholder surrender all use il ne poit annex ascun garranty a cest conveyance pur ceo que il est in mesme le degree quant all reputacion dell comon ley come un tenant a volunt et est bone counter plea al voucher adire que cesti que fesoit le feoffment avoit forsque estate a volunte et pur ceo per consequens le voucher est idle est null recompence serra gaine per ceo et donques le recoverye ne poit estre discontinuance pur ceo que ne fuit ewe vers tenant in taile mes vers le grauntee de son estate et donques apres son morte sans issue cesty in le remainder poit bien enter et issint son lease bone mes si il ussoit este trove per le verdit que le custome fuit que recoveryes poient estre ewe sur voucher ceo uste este barre de lestate taile mes icy est expressment trove le Contra FENNER cest estate taile est fait per lequitye dell statute de Westminster 2 et nemi per le custome pur ceo que ne fuit ascun estate taile all comon ley et divers demises in taile per coppie et le possession continuant accordant est sufficient evidence de prover lentaile sans ascun recoverye in formedon mes soit ceo estate per le comon ley ou per le custome donques secundum equum et bonum et in bon conservacion cest recoverye est barre a ceo car il est null droit mes si les parties ioyne poit estre done et est le comon courst et conveyance de lier estates tayled per recoveryes auxi cest garranty est sufficientment bone de recover le terre garranted et donques le recoverye in value ouster est perpetuall barre Car si estate taile soit allow de cest terre le mesnes auxi de ceo determiner serra allowe et per luy si tenant in taile de copihold soit le remainder in fee si un que avoit droit release ove garranty cest bon garranty et il conclude que quant Copieholder en taile ou en fee surrender all use uncor cesti que fait le surrender semper demmeurte tenant et nest hors de possession tanque admittance de celuy a que use le surrender fuit fait et issint le recoverye est discontinuance car recovery vers tenante pur vie est discontinuance de touts le remainders mes si soit per covin le lessor entra pur forfeiture come ad este agree devant cest temps auterment ils sont mise a lour accions mes si tenant in taile avoit uncor suffer recoverye ceo fuit discontinuance per que cesty en remainder est icy mise a son accion si le recovery ne soit perpetuall barre. POPHAM estate taile de Copiholde est sans le custome car null custome poit ceo garrante pur ceo que ne fuit tiell estate all comon ley mes si cest estate poet estre recover apres discontinuance et si briefe sur lestatute done remedye de recontinuer ceo ergo lequity dell statute done lestate et nient le Custome le recovery sans ascun voucher ouster est discontinuance car si tenant in taile grant totum statum suum et recovery est ewe vers le grauntee uncor ceo est discontinuance et lissue mise a son accion issint si tenant in tayle bargaine et vende le terre et recovery est ewe vers le bargainee ceo est discontinuance pur ceo que lestate est disaffirme per le recovery et novell estate gaine en le recoveror que doet auxi estre defeate per le [—?] le garranty faite per copiholder est bone sur que il prist cest diversity scilicet si Copiholder pur vie surrender in manus domini al use en fee ove garranty et le seignor admitt celuy a que use le surrender est fait secundum formam reditionis ceo garranty ne unques poit estre bone pur ceo que lestate primes extinguishe en le Seignor et apres admittance lauter est eines en le per de le seignor issint si copiholder est en fee et il surrender all use sans garranty et le seignor voile luy admitte ove garranty ceo garranty nest bone pur ceo que il nest enis en 2. case per le seignor car il est solement un instrument de conveyer ceo mes si copiholder en fee ou en taile surrender all use ove garranty ceo est bon garranty si le seignor fait admittance accordant pur ceo que lauter est enis en le per de le surrenderor et de cest estate a que garranty fuit annex et le Seignor Arundells case voile ceo prover disseisor graunte Copiholde le disseisee avoidra ceo car le tenante est enis de le disseisor mes si disseisor admitt un tenante accordant al le surrender dun auter le disseisee navoidra car quant all disseisor lauter vient enis in le post et per le ley et en le per de le surrenderor pur ceo cest recovery serra barre a lentaile per reason de cest garranty et voucher et il dit que de son conusance demesne il scavoit que tiell conveyance de docker lestate taile per recoverye fuit allowe de

Copieholde terre per le Cheife Justice son predecessorr icye et per Plowden pur 30 ans passe et que le garranty annexte a tiell estate varra solement a le customary terre et de ceo solement serra le recoverye in value en mesme le mannor sicome tenant in ancient demesne vouch et recoverye ewe null terre serra recover ou mise in execucion forsque auncient demesne terre contra sur garranty de charters et il dit que cest copiholde terre en cest latter temps ad este allowe tiells et touts priviledge come tenants de terre all comon ley car ad este tenus que possession fratris serra de Copiholde et tiels semblables et pur ceo en mults cases il est destre repute in equall degree ove terre all comon leye et nemi destre compare all tenant a volunte per mesme le reason le Comon ley workenge sur le Custome voile docker estates taile et ceo barrer a touts iours et sicome le custome ne done lestate taile neque est founded sur le Custome sed sur lequitye dell statute workenge sur le custome et cest equity done le meanes per formedon de ceo recontinuer eant discontinue per mesme le reason le Comon ley workenge sur le Custome liera lestate per le recoverye et le supposed recompense per que le recoverye est bone barre et cest le melieux exposicion car auterment mults garboiles per reason de mults de ceux conveyances devant fait ensuera sills serront ore evert, quere plus."

The same case is reported at large in BM Add. MSS 25,200, pp. 37b–39a. In the main, this report is the same as the one given above. However, the following excerpts from the second report may illuminate the meaning of portions of the first.

(i) From FOSTER's argument: ". . . . si ne soit un custome deins le mannor a voucher ne poet estre ascun voucher la Auxi un garranty est create per fait et ne poet annex al chattel ou meinder estate que franctenement sicome 21 H7 home nest rebutter per lease pur ans ove garranty nient pluis que voucher donques coment le copieholder ad estate de linheritance per le custome uncore il ad forsque estate ad volunt per le comon ley . . . et issint fuit lopinion de tout le court del comon bank Term. Michelmas darreine en case parenter [—?] et Pease que tiel recovery ove voucher suffer per tenant in taile nest barre per causa antedicta, scilicet que nul garranty poet estre annex a tiel estate uncore le case fuit rule encounter lissue en tayle pur ceo que il enter sur recoverer que ne poet faier car cest recovery est discontinuance . . . mes icy nest ascun discontinuance car le copieholder in tayle surrender que ne fuit discontinuance come ad este adiudge et donques cesty a que le surrender fait suffer le recovery et le copieholder in tayle vient eins come vouchee ayant riens en luy et pur ceo ne poet discontynue riens per cest entry en le garranty. . ."

(ii) From TANFIELD's argument: ". . . ascuns doubt si copiehold en tayle serra deins lequitie del statute . . . mes nest ascun question mes per custome home poet aver estate tayle en un copiehold quod fuit concessum . . . Ne poet estre per ascuns possibilitie un garranty annex a son estate . . . car le tenant in tayle surrender al seignor a son use per que son estate est drownde et donques nul garranty ne poet annex . . . et cesty que use le surrender fuit fait prist son estate del seignor et ne del tenant in tayle ergo [?] il ne poet aver un garranty del tenant in tayle per que il vouche luy Auxi il ad per le surrender forsque un use a que per le comon ley nul garranty poet estre annex et coment il ad apres un possession execute a ceo uncore ne poet aver garranty et donques si nest estre un garranty le voucher est voyed et issint nul barre intant que nul recompence poet vener al luy. . ."

(iii) From CLENCH's opinion: "Auxi ieo teigne que lestate tayle et le remainder est discontinue per le surrender del tenant en tayle et donques cesty en remainder ne poet enter."

(iv) FENNER's opinion entire: "En mon opinion cesty en remainder est tenus ne solement de son entry mes est barre de son droit per cesty recovery Judicandum est secundum equum et bonum et come prescripcion destate tayle de copiehold est destre maynteyne per lequitie del statute que create tiels estates Car le prescripcion exceede le statute intant que ne fuit estate tayles devant per mesme le reason tiel estate est destre barre per lequitie et rules del comon ley car come le equitie del ley maynteyne lestate lequitie del ley que est le recompence en valewe barre lestate auxi. Auxi un garranty poet estre al coppie hold car si soit un copieholder per tort et cesty que droit ad daver in tayle voyt confirme ove garranty et mort ayant assets de copiehold de inheritance deins mesme le mannor que discend al issue si ore lissue sue un pleint en nature de formedone il est cleare que il serra barre per ceo garranty ove assets per mesme le reason il poet estre vouche per que moy semble que le plaintiff doit estre barre."

47. Foss, *Biographical Dictionary,* pp. 168, 778.

48. BM Add. MSS 25,203, p. 463b: ". . . Et sur ambideux ceux evydences fuit tenus que si coppyhold soit graunt al un et lheires de son corps ceo est un taile deins lestatute de donis condicionalibus sans ascun speciall custome de garrant ceo."

49. BM Add. MSS 25,203, pp. 677a–b: "Nota sur un Evidens enter

Rooke et Wharton fuit agree per touts 4 Justices que poet estre un estate taile dun coppyholde sans ascun especiall custome car coppyholds sont deins lestatute de donis condicionalibus et ils diont que Litt prove ceo car il dit que lissue in taile dun coppyholde poet aver pleint en nature dun formdon en descender al comon ley et est impossible que il avoit formdon en descender forsque per lestatute de donis condicionalibus car avant cest statute ne fuit ascun formdon en le descender et un custome ne poet growe puis cest statute esteant deins temps de memory mes uncore il direct que cest matter serra trove specialment et sur mesme levidens fuit move le quel un surender per tiel coppyholder en taile serra discontinuance ou nient mes quant a ceo les Justices fueront devyde en oppinion scilecet 2 enconter 2 pur que tout le matter per assent del counsell dambideux parts fuit trove specialment."

50. See Coke, *Compleat Copy-holder,* secs. 47 and 48; Coke on Littleton, sec. 76. The seventeenth-century cases most worthy of note are Lee v. Brown, Popham's Reports, pp. 128–129, in which the King's Bench returned to the view that the Statute requires the cooperation of the custom, and Rowden v. Malster, Croke's Reports, III, 42–45, in which the Common Pleas affirmed the inapplicability of the Statute, 3–1.

51. Note 46 above.

52. See Scriven, *Copyholds,* pp. 44–52, for the later law.

53. See Coke, *Compleat Copy-holder,* sec. 34, for a general statement of the rule. The earliest decision I know of on the power of the *dominus pro tempore* is BM Harg. MSS 2, p. 15b, 4 Mary: "Nota que si home lessa manor pur ans in que sont copy holds et puis copy holder devye le termor del manor grant le terre per copye pur troys vies cest bon car le custom est per tout Angleterre que le seignor pur le temps esteant poit dimitter per copye &c. . ." For the rule that the usual custom may be prescribed against, see BM Add. MSS 25,188, p.46, 4 Elizabeth: "Nota que si home seisi dun mannor dont sont divers copyholdes dimittable pur vie ou pur ans & il less le mannor a un auter pur terme de vie le lesse poet fair demise per copy dun revercion a comenser per le mort le primer copyholder & cest assets bon coment que il neschua in le vie le lessee mes custome dascun mannor est al contrary & ceo ad este allow."

54. Dyer's Reports, p. 251a. BM Lans. MSS 1133, pp. 137a–139a, no. 20 is undated, but from the names of the judges clearly early, and from the facts almost certainly the same case as in Dyer. Dyer gives as a simple holding what the MS. reports as the opinion of two judges. Dyer also omits to report that the case contained an issue—whether the devisees

could grant copies without having an interest in the soil—sufficient to settle the case without reference to the widow's rights. The MS. report is as follows: "J. S. sease del manor de Dale en ffee devise per son darrein volunt que J. D. et S. C. poient faire coppies preignant fines a lur plus advantage pur le payment de ses detes et puis il devie J. D. et S. C. gard un court et font coppies a 3 homes pur vie successive secundum consuetudinuem manerii et puis un de les 3 devie et ils font novell coppies en revercion al R. D. a quel use les 2 primer surrender Et puis le feme J. S. recover en briefe de dower per defalt et mesme la terra sont assign pur son dower per que el enter et R. D. luy oust et el port briefe de tns [Trespass] et DIER er WALCHE diont que el bien avoid le coppie entant que el est endowe del melior possession baron et pur ceo si le baron mesme ou son heire eust graunt tell coppies devant le feme recover son dower quant el ad recover ceo el void ceo pur ceo que son title fuit devant le graunt del coppie aussy le graunt nest bon de ceux coppies car ils doient estre fait per le seignor del manor et que le Seignor del manor poet done authorite al auter home de faire coppies Issint quel fait ceux en le nosme del Seignor et pur ceo le ducke de Suffocke done comission pur fair lease pur ans de son terre et sil fait lease pur ans en son nosme demesne et nemy en le nosme del ducke et pur ceo adiuge void lease."

55. BM Add. MSS 35,940, pp. 304b–305a, Easter, 8 Elizabeth: "Home seise dun mannor ou sont copihoulds devise ceo mannor a ses executors de pay ses detts et devy et les executors lessont les terres per coppie pur paier les dettes et sa feme port briefe de dower de le mannor et fuit tenus per CARUS que le feme naver dower de les coppihould terres ne ouster les tenants per copie mes HARPOR al contrary mes le case ne fuit argued per le Court al ceo temps mes puis fuit adiudge que le feme ne avoid les coppies quel quere car issing le custome serra perd."

56. BM Lans. MSS 1133, pp. 137a–139a, no. 18: "Home sease dun manor en que sont coppieholders et customary tenants pur vie devise mesme le manor a diverse persons pur terme dans pur le payment de ses detts durant queux ans les devises graunt novell coppies de mesme le terre et aussy puis durant mesme les ans ils graunt le revercion de certen coppieholds et le particular tenant surrender en le court del manor al use del grantors per que les grantors fueront sease et surrender durant les ans et puis le feme le devisor port bref de dower vers lheir et ad iudgement de recover et cest manor fuit assigne a luy pur son dower per le vicount et fuit move per BROWNE si le feme avoid ceux copies faits per les devises et per BROWNE et WESTON el ne poet avoider ceux copies

car ils sont eins per le custome et nemy per les devises et pur ceo tell coppies fait per tenant pur ans ou pur vie ou disseisor sont bone et ne serra avoid car ceo quils font ils font come officers dexecuter un custome et si home soit seise dun manor a que villen est regardant et devi aiant feme et devie [sic] et le villein purchase terre et lheir enter ou si un gard eschete ou esglesse happen void et apres le feme recover le manor uncor le feme naver les terres purchase ne le gard ne la presentment et fuit agre que si le custome fuit que ils poient graunter coppies en revercion que donques ceux coppies en revercion sont aussy bone come en possession."

57. If the dowager receives only part of the manor, and especially if she receives only part of the copyholds, the question arises whether a severance from the manor has occurred such as to prevent the dowager from standing in the place of the original lord. There is probably no problem when the severance comes about by act of law, as in assignment of dower.

58. Coke's Reports, IV, 24a. BM Add. MSS 24,845, p. 313, is undated, but probably from the 1580's, judging from its position among other cases in the MS. The MS. report is as follows: "Baron seisis dun mannor ou sont copiholders pur vie et puis ascun del copiholders devie pur que le baron dimitt al auters per copie pur iii vies solonque custome del mannor et puis baron devie, feme avera dower de 3 parte del manor mes el ne avoyder les copies per curiam in communi banco."

59. Dyer's Reports, p. 270b. Also reported in BM Add. MSS 35,940, pp. 409a–410a: "Un Mannor deins que coppihoulds fueront per le Custome demisable pur vyes fuit done al baron et feme et al heire le barron que donques le barron a grant le Stewardshipp al J. S. le pere pur vie et al W. S. le fits habendum apres le mort le pere et il grant al eux X£ pur terme de lour vies per officium predictum executendo et donques le barron morust et un coppihoulder morust que le feme grant ouster al estranger et morust et le pere morust et le rent eeant arrere in temps le fitz et auxi le pere le fitz distrein pur tout in mesme coppihould et maintenera car come le feme quant al mannor fuit eins per title paramount le grant et issint el tenera discharge, uncore le copihoulder fuit eins desouth le title del grant come le feme avoit authority de faire novell coppies per le custome et ne serra eins per le feme solement sed serra subiect al le charge et eins del intier inheritance que fuit charge sicome home fait lease pur vye et donques grant un rent et donque le lessee pur vie et luy ioyne in un feoffment est le feoffment del tenant pur

vye et le confirmacion del lessor et durant le vye le tenant pur vye tenera discharge mes apres son mort serra eins per le lessor et tenera charge . . . [The court then discusses whether the son may distrain for rent not paid to his father, after which they resume the subject of the copyhold] . . . et WESTON et WELSH tient que si le Coppihoulder avoit surrender al use dun estranger que le Seignor admitt que il tenera discharge car il ad ceo del cesty que surrender et nemy le Seignor car nest forsque instrument de convey ceo et si le Seignor grant rent hors del demesnes uncore ceo ne charge les terrs in maines les Copihoulders quel BENDLOES deny . . ."

60. Moore's Reports, p. 94.

61. Leonard's Reports, I, 4.

62. BM Add. MSS 25,196, pp. 338b–339a: "Le Seignor Paget eant seisi del mannor de great Marloe in Comitatu Buckingham fait lease al Tho. Paget son frere pur 60 ans exceptant touts timber trees sur le dit mannor Tho. Paget fait son feme executrix et devi que prist a baron Carie et Carter per son comandement coupe certein ashes et Oakes deins le dit mannor et auters eux import et W. Paget fits le Seignor Paget port accion de Trespas vers Carter et les autres les defendants done in evidens a prover eux non culpable que le custome del mannor est que touts les copiholders del dit mannor poient couper timber cressant sur lour Copiholds pur repairer lour mesons sans ascun assignement [del Seignor] ou son baylie et per lassignement del Seignor ou son baylie ils poient couper timber cressant sur ascun del demesnes del mannor pur repairer lours dits measons et ils eant Copiholders per lassignment del baylie de Carie coupe les dits timber trees pur repracion de lour dits copihold mesons et fuit doubt si le baylie le lessee pur ans eant dominus pro tempore del mannor et les arbers eant except hors del lease poet assigne timber a les Copiholders del mannor our nemi et GAWDIE et FENNER disseront in opinion in ceo nul auter iustices adonques eant present in Curia . . . [The first speak to a point having nothing to do with the copyholders' right to the trees] . . . et per le melior oppinion quant les defendants pled non culpable a le trespas cest speciall matter de le custome in evidens ne voyle maintener lissue car les defendants nont ascun interest in larbers . . ."

63. Coke's Reports, VIII, 63–64; Brownlow and Goldesborough's Reports, pp. 231–232; Moore's Reports, p. 811.

64. Brownlow's Reports, p. 208.

65. There seem to be no later denials of Swaine v. Beckett.

66. Scriven, *Copyholds*, pp. 10–12.

67. Littleton, sec. 82.

68. Cf. the same principle in connection with discontinuance, executory interests, and warranty. See the argument of Ewans in Melwich v. Luther, note 78 below.

69. See, however, the argument of Harris in Melwich v. Luther, note 78 below, to the effect that the lord may always grant out of court if he chooses.

70. In the case as stated, A divorces himself from all interest in the land. By effect of the Statute of *Quia Emptores,* no tenure is created between A and B. Suppose, however, that A had enfeoffed B for life or leased to him for years. Although these transactions, by breaking the continuity of the custom, might destroy the demisability of the land by copy when it reverted to A, is there any reason not to consider the land still part of A's manor and to hold that A's manorial court still has jurisdiction for copyhold litigation at least? (As to other functions, the problem is of course more complicated because of the question whether A or B should have fines.) I know of no law on this point.

71. For both the classical definition and the conception of a "copyhold manor," see Coke, *Compleat Copy-holder,* sec. 31, and Calthrope, *Relation Between the Lord . . . and the Coppyholder,* pp. 9–14.

72. BM Lans. MSS 1133, p. 139a. The date given in the report is hard to read, but the case is certainly from 1574–1579, the years when Robert Monson sat on the court (Foss, *Biographical Dictionary,* p. 448): "Nota per touts les Justices del comon bank en 19 [?] Eliz que si coppiehold soit graunt a 3 successive et puis le manor est sever que uncor les coppies remain: mes Mounson ceo dowbt car sur tell case il dit il fuit clere [?] al channcery."

73. BM Add. MSS 24,845, p. 269: "Home purchasse le ffreehold dun copihold et puis le copiholder Releas al luy tout son droit et fuit move per SNAGGE si cest releas serra un surrender, et il dit que en le graund assurance que fuit passa que fuit ut dicitur enter le Roigne et Sir Christopher Hatton fuit prise que per cest alienacion linterest de copiholder ne fuit impeir quel fuit en manner graunt per le court mes Anderson dit que nul court poit estre tenus et nul court rolle poit estre fait . . ."

74. One reference indicates it was a Chancery case (BM Harl. MSS 1588, p. 154a: "[Hatton's Case] ou un copyhould in mesme manor fuit graunt al lui & rule in Chancery per Justices assistants la que il potuit tiendre un Court &c"). Other references indicate it was a Queen's Bench case (Jackson v. Neale, note 76 below; Moysier v. Walker, note 81 below;

and Gaye v. Kaye, note 83 below.) The principal issue for the interpretation of the case seems to have been whether it extended to new grants as well as admittance. Whether it involved severance of all the copyholds of a manor or only some is also unclear from the references.

75. Leonard's Reports, II, 208–209.

76. Croke's Reports, I, 394–395; Coke's Reports, IV, 26a. BM Add. MSS 25,200, pp. 80b–81a: "Le case fuit ouster le manor fuit done per le Roigne Domino Hunsdon en fee et le seignor lessa touts les copyhold a 2 pur mille ans et per ceux 2 le license [to lease] fuit done ANDERSON ceux 2 ne poient tener Court neque per ley neque per prescripsion quod fuit concessum per WALMESLEY & BEAUMOND mes OWEN dit que fuit adiudge in Sir Christopher Hattons case Seignor Chancelor in banke le roy et Auxi in lexchequer sur graunt de copyholds in fee de Wellingboron que il tener court uncore le roye ad le demeasnes ANDERSON ieo ne sacha ascun reason de ceo et ieo marveile sur que ground tiel Judgment fuit done . . . [In Pasch., 37 Eliz., the case was again moved at the bar by GLANVILL, who spoke as follows] Et ieo move que le lessee ne poet tener court car Chescun Court doit estre mainteyne per comon ley ou Custome per Comon ley a chescun mannor un Court baron est incident et cest part del manor ore lesse nest ore un manor et pur ceo nul Court per Comon ley donques ne poet estre per custome Car ne poet prescribe daver tiel Court pur ceo [que] nad este tiel court la de temps &c mes ieo graunt bien que en les Western parts et in auters liews poet estre tiel Courts pur dadmitter coppieholds tantum Anderson cest case poet estre sovent foits en question fuit le case de Hatton touchant son coppyholds in Wellinbroughe in County Northampton et fuit le Case dauters auxi et touts semble que le Court poet bien continue quant a cest purpose car auterment Chescun person act demesne poet destroy lestates de son Coppyholders . . . [The case was decided next Trinity Term on another point] mes a cest iour riens fuit parle del auter matter si le Court continue ou nemi."

77. BM Add. MSS 25,211, pp. 121b–122a: "In Replevin per Bright v. Forte que avowe come baylieffe al Margarett Stanley Countesse de Darby pur damage feasant et le case fuit un [The name is a blank in the MS] fuit seisi del Mannor de C . . . . et in Bradway [a place within the manor, comprising part of it] fueront Copiholders pur vies et il suffer recovery del Mannor except le terr in Bradway et puis cest part del Manor de Bradway discend al Countess . . . [She and her husband granted copies. The question was whether these grants were good. GLANVILL

argued that they were not, because when a manor is divided by the act of the party] ces copiholders sont auxi destroy et nemy semble al un copiholde dinheritance car sil sont sever del Mannor uncore ils remaine copiholde et le Seignor serra compell de graunter eux solonque le Custome car le Seignor nest forsque un meanes et instrument a passer le copihold . . . et cest diversity inter copihold inheritance et pur vie fuit accordant al case de Hatton Chauncellor et issint le case del Meredith del Copiholders de Stockingham fuit de copiholders denheritance mes pur nostre very case in 29 Eli. in cest court le case fuit que un feme fuit endowe de certaine copihold pur vie tantum per [que] ils fueront sever del Mannor et el graunt copiholds et adiudge void issint ad este resolve saepe in le Westerne circuite car le Duck de Somersett quant il avoit purchase plusors copiholds devant perteigne al severall Mannors voit compeller eux touts a vener al un Court et la il voit graunt per Copies quel ont este saepe Resolve destre void WILLIAMS contra [There are demesnes and services in Bradway which makes a manor, and there may be a copyhold court without free tenants] et le case de Sir Xopher Hatton ne poit estre respond car il sever les copiholds de Willingborough del Mannor et puis comand un de eux dappearer al un Court destre tenus pur ses copiholds quel refuse sur que il enter in son copihold et tenus in Banke le Roy que il poit garder un Court et issint touts fueront in oppinion in the case de Nele et Jackson . . . [ANDERSON speaks to a point of pleading. As to the matter in law, the judges do not want to give an opinion but advise the parties to compound. However GLANVILL] pria judgment pur le Countesse et ore touts forsque Owen agree (Owen eeant absent) que le graunt de copihold nest bon intant que ne fuit ascun tiel mannor de Bradway devant ne ore WILLIAMS et HARRIS mes nous avomus le record dun Judgment in Banke le Roy in le very point que le Coppy est bon et ceo est un Constantines case DREWE cest Judgment fuit secretment enter sans lorder del court et ieo aie parle ove EWENS baron del Eschequer que fuit del Councell in le case que dit a moy que puis le Judgment il port un Briefe derror de reverser ceo car loppinion del touts les Justices fuit enconter le Judgment per que le Copiholder que recover fuit content de prender le corne sur le terre et oustrement de perder le terre ANDERSON le case fuit sur un special verdict done devant moy et ieo ne intend que ceo serra adiudge per les Justices car la le copihold fuit in un vill in Hamshire et parcell dun Mannor in Dorsett et feoffment fuit fait dun copihold in Hamshire et pur ceo fuit distroy sans question [WALMESLAY and BEAUMOND agree. Judgment for avowant solely on the matter in law, without regard to the pleading point] . . . et a cest iour ANDERSON dit que si cest severrance ust este dun copihold del inheritance et le copiholder et ses heirs averont ceo mes ne poit unques surrender ceo issint que serra un perpetuity in le copiholder et ses heirs car surrenders sont per Customes et pur ceo doit estre in le court ou auterment nest bon quel BEAUMOND concessit . . ."

78. Croke's Reports, I, 102–103; Coke's Reports, IV, 26b. BM Add. MSS 25,196, pp. 127b–129a, is a much fuller report: "Deins un mannor la fuit un hamlet in quel fueront 3 copiholds parcell del mannor dauncient temps et le Seignor del mannor enfeffe estranger de cest parcell del mannor gisant in cest hamlett quel estranger puis tenust un court en et sur un auter mannor quil avoit et in ceo il graunt un de ceux copiholds arere per copie accordant al custome la used et ceo fuit fait sur le surrender dun auter copiholder in ceo court que avoit estate per copie de ceo copiehold per graunt de Seignor de primer mannor devant le disiointinge de ceux copiholds del mannor et le [—?] cest coppie bone ou nemi est le matter in eieccione firme Et HARRIS tenust ceo destre bone et que le feffee poet tener copihold Court a cest purpose solement de prender surrenders et graunt copies car le custome uncore remaine in ceux copihold terres coment que ne fueront parcell del mannor al temps del copie fait et comment que le grauntor de eux nad mannor alls auter purposes et ceo ad este le case de Sir Xofer Hatton Seignor Chauncellor que ore est ou il aiant conveians fait a lui de un quillett de copihold terres dun mannor poet graunter copies de ceo et tener court a cest purpose come ad este adiudge Et fuit dit per EWANS que per le severans de copihold terres de la mannor per le feffment le copihold est fait ingrosse et donques nul court mannor ne custome remaine de upholder ascun graunt per copie en apres de ceo terre Auxi cest copie desouth que le plaintiff claime est fait in le Court dun auter mannor in auter countie et est fait sur le surrender dun copihold la fait et est limitt al eux accordant al custome del mannor ibidem que est accordant al custome de mannor ou le copie fuit graunt et ceo ne garrant le custome destre bone et garranted per et accordant al custome del mannor et copihold terres del primer mannor car de ceo nest pled deins le copie et donques coment que est trove que cest terre fuit customarie terre et dimittable per copie accordant al custome del primer mannor uncore cest custome ne voile garrant ceo destre dimittable accordant al custom del 2 mannor et pur ceo le copie est void HARRIS le custome icy insue le terre come gavelkinde destre demittable per copie touts foits non obstant le disioint-

inge del manor come ad este adiudge devant cest temps in le case le Chauncellor Et auxi in 6 Eliz un feme aiant parcell dun copihold terres assigne a lui pur dower el de eux poet graunt copies in revercion assetts bien accordant al custome del mannor il nest destre doubt mes si le feffe de ceux terres customaries terres ust fait le copie al un court assemble al ceo purpose sur le copihold terre mes que ceo ust este bone et issint poet il graunter copies de ceo in quocunque lieu quil voile hors del court car le Seignor mesme poet graunter copies hors del Court in ascun lieu que il voile et donques quant il face ceo in son court dauter mannor serra entend ou les copiholds sont et ibidem la referr al copihold terres et nemi al darrein mannor et si soit admitt que les parols accordant al custome del mannor referr al darrein mannor donques pur ceo que nul custome est mostre in le mannor pur demiser in possession et revercion per copie ceux parols accordant al custome del mannor ibidem ou al meins cest parol ibidem serra prise come nugacion et sicome ils nussent este eins et les former parols serra assetts bone et pur ceux causes le copie est bone et de ceo oppinion fuit tout le Court per que ils done iudgement pur le plaintiff EWANS murmurant dit quil voile porter briefe derror sur ceo Et les Justices dissont quil poet issint faire in le nosme de diew Et in Hill 31 Eliz error fuit port in lexchequer Chamber accordant al Statute de 27 Eliz et error assigne in point de iudgement EWANS dit que le copie per le feffee ne poet estre bone pur divers causes car nest destre denie mes que le feffee nad mannor per le graunt de ceux 3 copiholds car coment que mannor poet estre severed per particion parenter soers come est 26 H8 ou per le demaunding del 3 part dun mannor per un feme pur sa dower come est 9 4 pur ceo sont per act in ley uncore per act de parties mesme nul mannor poet estre devided car sil poet le Seignor dun mannor poet faire tants mannors come il ad copiholds que seroit impertinent et donques si le feffee nad mannor il ne poet graunt copiholds accordant al custome del mannor et comment que soit issint que ou un ad mannor que nest mannor nisi in reputacion et nul mannor in droit entant que fault demesnes et free suitors et uncore copies la graunt sont bone uncore cest feffee nad ascun mannor in reputacion ne in facto mes solement ad inheritans in 3 copiholds que per nul means poet enable lui de tener court et graunt copies de ceo touts foits apres mes le feffment severant les 3 copiholds del mannor coment quil ne subvert le copie a ceo temps in esse uncore de ceo terre per le feffee nul novell copie poet estre fait car le custome uphold le copies cy longement que les copiholds continue parcel del mannor mes quant ils sont severed del mannor per feffment donques ils ont perde le custome que fait eux demittable per copie touts temps apres et al case de Sir Xofer Hatton que voit estre obiect encounter moy ieo die que coment que soit issint que le 2d copihold graunted sur surrender serra bone uncore ceo ne semble a nostre case car le primer copiholder limitast ceo al use dun auter et le Seignor nest que instrument a convey ceo al 2 copiholder et ne serra dit eins per le Seignor mes per le primer copiholder et ceo est prove le case 10 Eliz Dyer 2 270 que si Seignor dun mannor graunt hors de ceo un rent charge et puis copiholder denheritans de ceo mannor surrender al use destranger et le Seignor graunt a luy accordant al custome le 2 copiholder tiendra discharge de ceo rent mes si in le dit case del Seignor Hatton le copiholder ust devi sans heire ou copiholder ust solement surrender al seignor mesme ieo croy south correccion que le patentee ne poet graunt ceo arrere per copie et nostre case icy est peior que ceo car le primer copiholder in son possession fuit copiholder pur vie et surrender absolutement et le feffee sur ceo fist 2 copie quel ne poet estre bone le copihold eant determine per le absolute surrender et per ceo le custome determined et ore de necessitie le copiholder convient destre eins per le feffee et de son estate que neant able de faire copie le copie est void et per ceo si disseisor dun mannor prist surrender dun copihold al use dun auter et admitt le cestui a que use accordant le disseisee reenter il navera cest 2 copie car ne fuit fait per le disseisor dun novell copie car fuit nisi instrument de conveier launcient copie mes si copie escheat al disseisor et il fait novell copie le disseisee avoidra ceo sans doubt car lestate le disseisor ceo disproved et pur ceo touts estates derive hors de ceo issint in nostre case pur ceo que le feffee per le absolute surrender ad le terre et entant que nad mannor ne court il ne poet create novell copie le 2 copie per lui graunt est void Et a ceo que percase voit estre obiect que ceo copie eant fait sur le surrender de 2 homes quel avoient estate pur lour 2 vies que durant les vies les 2 homes le seconde copie serra bone a ceo ieo die que si le surrender ust este fait per eux al use le 2 copiholder il voit estre issint mes le surrender icy est absolute per que le feffe nad power de faire novell copie durant le vie de le 2d a que il pleist et coment quil puist uncore nest icy trove que les 2 homes que surrender sont ou fueront al temps de eiectment in vie et donques le iustification desouthe le copie void Auxi coment soit admitt que le feffee puist aver graunt copie accordant al custome del primer mannor uncore a son mannor in auter county il ne poet graunt accordant al custome del mannor ibidem car ne fuit unques parcell de ceo mannor Auxi coment que le copie fuit bone uncore icy le copiholder ne poet faire lease pur un ann per fait come icy il ad sans custome de garrant et pur ceo il est forfeit de son copihold car per ceo il ad prise sur lui daver estate al comon ley lou le qualitie de ceo est forsque a volunt et coment que nest forfeiture sans custome alledge de nostre parte de faire ceo forfeit come il voil estre obeict uncore le lesse entrant per force de cest lease est disseisor et nemi un lessee car si tenant a volunt al comon ley fait leas pur ans lessee enter nest termor mes disseisor et coment que lessee vers estranger poet aver eieccione firme sur ceo lease uncore vers le Seignor mesme que ad lenheritans ou vers le defendant icy queux sont servants al cesti que ad lenheritans cest accion ne voile giser per que le plaintiff nad cause de recover et cur ceo le iudgement erronious et priomus que poet estre reverse HARRIS econtra et dit que non obstant le severans de ceux 3 copies del mannor per feffment uncore le primer custome annex al terre que fait ceo demittable remain in quorumcunque maines que ceo vient car customes que va al tenancy remain et sont allowable in touts Courts et cesti que vient al terre prendra hold de cest custome come est 2 E4 6 per Lit. contra de customes que courge ove seignories car la per escheat del terre ou severans de Seignorie le custome est auxi ale come est 14 H4 et coment que in veritie le feffee nad mannor ne poet tener court baron in touts respects uncore poet assembler les copiholders queux sont in possession et la poet prender surrenders et faire novell copies accordant al primer custome et a cest purpose le Court teng et Copies graunt sont bone car in divers lieus ou nul mannor est uncore le Seignor que ad forsque un quillett de Copiholds est assetts bone de faire copies et les copies sont bone issint faits et ont este allowed divers foits in touts Courte et ieo ne doubt mes in le dit case del Seignor Chauncellor si copihold escheat il poet faire novell graunt per copie et uncore nad il mannor ne in veritie ne in reputacion per le grant de ceo quillett de copiholds et coment que le feffee ne poet faire novell copie uncore sur le surrender dun copie in esse il poet faire auter copie come icy fuit fait et al meins durant le former estate surrendered le primer custome remaine et copie bone et coment que nest trove quils sont in vie uncore pur ceo quil nest trove quils sont morts serra intend in vie Et al obieccion que ad este fait pur ceo que cest copie est fait habendum secundum consuetudinem mannerii ibidem que referr al hamlett car ceo est darreinment nosme a que ibidem veignant apres referera et nemi al darrein mannor que est in le margent del copie et coment quil duist estre issint intend uncore ceo ne serra hurt al copie car si le copie ust este fait al eux secundum consuetudinem sans disont manerii ibidem ou si le copie ust este graunt a eux et les parols secundum consuetudinem ussent este lesse hors uncore le copie per ceo nust este le peior car si le copie soit fait in estate accordant al length limited per le custome del mannor ceo est le substans del copie et pur ceo sera le copie bone coment que nad ceux parols secundum consuetudinem manerii et donques le mittinge eins de eux est forsque surplusage si ascun contrarietie ou impossibilitie soit uncore per ceo nest le copie que est sans ceo bone in substans impaired et pur ceo si le Seignor a son mannor de D. graunt copie pur 3 vies que estate est garranted per le custome et puis il ad al ceo secundum consuetudinem manerii de Hale cest surplusage ou nugacion ne noiera le copie que in substans fuit bone accordant al custome del mannor de Dale Issint labbot de Glaston ad divers mannors et appellast les tenants de ceux mannors al Glaston et al Court teng la graunt copies in chescun de ses mannors secundum consuetudinem manerii ibidem ceo referr al custome del mannor ou le copihold gist et nemi accordant al mannor de Glaston et les customes la et a ceo que ad estre obiect que le copie fuit graunt hors del terre in le court dun auter mannor et in auter county il dit que le Seignor mesme hors de ascun Court poyt granter copies et issint poyt le Seneschall mesme come est in 2 E6 Brooke novel cases 387 et est comon course et usage que le Seignor dun mannor que gist in Devonshire poet graunt copies icy in Seriants Inn sil voil et ceo serra bone Et quant a ceo que ad este obiect que copiholder ne poet faire lease pur ans mes il serra forfeit il nest issint car touts copiholders poient faire lease pur un an assets bien et sil per le custome del mannor soit forfeit ceo doit estre trove et avere de lauter part et coment que le copiholder ad forsque a volunt le Seignor del mannor uncore il est solonque le custome estate setled nient determinable come estate a volunt al comon ley est et pur ceo il poet bien faire lease pur ans et ceo lessee avera eieccione firme vers le Seignor mesme sil lui eiect auxi bien come le copiholder mesme puit aver ew trespass vers le Seignor per que per touts cy causes il pria que le iudgement poet estre affirmed."

79. In Bright v. Forte, note 77 above, Drewe reports a conversation he had with Ewens (Ewans) who was of counsel in "Constantine's Case." Ewans said he brought a writ of error to reverse the judgment of the Queen's Bench, which is what he did in Melwich v. Luther. In addition, Anderson's mention of the fact that the two manors were in different counties corresponds to a fact in Melwich v. Luther.

80. Croke's Reports, I, 252; Coke's Reports, IV, 24b.

81. BM Add. MSS 25,198, pp. 78b–79a: "En evidence al Jurye en eieccione firme sur lease pur ans fait per Copiholder fuit agree per Gawdye Clenche et Fenner que lessee pur ans de copiholde severed del mannor poet prender surrenders ou graunt copies et faire seneschall de tener Courts pur cest purpose et cest courte est appele une Courte de Survey et toute est bone mes il ne poet tener Courte baron pur defalte de suitors et le case de Sir Christopher Hatton fuit cyte destre rule accordant . . ."

82. BM Add. MSS 25,200, p. 116a: "FENNER . . . ad este adiudge que il poet in 23 El & adiudge que il poet accept surrender al uses et faire estates accordant POPHAM coment ne soet ascun manor in presice termes del ley uncore sil soiet un manor in reputation un prescription pur demise per copy poet estre mainteine auterment plusors copihold estates in Engleterre specialment in le westerne parts serront subverte & destroy et la sont plusors manors per reputacion quel consist tantum de copiholders sans ascuns franktenants & est dure a defeat lour estate quaere intant que le seignor ne poet tener un court come semble et in court baron les suitors que sont franktenants sont judges & sans iudges ne poet estre un court et donque quaere coment un surrender poet estre la mes . . . [illegible word] que nest court barron mes serra quasi un court de Jury [Survey?]."

83. BM Add. MSS 25,203, p. 59b: ". . . coment les Coppyholds sont sever del Manor uncore cesty que ad le franktenement de eux poet garder un courte et graunter coppyholds car nest requisite que soet un courte baron et dit que issint agree en un case concernant les Coppyholders de Wallingborne . . ."

84. Coke, *Compleat Copy-holder,* secs. 31, 34, 37; Scriven, *Copyholds,* pp. 11–12.

TABLE OF CASES

INDEX

HARVARD HISTORICAL MONOGRAPHS

1. Athenian Tribal Cycles in the Hellenistic Age. By W. S. Ferguson. 1932.
2. The Private Record of an Indian Governor-Generalship: The Correspondence of Sir John Shore, Governor-General, with Henry Dundas, President of the Board of Control, 1793–1798. Edited by Holden Furber. 1933.
3. The Federal Railway Land Subsidy Policy of Canada. By. J. B. Hedges. 1934.
4. Russian Diplomacy and the Opening of the Eastern Question in 1838 and 1839. By P. E. Mosely. 1934.
5. The First Social Experiments in America: A Study in the Development of Spanish Indian Policy in the Sixteenth Century. By Lewis Hanke. 1935.*
6. British Propaganda at Home and in the United States from 1914 to 1917. By J. D. Squires. 1935.*
7. Bernadotte and the Fall of Napoleon. By F. D. Scott. 1935.*
8. The Incidence of the Terror during the French Revolution: A Statistical Interpretation. By Donald Greer. 1935.*
9. French Revolutionary Legislation on Illegitimacy, 1789–1804. By Crane Brinton. 1936.
10. An Ecclesiastical Barony of the Middle Ages: The Bishopric of Bayeaux, 1066–1204. By S. E. Gleason. 1936.
11. Chinese Traditional Historiography. By C. S. Gardner. 1938. Rev. ed., 1961.
12. Studies in Early French Taxation. By J. R. Strayer and C. H. Taylor. 1939.
13. Muster and Review: A Problem of English Military Administration 1420–1440. By R. A. Newhall. 1940.
14. Portuguese Voyages to America in the Fifteenth Century. By S. E. Morison. 1940.*
15. Argument from Roman Law in Political Thought, 1200–1600. By M. P. Gilmore. 1941.*
16. The Huancavelica Mercury Mine: A Contribution to the History

of the Bourbon Renaissance in the Spanish Empire. By A. P. Whitaker. 1941.

17. The Palace School of Muhammad the Conqueror. By Barnette Miller. 1941.*
18. A Cistercian Nunnery in Mediaeval Italy: The Story of Rifreddo in Saluzzo, 1220–1300. By Catherine E. Boyd. 1943.*
19. Vassi and Fideles in the Carolingian Empire. By C. E. Odegaard. 1945.*
20. Judgment by Peers. By Barnaby C. Keeney. 1949.
21. The Election to the Russian Constituent Assembly of 1917. By O. H. Radkey. 1950.
22. Conversion and the Poll Tax in Early Islam. By Daniel C. Dennett. 1950.*
23. Albert Gallatin and the Oregon Problem. By Frederick Merk. 1950.*
24. The Incidence of the Emigration during the French Revolution. By Donald Greer. 1951.
25. Alterations of the Words of Jesus as Quoted in the Literature of the Second Century. By Leon E. Wright. 1952.*
26. Liang Ch'i Ch'ao and the Mind of Modern China. By Joseph R. Levenson. 1953.
27. The Japanese and Sun Yat-sen. By Marius B. Jansen. 1954.
28. English Politics in the Early Eighteenth Century. By Robert Walcott, Jr. 1956.
29. The Founding of the French Socialist Party (1893–1905). By Aaron Noland. 1956.
30. British Labour and the Russian Revolution, 1917–1924. By Stephen Richards Graubard. 1956.
31. RKFDV: German Resettlement and Population Policy, 1939–1945. By Robert L. Koehl. 1957.
32. Disarmament and Peace in British Politics, 1914–1919. By Gerda Richards Crosby. 1957.
33. Concordia Mundi: The Career and Thought of Guillaume Postel (1510–1581). By W. J. Bouwsma. 1957.
34. Bureaucracy, Aristocracy, and Autocracy: The Prussian Experience, 1660–1815. By Hans Rosenberg. 1958.
35. Exeter, 1540–1640: The Growth of an English County Town. By Wallace T. MacCaffrey. 1958.
36. Historical Pessimism in the French Enlightenment. By Henry Vyverberg. 1958.

37. The Renaissance Idea of Wisdom. By Eugene F. Rice, Jr. 1958.
38. The First Professional Revolutionist: Filippo Michele Buonarroti (1761–1837). By Elizabeth L. Eisenstein. 1959.
39. The Formation of the Baltic States: A Study of the Effects of Great Power Politics upon the Emergence of Lithuania, Latvia, and Estonia. By Stanley W. Page. 1959.*
40. Conservation and the Gospel of Efficiency: The Progressive Conservation Movement, 1890–1920. By Samuel P. Hays. 1959.
41. The Urban Frontier: The Rise of Western Cities 1790–1830. By Richard C. Wade. 1959.
42. New Zealand, 1769–1840: Early Years of Western Contact. By Harrison M. Wright. 1959.
43. Ottoman Imperialism and German Protestantism, 1521–1555. By Stephen A. Fischer-Galati. 1959.
44. Foch versus Clemenceau: France and German Dismemberment, By Jere Clemens King. 1960.
45. Steelworkers in America: The Nonunion Era. By David Brody. 1960.
46. Carroll Wright and Labor Reform: The Origin of Labor Statistics. By James Leiby. 1960.
47. Chōshū in the Meiji Restoration. By Albert M. Craig. 1961.
48. John Fiske: The Evolution of a Popularizer. By Milton Berman. 1961.
49. John Jewel and the Problem of Doctrinal Authority. By W. M. Southgate. 1962.
50. Germany and the Diplomacy of the Financial Crisis, 1931. By Edward W. Bennett. 1962.
51. Public Opinion, Propaganda, and Politics in Eighteenth-Century England: A Study of the Jew Bill of 1753. By Thomas W. Perry. 1962.
52. Soldier and Civilian in the Later Roman Empire. By Ramsay MacMullen. 1963.
53. Copyhold, Equity, and the Common Law. By Charles Montgomery Gray. 1963.

* Out of print.